Mac OS® X Lion™ Server

PORTABLE GENIUS

D1056763

Mac OS® X Lion™ Server

PORTABLE GENIUS

by Richard Wentk

WILEY

John Wiley & Sons, Inc.

Mac OS® X Lion™ Server Portable Genius

Published by
John Wiley & Sons, Inc.
10475 Crosspoint Blvd.
Indianapolis, IN 46256
www.wiley.com

Published simultaneously in Canada

ISBN: 978-1-118-03173-5

Manufactured in the United States of America

10 9 8 7 6 5 4 3 2 1

For general information on our other products and services or to obtain technical support, please contact our Customer Care Department within the U.S. at (877) 762-2974, outside the U.S. at (317) 572-3993 or fax (317) 572-4002.

Wiley publishes in a variety of print and electronic formats and by print-on-demand. Some material included with standard print versions of this book may not be included in e-books or in print-on-demand. If this book refers to media such as a CD or DVD that is not included in the version you purchased, you may download this material at http://booksupport.wiley.com. For more information about Wiley products, visit www.wiley.com.

Library of Congress Control Number: 2012933403

WILEY

About the Author

Richard Wentk covers Apple products and developments for *Macworld* and *MacFormat* magazines and also writes about technology, creativity, and business strategy for titles such as *Computer Arts* and *Computer Music*. As a trainer and a professional Apple developer, he has more than 15 years of experience making complicated technology simple for experts and beginners alike. He lives online but also has a home in Wiltshire, England. For details of apps and other book projects, visit www.zettaboom.com.

Credits

Acquisitions Editor
Aaron Black

Project Editor
Martin V. Minner

Technical Editor
Paul Sihvonen-Binder

Copy Editor
Gwenette Gaddis

Editorial Director
Robyn Siesky

Business Manager
Amy Knies

Senior Marketing Manager
Sandy Smith

Vice President and Executive Group
Publisher
Richard Swadley

Vice President and Executive Publisher
Barry Pruett

Project Coordinator
Patrick Redmond

Graphics and Production Specialist
Andrea Hornberger

Quality Control Technician
Rebecca Denoncour

Proofreading and Indexing
Sossity R. Smith
Potomac Indexing, LLC

For Betty.

Anima magis est ubi amat, quam ubi habitat.

Acknowledgments

Although this book has my name on the cover, it's been very much a team effort. I'd like to thank acquisitions editor Aaron Black for dealing gracefully with an unexpected change of direction halfway through the project, and project editor Martin V. Minner for continuing patience, support, and good humor. Sincere thanks are also due to the rest of the team at Wiley for their hard work behind the scenes, especially copy editor Gwenette Gaddis and technical editor Paul Sihvonen-Binder.

Alexa, Hilary, Michael, and Annette helped with support, entertainment, pasta, nights out at the opera—and occasional suggestions, some of which were helpful.

Software has always been about networks, especially networks of people. Online communities and blogs have become an invaluable part of the support process, and thanks are due to the countless individuals who volunteer their time and expertise to help others.

Finally, thanks ever to Team HGA—soon . . .

Contents

chapter 4

How Do I Set Up a Web and
E-mail Server?   66

chapter 5

How Do I Enhance Collaboration
with Wikis, Blogs, and Chat?   94

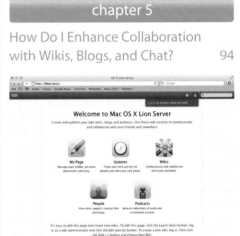

chapter 6

How Can I Share Files, Calendars,
and Contacts?   126

chapter 13

How Can I Fix Problems and Get More from Lion Server?   314

appendix a

Lion Server Extras and Alternatives   338

Introduction

What is a server, and why do you need one? The simplest possible answer is that, with a server, you can do many of the things you're used to doing online, including sending and receiving e-mail, putting up web pages, and running chat rooms—but instead of relying on a third party, you can provide and manage these services yourself, using your own hardware and software.

There are challenges and rewards in setting up and running a server.

The challenges are obvious, with new concepts to learn and new skills to master.

The rewards depend on your motivation. These are some possible applications:

- **Keeping e-mails private and safe within your home or small business.**
- **Setting up an online business with custom web software.**
- **Creating podcasts and distributing them automatically.**
- **Mastering networking technology for its own sake.**

Apple's OS X Lion Server meets all these needs and others. Compared to enterprise-level server products, it's exceptionally affordable and relatively easy to set up. It also includes powerful features for secure sharing of e-mails and web pages, easy private chat, secure network access, and podcast creation.

Although Lion Server is powerful, this book is written for beginners. You need to be comfortable using a Mac and familiar with essential software such as Finder and System Preferences. However, everything else you need to know is explained to you here. You learn about key concepts in network technology and work through step-by-step instructions to help you set up all of Lion Server's elements.

Although setting up Lion Server is more challenging than basic Mac mastery, after your server is working, you'll have learned more about your Mac than you expected. And you can use a new set of Mac-based tools for fun—and for profit.

How Do I Install
Lion Server?

Mac OS X Lion

To set up the installation of Mac OS X 10.7, click Continue.

Continue

For Mac OS X Lion and Lion Server, Apple no longer offers disk-based media for installation and no longer supports the .dmg file format that users of previous versions of OS X have used. Instead, purchase and installation are managed by the Mac App Store. This simplifies purchase for some users but complicates it for others. This chapter explains how to buy and install Lion Server, and it includes timesaving tips about installation on multiple computers and reinstallation.

Choosing a Mac for Lion Server

OS X Lion Server can run on any Mac compatible with OS X Lion. But because Lion Server doesn't have the same performance requirements as a standalone Mac, some Macs are more suitable than others. When you choose a Mac for Lion Server, the ideal specification and form factor may not be the same as your perfect standalone Mac.

Choosing a processor

Lion and Lion Server require a 64-bit Intel processor. Older G-series processors aren't suitable. Nor are Rev A Intel Macs with a 32-bit Core Duo processor. At a minimum, Lion Server Mac needs a Core 2 Duo or i-Series processor.

Slower, older processors are good enough for light home use. For small office use, aim for a more powerful i-Series multi-core processor. Because Lion Server doesn't spend much time generating graphics or calculating floating-point numbers, an i5 or even an i3 processor should be adequate. For light commercial applications, consider a fast Mac with an i5 or i7 processor.

Selecting memory

Lion Server will run in 2GB of RAM, but 4GB is a workable minimum. When a computer lacks RAM, it can *thrash*—write stale information to disk while trying to load information that users are asking for. This can create long pauses.

Users of standalone computers can get used to this, especially when there's a visual indication to tell them to wait. But long pauses are less acceptable on a server. Web pages may fail to appear on demand, and other services may stall without warning.

For best performance, a server needs more RAM than a standalone Mac. A computer with 4GB of RAM should be adequate for very light home use. For small office applications, aim for 8GB. And 16GB is recommended for a larger office or a business running a small commercial web server.

Selecting peripherals

As a network product, the only essential peripheral needed for Lion Server is an Ethernet socket. Most Macs have one.

You can manage Lion Server remotely without using a monitor, mouse, keyboard, or trackpad. But you must connect them for initial installation. After installation, you can disconnect them and use them with another Mac. Because Lion Server is designed to be administered remotely, there's no advantage to using it with a large monitor unless you also plan to use your server as a general-purpose Mac.

Lion Server no longer supports the print server available in Snow Leopard Server. But almost any Mac can be used as a basic print server. So if your home or office needs a printer, you can locate it next to any Mac on the network.

External backup storage is a useful optional extra. Depending on the size of the network, it can be useful to add an Apple Time Capsule, shown in Figure 1.1, or some competing NAS (Network Attached Storage) server. Alternatively, to save costs, you can simply attach an external USB drive to the server Mac and set up Time Machine to use it for backups.

1.1 Don't forget that you may need to add extra hardware to your server, such as a Time Capsule backup disk for use with Time Machine.

Selecting a form factor

Lion Server doesn't have to run on server hardware, but some Mac form factors are more suitable than others.

Running Lion Server on a laptop

You can run Lion Server on a laptop, such as the Mac Book Air models shown in Figure 1.2. In theory, it's possible to create a mobile server that can be carried by one person and accessed remotely by others. But the patchy availability of mobile bandwidth in most locations makes this an unlikely option. Even where wireless bandwidth is available, Lion Server is more efficient when it's physically connected to a network using cabling—preferably gigabit Ethernet for maximum performance.

1.2 Although you can run Lion Server on any recent Mac laptop, this doesn't usually create an ideal network server.

Generally, Lion Server isn't a practical choice for less experienced laptop users or for anyone who wants to build a relatively simple network. But it can offer intriguing possibilities for developers and advanced users with network experience.

Running Lion Server on an iMac

At first sight, an iMac, shown in Figure 1.3, appears to be the ideal Mac for a home server. You can set up Lion Server to share music files, notes, calendars, and other information. You also can pre-filter and monitor e-mail, and you can create a custom family chat server that is invisible to the rest of the Internet.

Performance can be an issue. If the family iMac is heavily used, it may not have the power to operate as a full-performance stand-alone Mac and a server at the same time. Because family network applications aren't

1.3 An iMac can be a practical home and small office server, as long as you don't underestimate the required performance.

usually demanding, this may not be a problem in practice. But if you plan to use your iMac for heavy gaming, video editing, advanced photo editing, and other more challenging applications, consider an iMac with more memory and a more powerful processor than you would otherwise use, to allow for simultaneous standalone and network use.

Running Lion Server on a Mac Mini

The Mac Mini, shown in Figure 1.4, is a small and convenient solution for small office and home use. But Mac Mini models aren't outstandingly powerful, so they're not recommended for mid-weight commercial applications.

You can use a Mac Mini to share photos and media with friends, family, and coworkers and to host a low-traffic blog or an eCommerce site with limited traffic. But a Mac Mini won't cope with the tens of thousands of page impressions needed to run a popular blog or with the background services needed to run a busy shopping site.

However, it can still be a good choice as an affordable hobby and home media server or as a small office web server and storage manager that can be accessed remotely when working away from base.

1.4 A Mac Mini is ideal for light and medium performance applications, but may struggle as a professional web server for eCommerce.

Running Lion Server on a Mac Pro

Now that Apple no longer supplies Xserve hardware for commercial and industrial networking, a Mac Pro, shown in Figure 1.5, can be a practical substitute for lightweight commercial applications. Unfortunately, Lion Server isn't ideal for heavy-duty corporate, educational, and commercial networks.

Many of the enterprise features in Snow Leopard Server have been simplified, deprecated, or removed. Experts can continue to manage some of them from the command line, but this makes Lion Server more difficult to work with than Snow Leopard Server. For high-performance web applications, consider other solutions, especially the Mac version of the free and widely-used LAMP package (Linux, Apache, MySQL, and PHP; see Appendix 1).

1.5 A MacPro is a good choice as a medium performance server for office and light commercial use.

A Mac Pro running Lion Server continues to be a good option for mid-weight applications, such as a network for a larger single office with a few tens of users. Because ultimate performance isn't needed, it's possible to run Lion Server successfully on a mid-range Mac Pro, enhanced with extra memory.

But because of the changes to Lion Server, and because Apple is deliberately moving out of the enterprise market, Lion Server isn't ideal for heavy-duty commercial and enterprise applications. The high performance of a very powerful Mac Pro is likely to be wasted, and cheaper and more efficient solutions may be available elsewhere.

Installing Lion Server

Lion Server has three components, and installation isn't a single-click process; you must download and install the components separately.

Genius

If you buy Lion Server from the App Store, you won't be told about Server Admin Tools, and it's not obvious that one third of the full package is missing!

These are the three components:

- **OS X Lion.** Because Lion Server is an add-on for OS X Lion and not a separate product, you must be running a copy of Lion before you can install Lion Server.

- **OS X Lion Server.** Lion Server is packaged as a further purchase and download. It launches a dual-purpose application called Server App, which downloads the latest updates to Lion Server, installs them automatically, and then displays a control panel. After installation, you administer (manage and control) Lion Server using the options in the control panel.

- **Server Admin.** Server Admin - known formally as Server Admin Tools, and shown in Figure 1.6, is an optional but strongly recommended free extra application. It's aimed at more experienced network managers, but it can be installed by anyone who wants it, and is an essential add-on for readers of this book. Unlike Lion and Lion Server, it isn't distributed through the App Store. Nor is it mentioned in Server App. You must download and install it manually from Apple's support web site.

Note

Server App is a somewhat simplified descendant of Server Preferences in Snow Leopard Server. Similarly, Lion Server's Server Admin is a simplified version of the more powerful and complete Server Admin application available in Snow Leopard Server. It's not clear why Apple removed some of the more useful features from Server Admin, but if you have experience with Snow Leopard Server, you may be surprised by some of the changes.

Genius

Experts also can manage Lion Server from the command line using Terminal and the Bash shell. Command-line management gives you powerful and direct control over Lion Server's features, but it requires specialized skills and knowledge that make it a challenging option for beginners. There's more about command-line management in Chapter 13.

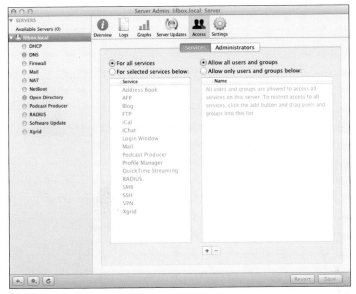

1.6 Although it's not advertised, the Server Admin application is very much part of the Lion Server package.

Purchasing Lion

If you bought a Mac after July 2011, it almost certainly came with OS X Lion preinstalled. Earlier Macs were shipped with OS X Snow Leopard. If you're still running OS X Snow Leopard, you can install Lion in three ways:

● **From the App Store, as shown in Figure 1.7, for $29.99 (£20.99 in the UK).** The Mac App Store first appeared in Snow Leopard 10.6.6 and is available in all subsequent versions. You can pay for items with your iTunes account details, or you can sign up for a new account. Lion is a heavily advertised application and is usually prominently featured on the App Store's front page.

9

● **Using Apple's USB drive installer, which is available from the main online Apple store (www.apple.com) for $70.** OS X Lion is a 3.5GB download. If your location lacks fast broadband or is limited to dial-up, you can buy a USB drive as a convenient physical alternative.

● **With a custom USB drive or DVD installer.** Although the Lion Installer deletes itself after running, it's possible to extract the installation .dmg file from it before it runs and create a custom bootable source for installation and reinstallation. For details, see later in this chapter.

1.7 Lion Server is the first version of OS X distributed through the App Store.

Installing Lion

The Lion Installer is very straightforward. After downloading, it appears in the Dock on Snow Leopard, and you can double-click it to start the installation process. After you select a language and a target partition, the rest of the installation is automatic.

If you select a target partition that boots Snow Leopard, Lion automatically performs an upgrade. If you select an empty partition, Lion performs a clean install.

Genius

If you don't have fast broadband, you don't want to download OS X Lion more than once. Look for instructions later in this chapter for making a custom installer that doesn't require an App Store download.

Installing Lion Server

Lion Server is a separate purchase from the App Store. In practice, Lion Server means the Server App administration tool and a collection of services—a web server, e-mail manager, chat server, and others—that run behind the scenes and remain invisible until accessed by network users.

1.8 Downloading Lion Server from the App Store is the first stage in a longer process.

After you pay for and download Lion Server, it installs a small and minimal version of Server App automatically, as shown in Figure 1.8. This minimal version of Server App is an installer for the full version. When you launch it for the first time, it downloads around 200MB of the latest updates for Lion Server and installs them for you.

The installation process is minimal. You must click Continue after launching it, but otherwise there's literally nothing to set up, as shown in Figure 1.9. The installer makes some assumptions about useful default settings, but doesn't ask you about them. It's likely you'll want to change them almost immediately, as shown in the rest of this book.

1.9 Server App downloads an expanded version of itself and creates default server settings.

11

Installing Server Admin Tools 10.7

After Server App is installed, you can install Server Admin Tools, also known as Server Admin. Server Admin is an alternative management tool for Lion Server and provides more sophisticated and powerful access to some of Lion Server's features. You can use Lion Server without Server Admin; it's a useful tool to have. It's especially helpful if you have experience with Server Admin on Snow Leopard Server or moderate to advanced network-management skills gained with other kinds of servers.

Caution Server Admin was a prominent feature of Snow Leopard Server, but it's now officially deprecated. It's likely that future releases of OS X Server will lose Server Admin altogether. It may even be withdrawn before the end of Lion Server's life.

You can download Server Admin 10.7 from http://support.apple.com/kb/DL1419, as shown in Figure 1.10. It's around 200MB. Run Software Update after installation to download and install the most recent version.

Although some official Apple help pages suggest otherwise, Server Admin *isn't* listed in the main Apple software support download collection.

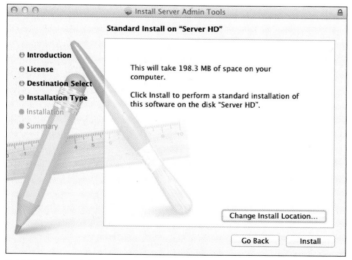

1.10 The Server Admin installer is a standard Mac .dmg file. Double-click it to install it. The installation process doesn't have any settings or options.

Note

If you're a beginner, Server Admin can seem bewildering. The secret is to use it in a task-based way, rather than trying to master the entire application immediately. This book doesn't introduce every feature in Server Admin in detail, but it does refer to it when it makes it easier to perform a specific task.

Reinstalling Lion Server

It's often useful to install Lion Server on multiple computers. It's also useful to be able to reinstall Lion Server from scratch, especially when you're experimenting with it. Certain features remain somewhat fragile, and it's possible to leave parts of Lion Server in a non-operational state by accident; assume that you'll need to reinstall at least once before you get Lion Server running reliably. For both installation and reinstallation, the App Store delivery process can be slow and inconvenient. This can be a showstopper problem if you don't have a fast broadband connection. Outside urban areas, download speeds can be as low as 1MB/s, and it can take more ten hours to download the full 3.5GB. If you have dial-up only, App Store delivery is completely impractical.

However, you can save download time by creating a custom installer for Lion and including the Server Admin download for manual installation. Server App typically requires a further download, so this isn't a complete solution. Still, it can save you time over the time needed for three full downloads.

Genius

Lion includes a recovery and reinstall feature, which you can access by holding down Option-R as you restart. The recovery feature includes access to Disk Utility, the ability to change startup disks, and an option to reinstall Lion. Unfortunately, the latter downloads the full installer from Apple's servers, so this is an inconvenient solution for users with limited bandwidth. However, if you have two Macs you can use an advanced feature called NetBoot to create a backup of a full installation. You may want to create multiple versions for reinstallation—for example, a completely clean version, a version with some basic features set up and basic users added, and so on. A full description of NetBoot is outside the scope of this book, but Chapter 13 provides an introduction.

Genius

If you have slow broadband or dial-up, you can save time by making a trip to an Internet Café or public WiFi hotspot and performing the initial download there. After you have the installer files on disk, you can follow the instructions in the rest of this chapter to create your own custom installer.

Creating a custom USB installer

In outline, creating a custom installer is a three-stage process:

1. **Create a bootable USB drive.**

2. **Extract the Lion installer files from the App Store downloads.**

3. **Create a restore partition with the installer files on the drive.**

When Lion boots, it can load the files from a bootable drive and launch the installer.

Let's go through these stages in detail.

Caution

The instructions in this chapter are correct for Lion 10.7.1. In the future, Apple may decide not to allow users to make their own bootable media, so it's possible the process may no longer work in later versions. There's no way to predict if or when this will happen. For the latest information, check your favorite Mac blogs and message boards online.

Creating a bootable USB drive

Many Macs no longer support optical drives, and USB drives are relatively cheap and robust. So for many installations, a bootable USB drive is the ideal medium for installation.

Any USB drive can be used for booting, but the boot process works only with drives that have been formatted in a special way. Specifically, the drive must use a "GUID Partition Table."

Genius

GUID is an acronym for Globally Unique Identifier. (You probably don't need to know this.)

Disk Utility includes the tools you need to create this. Follow these steps:

1. **Launch Disk Utility.**

2. **Select the USB drive from the list at the left.**

3. **Select Erase from the tabs at the top.** Select the Mac OS Extended (Journaled) format from the menu. Leave the name field unchanged. Click Erase to delete everything on the drive.

4. **Select Partition from the tabs at the top.**

5. **Select 1 Partition from the Partition Layout menu.**

6. **Select Options under the partition diagram.** Click GUID Partition Table, as shown in Figure 1.11, and OK.

7. **Click Apply.**

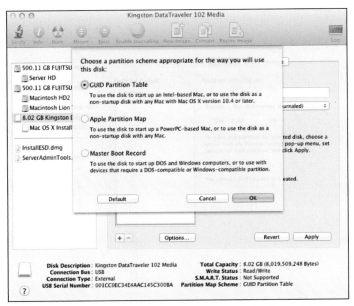

1.11 Formatting a USB drive with a GUID partition makes it possible to boot from it.

This creates an empty bootable USB drive with no files in it. The next step is to install the installer files into the drive with Disk Utility, after extracting them from the installer package.

The Lion installer is a standard Mac .dmg file, but it's buried inside the package downloaded from the App Store. Luckily, it's easy to extract the installer from the files around it.

 Copying the files into the drive with Finder doesn't make them bootable. You must use Disk Utility instead.

Note

Caution Note that you must perform the next steps *before running the Lion Installer*. The installer deletes itself when it completes, and the only way to recover it is to download it again and begin from scratch.

Extracting the Lion installer file

The Lion installer appears as a standard app package. You can use Finder's Show Package contents to find the .dmg file in the package and then load the file directly into Disk Utility.

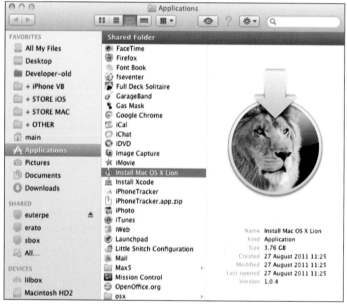

1.12 Locate the OS X installer package in your Applications folder; find it *before* you run it.

Follow these steps:

1. **After the App Store download completes, find the package in your /Applications folder, as shown in Figure 1.12.** It's usually named Install Mac OS X Lion.

2. **Right-click the package, and select Show Package Contents.** This opens the application and allows you to view the files inside it.

3. **Select Contents ⇨ Shared Support.**

4. **Right-click the InstallESD.dmg file.** This is the file that installs Lion.

5. **Select Open With... Disk Utility, as shown in Figure 1.13.**

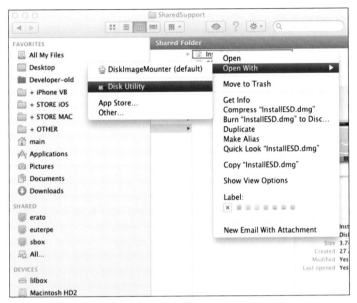

1.13 Finding the InstallESD.dmg file before loading it into Disk Utility.

You have now prepared a USB drive for the installer and loaded it into Disk Utility. The final step is to copy the installer .dmg file to the drive. Counter-intuitively, this means using Disk Utility's Restore feature.

Creating a bootable installer

The Restore feature copies files to a drive in a special bootable format. To copy the files to your empty USB drive, follow these steps:

1. **Select the Restore tab from the top of the pane.**

2. **Drag the InstallESD.dmg file from the list at the left to the Source field.**

3. **Drag the bootable partition from the USB drive at the left to the Destination field, as shown in Figure 1.14.**

4. **Select Restore.** Disk Utility performs the copy.

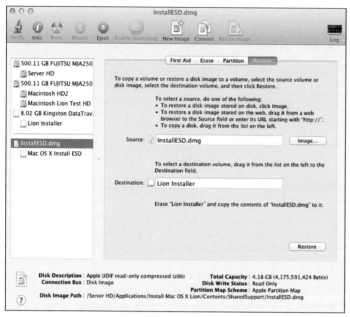

1.14 Copying the InstallESD.dmg file to your USB drive.

Your custom installer is almost ready. You can now copy the Server Admin installer .dmg file to it with Finder. As mentioned earlier, Server App/Lion Server remains a manual download.

Using your USB installer

To boot from your installer, leave the USB drive in its socket and restart your Mac. Hold down the Alt key as it boots. You see a new USB boot option. Select it from the icons to boot from it, and Lion Installer begins automatically.

You can now set an installation target. If you want to upgrade an old copy of Snow Leopard Server, select the old Snow Leopard partition. For a clean install, erase the partition first in Disk Utility.

After installation, you can install Lion Server/Server App in the usual way from the App Store and then double-click the Server Admin .dmg file on the USB drive to install Server Admin manually.

Caution

Erasing a partition deletes everything on it. Your data *will* disappear permanently, with no hope of recovery. Check and double-check that you're not deleting anything essential before erasing. Check also that you have at least two backup copies of very valuable data on independent disks.

Caution If you have a working USB installer, you can erase your Mac's boot partition and do a clean reinstall of Lion to it. It's a *very* good idea to check the installer with a test boot before you do this; otherwise, you could be left with a useless Mac. If you have the disk space, it's useful to create a small rescue partition with a working copy of Lion to keep as a backup in case of problems.

Creating a custom DVD installer

It's easier to create a DVD installation disk than it is to create a bootable USB drive. Follow these steps:

1. **Follow the steps in the previous section to find the InstallESD.dmg file and load it into Disk Utility.**
2. **Insert a blank DVD disk into your Mac's disk slot.**
3. **Click the Burn icon at the top of Disk Utility.**

Wait while the disk burns. You can then boot from it using the same Alt boot selection sequence as for a USB drive. Because the InstallESD.dmg file barely fits onto a single disk, you must burn the Server Admin .dmg installer to a separate blank DVD or CD and load it separately.

Genius The easy way to create a custom DVD or USB installer is to use the Lion Diskmaker utility, available as a free download from http://blog.gete.net/lion-diskmaker-us. It doesn't work with all Macs in all circumstances, which is why this chapter includes instructions for creating installers manually. But when it works, it's almost a one-click installer creator.

Caution Getting all of the features of Lion Server working can be challenging, and it's important to set up some features before others. Before attempting to set up further features you should read—or at least skim—the rest of this book to see which features you're likely to want. You can then work through the final summary check list in Chapter 13, enabling features in the order listed there. If you don't do this, you'll find that some features can't be reset to a useful default, and you'll need to perform a clean install and start again.

How Do I Start Building a Network?

You can use Lion Server to create different kinds of networks. For example, you can build a secure office network that isn't visible on the Internet. Or you can create a network around a home or office web server that can be visible to Internet users while other network features stay hidden. Before you can make these options work, you must set up a small selection of core network services. Lion Server does some of this setting up when you install it. But for the most reliable results, you must complete the process manually, which means finding out more about network technology.

Understanding Networks

A server isn't like a stand-alone computer. When you use a stand-alone computer, you usually launch applications that are kept on its hard drive and save data to the same hard drive. The key feature is that almost everything happens locally.

A network server works differently. It provides *services* to network users. Lion Server provides a selection of useful services that make it possible to share files, share a calendar and address book, create and edit web pages, create and edit wikis, and so on.

Services aren't applications. They don't usually have windows and menus of their own. Instead they run on a server Mac at the center of the network, and they can be accessed in various ways: from a web browser, from the command line, from Finder or some other file browser, and even from mobile devices.

A key feature of network services is that you can use them wherever network access is available. Potentially, you can make them accessible to the entire Internet. Or for maximum security, you can choose to keep them inside a private network.

Lion Server manages these differences by running in three different ways, one for each type of network:

- **Local.** A local network provides services for a home or office, but it's hidden from the Internet. Users can access the Internet in the usual way, and they can view pages, wikis, and other information on the server at the center of the network. But no one can access these services from the Internet.

- **Private.** A private network is similar to a local network, but users can log in to the network over the Internet from a remote location to access its services. It remains private because user access is controlled by a system of network login accounts.

- **Public.** A public network includes services that are visible to local users and to all Internet users, such as a web server.

Setting up Lion Server to support one of these network types is easy. But before you can do it, you must set up your network to make sure Lion Server fits into it correctly, Figure 2.1 shows the server's configuration and information pane, and there are detailed instructions for setting the network type from this pane later in this chapter.

Genius

A public network is usually a hybrid; for example, you can make a web server visible to the Internet, but keep other network services local or accessible only via passwords. If you plan to create a public web server, you can maximize security by running it on a separate Mac or even on a separate network. Mixing public, private, and local services on the same server is less secure than keeping it physically independent.

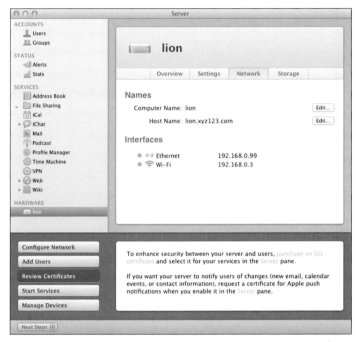

2.1 Before you can build a network around Lion Server, you must configure some basic features.

Getting started with core network services

To keep all three types of networks running smoothly, Lion Server relies on low-level network services. In the same way that a stand-alone computer does lots of work behind the scenes to keep your applications running—managing memory, sending and receiving Internet traffic, and so on—network services perform similar tasks for a network. These services are invisible to most users, but when they're working properly, computers can exchange information locally and over the Internet. When they're not working, the network is useless.

Understanding network addresses

Although the details of low-level network plumbing can get complicated, these services do a simple job: They make it possible for computers to find each other and exchange information.

In the same way that you need a phone number, postal address, or e-mail address before you can contact someone, computers use a related system of addresses when they communicate. And just as humans use different kinds of addresses to reach each other, computers do too.

You'll find three different kinds of addresses on a network:

- **A MAC (Media Access Control) address.** This is a string of six hexadecimal numbers, such as 7c:6f:92:f1:7d:51. It's the physical address of a specific hardware connector, such as an Ethernet socket, a WiFi connection, or a Bluetooth link.

- **An IP (Internet Protocol) address.** Also known as an IP number, this is four numbers between 0 and 255 separated by periods, such as 192.168.0.12. Every MAC address is associated with a unique IP address.

- **A domain address.** This consists of words separated by periods: for example, lion.local or www.myexcellentserver.com. Domain addresses are used because they're easier for humans to remember than IP addresses.

These addresses are partly interchangeable. For example, if you want to view a website, you can type the standard www.aserver.com address into your browser. But you also can type in the IP address (if you know it), and the web page appears in the usual way, as shown in Figure 2.2.

Note Hexadecimal numbers (base 16—also known as "hex") are used by computer designers because they're more convenient for computer design and programming than decimal numbers. Hexadecimal numbers are made of the digits 0-9 *and* the letters a-f. They're a simple way to count from 0 to 15 without having to use another digit. If you're not a programmer, you don't need to learn how to count in hex or use it for arithmetic. But because they're used in MAC addresses, it's useful to recognize them.

Caution MAC addresses have nothing to do with Macs! They're linked to specific hardware on each computer. Other types of devices, including cell phones and tablets, also have MAC addresses and use those addresses for network connections.

24

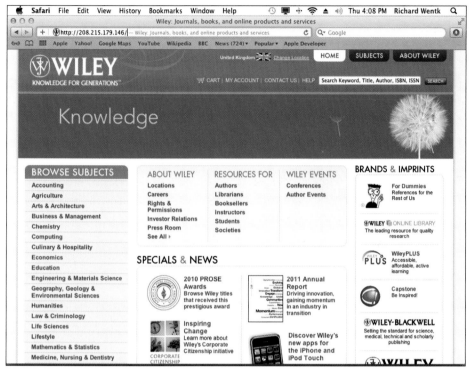

2.2 Domain names are for human convenience only. Behind the scenes, the Internet uses IP addresses for all traffic, including web traffic.

Understanding private and public addresses

Two further wrinkles apply to IP addresses. An IP address can be public or private. A public address is valid on the entire Internet. For example, when you use a browser to view the www.wiley.com website, the browser secretly consults an Internet address directory called a DNS (Domain Name System.) It finds the IP address of the Wiley network, which is 208.215.179.146, and then it downloads a web page.

A private address is valid only on a local network. Traditionally, all small networks use a limited and preselected range of IP addresses, from 192.168.0.1 to 192.168.255.255, as shown in Figure 2.3. Because these addresses are private and the networks that use them aren't connected to each other, there are no address conflicts.

The second wrinkle is that 127.0.0.1 is a special address. It's always equivalent to "this computer"—whichever computer you're using. The equivalent domain address is "localhost."

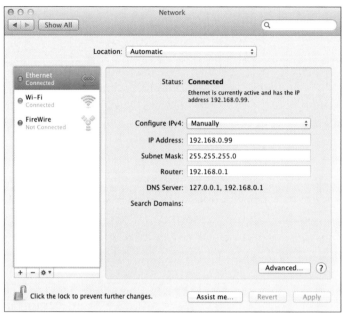

2.3 If you open System Preferences ⇨ Networking and select Ethernet, you usually see that your Mac is using local addresses already.

If you set up a web server on any computer and want to view the web pages it's serving, type **http://127.0.0.1** or **http://localhost** into your web browser. If the web server is working correctly, it generates a page for you.

Genius

It may seem strange that all small networks use the same addresses, but there's a good reason for it; there simply aren't enough addresses in the full IP address range of 0.0.0.0 to 255.255.255.255 to give every computer on every network in the world a unique address. Some duplication is unavoidable, and for arbitrary historical reasons, the 192.168.X.X range was chosen. (X stands for any number between 0 and 255.) On very small networks, the range of addresses used in practice is even smaller—typically 192.168.0.X, giving a total of 256 addresses, which is very small subset of the possible number, but still enough for most homes and small offices. Corporate networks use private addresses with a different, larger range—typically 10.X.X.X—but you won't usually see this option at home or in a small office.

Genius

If you want to find the IP number for any website, search for "find ip address" to see a list of sites that can report your own IP address or for any domain. If you've never done this, it's a good idea to experiment with these services to get some hands-on experience of converting domain names into IP addresses. The Internet's DNS technology does the same translation for you automatically, and Lion Server includes a simplified version of the same service, as you'll see later in this chapter.

Using public and private addresses in practice

It's useful to understand exactly what happens when you try to view a web page, because most networks, including the one you're about to set up, work in a similar way. Although the example sequence below illustrates what happens when you access a web page, as shown in Figure 2.4, a similar sequence happens for other network services, including chat and e-mail. The sequence is similar for remote and local networks, and it must work correctly.

2.4 The lookup process is the same for web pages served from a local web server or from the Internet.

The steps are necessary to reach a web page:

1. **Type the address of a web page into your browser.**

2. **Press Enter.** The browser converts the domain name in words into a public IP address by looking it up in a vast table of addresses. (The Internet is held together by a system that manages these look-ups for all Internet traffic.)

3. **The browser sends a web page request to that IP address.**

4. **A network server at that address receives the request.**

5. **The server recognizes the web request (web requests have a unique signature) and looks up the *local* address of the web server on the network.**

6. **It forwards the request to the web server on the local network.** In reality, the request arrives at a physical network port defined by the web server's MAC address.

7. **The web server sends the data for your web page back to your browser, which displays it.** In practice, a single page usually makes multiple requests, but each request works the same way.

ISPs and web-hosting companies use more or less the same technology as home and small business networks. When a network is set up correctly, each step in this process happens automatically. You don't have to worry about it, and your users don't either; it just works.

But some assembly is required before it works smoothly. Let's look at what this means in more detail.

Using core services in theory

The core services that manage addresses are named with an alphabet soup of acronyms. The names can seem intimidating at first meeting, but you don't need to become an expert to use them. As you'll see later in this chapter, there's an easy way to get them working with almost no effort. But it's still useful to know what these services do.

These services are available:

- **DNS (Domain Name System).** DNS converts domain addresses to and from network addresses and IP numbers. Users can type www.myexcellentserver.local into a web browser, and the DNS service on the network finds the IP number for that domain automatically. Depending how the DNS service is set up, this may mean looking up the address from a local table or from the Internet.

- **DHCP (Dynamic Host Configuration Protocol).** DHCP assigns IP numbers to MAC addresses. The "dynamic" part means that IP numbers are usually assigned as needed; when a computer boots, it asks the DHCP server on the network for an IP number for each MAC address it uses. It then keeps the same number (or numbers) as long as it's active. When a computer disconnects from the network, DHCP recovers the numbers and makes them available to other computers.

- **NAT (Network Address Translation).** On public networks, NAT converts IP addresses into local addresses. NAT is a more advanced network feature and is covered in Chapter 10.

Setting Up Core Services

It's obvious from the example that your network must be able to translate domain names into IP addresses and then translate IP addresses into MAC addresses. At the heart of every network, these three services manage the local addresses of computers on the network and translate between the different types of addresses that are used.

Setting up core services the lazy way

As you might expect, Lion Server can provide DNS, DHCP, and NAT services to a network, as shown in Figure 2.5. If you run Server Admin, these features are available. But don't try setting them up, because getting them working can be a challenge, and there's a simpler way to add them to your network. If you've already built a network around a router or WiFi access box, you may have set them up successfully without knowing.

Most ADSL or cable modems, WiFi distribution boxes (including Apple's AirPort series), and small-network routers include these services for free. When you set up your router or modem, DNS and DHCP usually start working immediately.

- **If you follow the instructions your ISP gave you to set up your router, you get full local and Internet DNS.**
- **DHCP is typically set up with useful defaults, so it just works with no setup at all.**
- **NAT usually isn't set up, but you can set it up manually if you need it.** For more details, see Chapter 10.

A typical home or small office network has at least one device that can manage these services. There's no advantage in turning off these services on that device and making them run on Lion

Server instead. So if you're using a suitable device, you can make life simpler for yourself by ignoring these features in Lion Server and using external hardware to manage them.

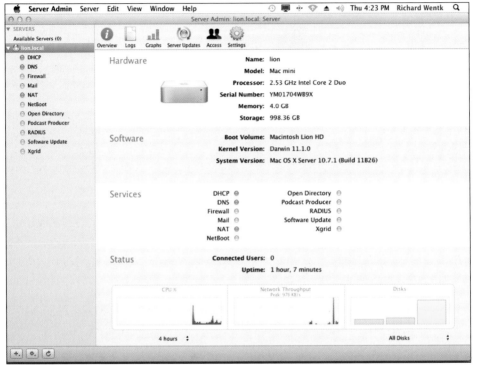

2.5 You can find setup options for DNS, DHCP, and NAT in Server Admin. But you don't need to use them, and they're best left to experts.

Setting a fixed IP address for Lion Server

You must make one adjustment to the network and to Lion Server before it can start working for you.

Because Lion Server provides some of the services on the network, it needs a fixed IP address. If you use DHCP to give it an address automatically, the address may change every time you boot the server. This is a bad thing, and it guarantees that Lion Server won't work correctly.

So you must set DHCP on your network device to make sure it always supplies the same address to your server Mac. Making sure a computer always gets the same address is a standard feature of DHCP; it's called "assigning a fixed IP address."

Unfortunately, literally hundreds of different network devices are available, and I don't have room in this book to give detailed instructions on how to set up a fixed IP address in all of them.

Genius

If DHCP isn't working on a network, computers assign themselves IP addresses in the range 169.254.X.X. If you see a computer using an address in this range, you can be sure that DHCP isn't set up properly; for example, you may have enabled the DHCP service in Lion Server, and it's conflicting with the DHCP service in a network device.

Note

Apple's own AirPorts are a popular choice with users of Lion Server, and include a simplified set-up procedure. But it's important to understand that you can use almost any router—which is why this chapter includes a non-Apple example.

The instructions that follow are a sample for one common type of router: a Netgear DG834G. Setting up a fixed IP address on another device requires similar steps. The web pages, settings, and dialogs you see will look different, but the underlying features will be similar. You should be able to find and modify the settings you need by combining the instructions that follow with the instructions that came with your device:

1. **Log in to your router or other device from a web browser.** Network devices don't always have domain names, so you may have to type an IP address into your web browser—for example, http://192.168.0.1. You can find the IP address you need to use in the device instructions.

2. **Supply the username and password.** Again, you find these in the device instructions. After you log in, you see a setup page with features similar to those in Figure 2.6.

Genius

If you haven't changed the default name and password for your device, do it now, and don't forget to save the new details. Hackers love to try default login details on network devices. If you don't change them, you could be leaving your network open to abuse.

3. **Find the DHCP settings from the main menu options.** They're often called DHCP settings or LAN IP setup, or they may use some related wording.

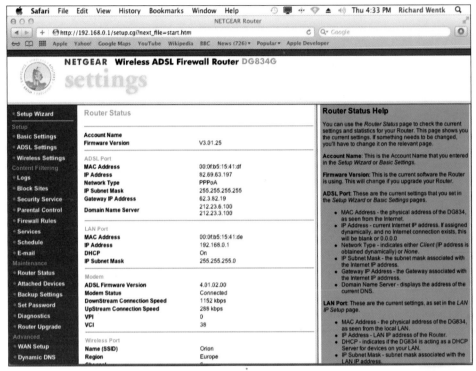

2.6 When accessing a router's settings, you almost certainly won't see this page, but you should see a similar page.

4. **Find the address reservation or static IP feature.** In the example shown in Figure 2.7, the feature is called Address Reservation. Note how the network device lists the Device Name (similar to the domain name), the IP Address, and the MAC address for every connected device.

5. **Use an Add or Reserve option to start the reservation process.** In this example, you can select the device for which you want to reserve an IP address from a list. Many devices offer the same option.

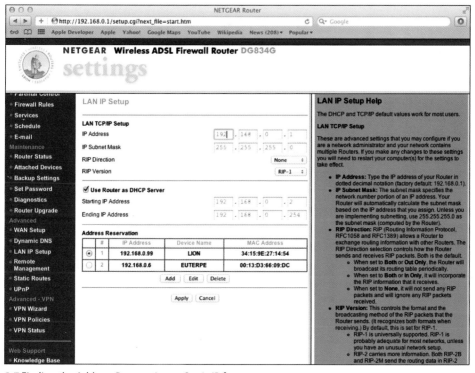

2.7 Finding the Address Reservation or Static IP feature.

6. **Specify a fixed IP address, as shown in Figure 2.8.** This tells the DHCP service in the device to *always* assign the same IP address you specify to the MAC address of the Mac on which you're running Lion Server. The exact IP address doesn't matter, as long as it's unique. This example uses 192.168.0.99.

7. **Click through any confirmation buttons or dialogs.**

8. **Restart the Mac on which you're running Lion Server.**

9. **Select System Preferences ⇨ Network.** Click Ethernet. You should see the details in Figure 2.9. The IP Address field should match the number you entered in Step 6.

33

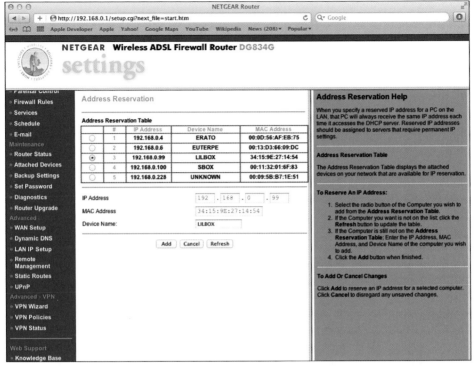

2.8 Setting a fixed IP address for a given MAC address on a given computer, which must be your Mac server.

IPv6 vs IPv4

The instructions in this section apply when a network uses an addressing system known as IPv4 or Internet Protocol version 4. This is a creaky and antiquated technology that is still widely used and will continue to be widely used for the lifetime of this book.

Lion Server supports a newer addressing system known as IPv6. IPv6 supports a wider range of addresses, so there's no need to make a distinction between private and public network addresses.

IPv6 addresses use eight groups of four hexadecimal digits; for example:

2001:0db8:85a3:0568:9142:8a2e:0370:7335

Few devices support IPv6, but Lion and Lion Server both include a Configure IPv6 setting in the Network pane in System Preferences, under the TCP/IP tab. If your network uses IPv6, you should be able to leave this option set to Automatically, and the network should manage address assignments for you without further setting up.

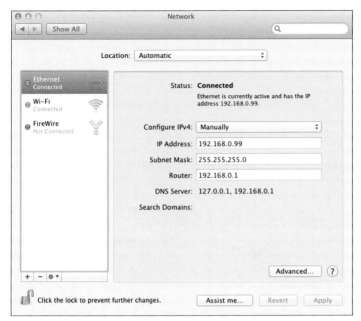

2.9 When you restart and check the assigned IP address in the Network pane in System Preferences, it should match the address you specified.

Genius

Make sure you connect and turn on every computer, file server, and other item that uses your network before you attempt this stage. If your network device is smart enough to display a list of devices with associated MAC addresses and names (and most are), it's easier to find and select an IP address that isn't already being used by some other item. If two items on the network try to use the IP same address, neither will work reliably.

Note

If your DHCP device can't list network items, you can find your server Mac's MAC address manually by choosing System Preferences ⇨ Network ⇨ Ethernet and selecting the Hardware tab at the far right. On less advanced DHCP devices, you may need to type the MAC address manually before you can assign a fixed IP address to it.

Selecting a Network Type

Now that your network can find addresses, you can select a network type in Lion Server. You also can use this feature to change the network name—known as the *host name*—of the computer running Lion Server. The network name is related to the domain name, as you see later in this section. Your users will use this name to access the web server, wiki, and some other network features of Lion Server.

It's a good idea *not* to change the host name or the computer name after it's been set. Lion Server may become less reliable if you do this, and changes may confuse your network users.

However, it's possible that you may want to change the host name while setting up your network for the first time, so it's useful to know the option exists.

Whether you're creating a local network, a private network, or a public network, the first steps are as follows:

1. **Launch Server App, if it's not already running.**

2. **Select your server from the list under the HARDWARE icon at the bottom left of the list on the right.** On most networks, you will have only one server to choose.

3. **Select the Network tab at the top of the right pane, to show the dialog in Figure 2.10.**

2.10 To select a network type or change the computer name, start here.

Genius

The next few sections seem very simple, but there's more going on than meets the eye. When you set up a network type, Lion Server starts its internal DNS service running and creates an address table that makes it possible for the server to access its own services and for other computers on the network to access the server. You can attempt to set up DNS manually using Server Admin, but it's a complex process, and it's easier to leave Server App to do it. Occasionally, experts may find that Lion Server's default settings don't exactly match their needs. If you have experience with setting up DNS manually, you'll find it useful to check the settings in Server Admin after changing the host name to reassure yourself that DNS has been set up to meet your needs.

Changing the computer name

This is a simple operation, but you shouldn't need to do it often, if at all. Select the Edit button to the right of the Computer Name field, and fill in the two details shown in Figure 2.11. For consistency, the two details should match. For best reliability, click the Edit button to the right of the Host Name field after you make the change and follow the steps listed in the next section.

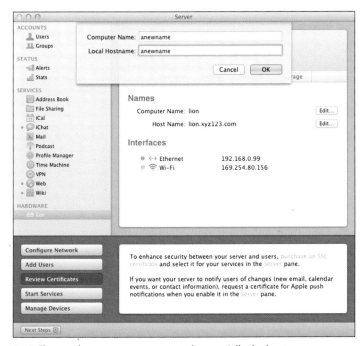

2.11 Change the computer name—and potentially the host name.

Changing the host name and selecting a network type

You also can change the host name independently of the computer name. Slightly confusingly, this option is also used for selecting a network type. Follow these steps:

1. **Select the Edit button to the right of the Host Name field.**

2. **If a page of text with no options appears, click Continue.**

3. **If you see the dialog shown in Figure 2.12, select an Ethernet port instead of WiFi or any other alternative.** If your server Mac has more than one Ethernet port, select the default.

4. **Select one of the options from the dialog shown in Figure 2.13, and follow the steps in each following section.** This dialog suggests it sets only the host name, but in fact it also makes important changes behind the scenes to set up each type of network.

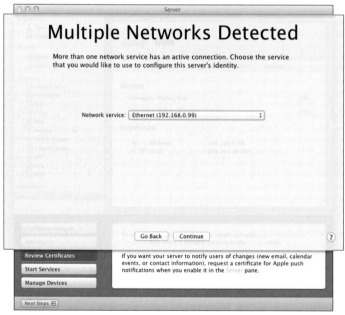

2.12 Select the physical connection to your server. Use Ethernet where possible.

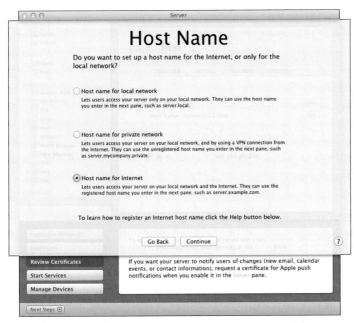

2.13 Select a network type. You can change the network type later if you need to by selecting a different option here.

Caution Although you can set up a cable-free WiFi-only network around Lion Server, it isn't likely to be fast or efficient. You get better results if you connect your server Mac to desktop computers on the network with Ethernet cabling. Laptops can use Ethernet or WiFi, depending how physically convenient it is to set up the former.

Setting up a local network

Selecting the Host name for local network option sets up Lion Server to run a local network. When you click Continue, you see the dialog in Figure 2.14, which includes the features of the Change Computer Name dialog and also gives you another chance to define the Network Address—the physical connection to the server.

You usually won't want to change the computer name. But it's useful to set the host name to make it clear that it's hosting a local network. Traditionally, this means using the computer name followed by .local.

39

Select Continue after you change the host name, and wait a few seconds. Lion Server is now ready to run as a local network server.

2.14 Create a local network. Give the host name the .local suffix, as shown.

Setting up a private network

To set up a private network, repeat the steps in the previous section, but use the .private suffix instead of .local. If your server is called lion, name it lion.private. That's all you need to do. Select Continue as in the previous example, and Lion Server is ready to run as a private network.

Although this sets up the core services for a private network, it doesn't make your network securely accessible from the outside. To use your network remotely, you must set up another service called VPN (Virtual Private Network). For details, see Chapter 12.

Getting started with a public network

To create a public network, repeat the steps as before, but this time type a full server and domain name into the Host Name field. If you don't already have an Internet domain name registered for your server, skip ahead to Chapter 10 and follow the steps there. If you do, type the domain name here. Optionally, you can prefix the computer name as suggested in the note on the dialog. But it's simpler to set up a web server and other features if you use the domain name without a prefix, as shown in Figure 2.15.

2.15 Set up a public network. Use a full domain for the host name, as shown here.

Because external access requires NAT features, there's some extra work to do before your server is visible online. For more information, see Chapter 10. But you've made the first steps toward creating a public server, and Lion Server is now configured in a way that can use NAT to create a public server that is visible on the Internet.

Testing the network

The easiest way to test your new server is to get the web features running and check that you can view web pages on the server and on the network. For details, see Chapter 4.

How Do I Create Users and Groups?

Before users can access the features of Lion Server, you must create network login accounts for them. Lion Server's Users and Groups tool in Server.App includes all the features you need for basic account creation and management. You can create individual user accounts, set and reset passwords, and group users together for convenience and workgroup collaboration. Each group of users can have its own wiki and shared folder. Members of a group also can become automatic iChat buddies.

Getting Started with Users and Groups

If you've used OS X before, you're familiar with the Users & Groups pane in System Preferences. These login accounts are *valid for one Mac only.* They include various optional features, such as parental controls, and a list of the software that is preloaded for each user when they log in.

If you set up a user account on one Mac and try to log in with the same details on another Mac, you're not allowed to, because the other Mac doesn't know who you are.

Understanding network user accounts

A network user account gives users access to the services that run on the network server. Network accounts are valid on any Mac connected to the network, and they use a web-based login system, which is completely different from the standard stand-alone Mac login, as shown in Figure 3.1.

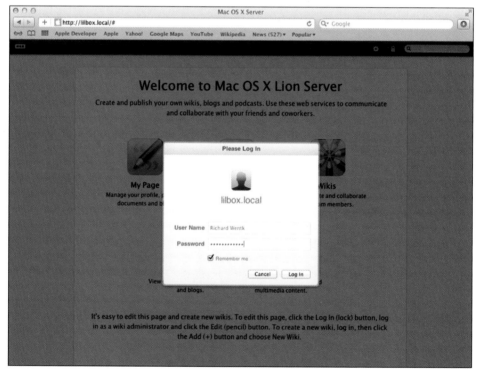

3.1 Lion Server's web-based network login isn't the same as the standard Mac user login.

When a user logs in to the network, he or she can create and edit a personal profile page, share documents, pick up e-mail, and create blog entries. Network users also can view the profiles, blogs, and shared documents created by other users, collaborate on wikis, access podcasts uploaded to the network, and work with the shared calendars and address books. These features run on the network server, the Mac at the center of the network running Lion Server.

It's important to understand the relationship between standard Mac accounts and network accounts. The differences might seem obvious, but there's an extra wrinkle: There are two types of network accounts.

A *local* account, shown in Figure 3.2, is a hybrid account. It's a network account, valid for web log-ins via any Mac on the network. But it's also a standard Mac user account, and it allows users to log in directly to the server if they're sitting in front it.

3.2 Local network accounts are also standard user accounts on the server Mac.

A *managed network account* offers access to network features only. It's more secure, because it doesn't give users the power to log in to the server.

Local accounts are the default option for Lion Server. If you want to set up managed network accounts, you have to do a small amount of extra work before you begin creating users; specifically, you have to enable a feature called Open Directory, which is introduced later in this chapter.

Understanding network groups

In the same way that it's useful to group users together on a single Mac and make changes to all their settings with a single action, it's useful to group network users together. Network accounts have more features and options than standard Mac accounts, so this feature is more useful than the groups on a stand-alone Mac.

Groups also can be local and managed, and they work in the same way as local and managed users. A local group is valid on the network and the main server Mac. A managed group is available only on the network, as shown in Figure 3.3.

3.3 This workgroup is a network managed group and is available only on the network. Team A and Team B are local groups.

Managed groups also support *group profiles*—hardware and software settings that control what users can do with their Macs and iDevices. This chapter explains how to get started with users and groups. For information about working with group profiles, see Chapter 8. You may want to skim Chapter 8 now to see if you need this feature before you begin creating users.

Caution

Some users make the mistake of assuming that Lion Server creates a virtual Mac for every user. Unfortunately, this isn't how Lion Server works. Instead, it runs common services on a server and makes them accessible from Macs on the network. Although Apple is moving toward giving every user access to his personal applications and settings from any Mac on the network, the evolution of the technology to make this effortlessly practical may take years. For now, this option remains science fiction.

Getting Ready to Create Managed Network Accounts

If you don't need to worry about the security risk, or if you run a very small home or family network where it doesn't matter, you can skip this section and create local accounts for your network.

If you want to create managed network accounts, you must set up Open Directory on your server. On a simple network, you can use the network accounts feature built into Server.App, following the steps later in this section.

Genius

You can make life simpler by using either local accounts or network managed accounts. Although it's possible to work with both types of accounts, it isn't easy and is likely to waste time. Because managed accounts are more powerful and more secure, they're a better choice for most applications, with the exception of very simple home and family networks with one main living room Mac.

Note

Server Admin includes more advanced control of Open Directory. You can ignore this feature on a small and simple network, because you're unlikely to need it.

1. **Launch Server.App if it's not already running.** Click the Next Steps button at the bottom left of the window. Click Add Users, and select the link labeled "manage network accounts" in the text box at the bottom right, as shown in Figure 3.4.

2. **Click Next to skip the help box that drops down.**

3. **Enter a password for the diradmin account, and repeat it in the Verify box.**

Caution Don't change the account name. It must be diradmin, or Open Directory won't work correctly. Don't forget to make a note of this password! You will need it while setting up other parts of Lion Server.

4. **Enter your organization name and administrator e-mail address, as shown in Figure 3.5.** The name and e-mail address are difficult to change, so make sure you get them right first time. It doesn't matter if the e-mail address doesn't exist yet. You learn how to create it later.

3.4 Navigating to the manage network accounts dialog.

5. **Click Next, and Set Up to create the new account and set up Open Directory.** Now wait. It can take a few minutes for Server.App to configure and start Open Directory.

6. **You should see a confirmation window telling you that the preceding steps have been successful.**

Note You may be wondering why the diradmin account never appears in the User list. In fact, it's not a user account at all; it's a special extra account used internally by Open Directory. Experts can use this account to manage Open Directory directly.

3.5 Defining the organization name and administrator e-mail address.

Genius If you see an error message after creating a diradmin account, quit and restart Server. App. There are various reasons an error can appear at this point. One common reason is that you haven't yet installed a valid security certificate. Quitting and restarting Server.App doesn't fix this problem, but it resets Lion Server to the point where it can manage users and groups effectively.

Server Admin includes more advanced Open Directory management options, as shown in Figure 3.6. Experts can use them to link Lion Server's Open Directory features with existing user lists on other computers, but you can ignore them on a simple network.

3.6 Server Admin includes advanced Open Directory options. You can ignore them on a simple Apple-only network.

Understanding Open Directory

Open Directory is a technology developed for large corporate networks that needed a relatively simple way to manage a single network-wide database linking usernames, software permissions, and network permissions.

With Open Directory, a user can log in on any computer on the network, and the network loads her permissions and other details from the shared database. Users can access the network from any computer on the network, including a remote one, and Open Directory makes sure they're identified correctly and that they're not suddenly given privileges and access to features they shouldn't have.

A full version of Open Directory can share permissions across mixed networks that use Mac, Windows, and Unix/Linux computers. Setting up Lion Server to share this information reliably is a complicated process. Fortunately, it's not essential for simple Apple-only networks. Although Open Directory works behind the scenes to manage user accounts, Server.App's simplified management hides most of its complexity.

Creating and Managing User Accounts

Creating a single user is almost effortlessly easy: You define the name, e-mail address, and password. Lion Server even includes a password generator, so you don't need to think of passwords for yourself.

Genius

If you already have an older server running Open Directory, click Next Steps at the bottom left of the Server.App window, and select Add Users. If Open Directory is working correctly and is accessible, you should see some text with a link labeled "connect to it." Click the link, type the server name or IP address, and follow the instructions to load information about existing users and groups. This saves you having to retype the information into Server.App.

Note

Many of the features in Lion Server refer to the user and group lists. Unfortunately, not all of them respond immediately when you add a new user. For best results, turn off other services before you add or remove users or groups, then restart them after your edits. In extreme cases you may need to reboot the server before changes register. It's possible future versions of Lion Server won't need these steps.

Creating a new user

To create a user, follow these steps:

1. **In Server.App, select Users at the top left.**

2. **Click the + icon at the bottom left of the Users window.**

3. **Type a full name, as shown in Figure 3.7.** If this user is included in an address book, use the name as entered there.

4. **Press Enter.** The Account Name field, used by Lion Server internally, is filled in automatically.

5. **Type an e-mail address.** This address is visible to other network users, and typically uses your domain name—for example, anewuser@mydomain.com.

6. **You can either type a password of your own or click the key icon at the right of the password field to auto-generate a password, as described later in this chapter.**

Genius

You should have a consistent policy for translating first names and surnames into e-mail addresses. firstname.surname@mydomain.com is a popular choice—for example, John Smith translates to john.smith@mydomain.com. Because e-mail addresses must be unique, you also should have a policy for dealing with situations where users have identical names. The ideal policy is simple, distinctive, and easy to remember. firstname.middleinitial.surname is a popular extended option. So is firstname.surname twodigitnumber@mydomain.com—for example, john.smith02@mydomain.com.

7. **Retype the password you entered in the previous step into the Verify field.** (Don't use cut and paste—it makes it harder to spot a typo in the password.)

8. ***Don't* click the Allow user to administer this server option, unless you want this user to have network administrator privileges.**

9. **Click Done.** Wait a minute or so while Lion Server updates its database.

10. **Optionally, you can click Users again to confirm that the new user has been added.**

3.7 Adding a new user.

Working with passwords

The ideal password is so easy to remember that it doesn't need to be written down and is impossible to guess or to hack—and because these are impossible requirements, it doesn't exist.

As a network administrator, it's up to you to trade off security against user-friendliness and to estimate the extra work you need to do when passwords are lost or forgotten against the value of access to individual user accounts.

Auto-generating a memorable password

The password generator built into OS X makes it easy to manage this trade off, by selecting either Memorable or Random passwords. (The other options are less useful, so you can ignore them.)

Follow these steps to create a memorable password:

1. **Click the key icon mentioned in Step 6 in the preceding example to show the Password Assistant application.**

2. **Select the Memorable option from the top menu for passwords that include two words, one digit, and one punctuation character, as shown in Figure 3.8.**

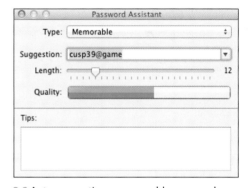

3. **Optionally, make the password longer to improve security further. Passwords of 31 characters are very difficult to crack.**

4. **For alternative passwords, click the Suggestion menu and select another password from the menu.**

3.8 Auto-generating a memorable password.

5. **When the quality bar is green, the password is secure enough for basic security.**
   Highlight it to copy it into a password field, and continue creating a user as before.

Auto-generating a random password

For a more secure random password, work through these steps, but select the Random type from the top menu, as shown in Figure 3.9. This creates a very secure password. Most humans find a random password impossible to remember, but these passwords are so secure that they're very difficult to crack using a direct computer attack.

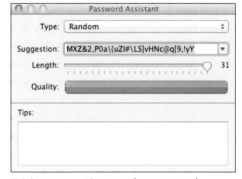

3.9 Auto-generating a random password.

Genius

A random password isn't necessarily more secure than a memorable one, because users still need to write it down, store it in their browser's autocomplete list, or keep some other record, which is less secure than the password itself. Memorable passwords are adequate for most applications, unless you have serious reasons for believing that your network will be attacked by hackers from outside. For more secure applications, using a very high security password is best, a random 31-character password managed by an online password manager such as LastPass. (http://lastpass.com). Access to LastPass must be managed carefully, but a good password manager makes it easy to recall any password, no matter how complex.

Listing user accounts

The users list, which is accessed by clicking Users at the top left of Server.App, displays extra useful information about each user, with a combination of numbers and icons.

Three different types of icons give you further information about users. If you replace the default icons with a custom image, as described later in this chapter, some of these details change. But it's useful to know what the defaults mean, as shown in Figure 3.10 and listed in Table 3.1.

3.10 Viewing the users list. Antonio Vivaldi is a network managed user.

Table 3.1 User Account Types

User Type	Description and Default Icon
Master administrator	This is the main administrator account, with master access privileges to all network features. This account has User ID 501 and is listed with a special icon that combines a black silhouette over graphics derived from Apple's standard network icon.
Local user	This is a normal user account stored locally on the server. It's listed with the default black silhouette icon.
Network managed user	This is a user account managed by Open Directory, either on the main server Mac or on another computer. This type of account is listed with a black silhouette behind a light blue globe.

Editing user accounts

You may occasionally need to edit a user account after it's created. You can do the following:

- **Change the user name.**
- **Change the e-mail address.**
- **Enable or disable network administration privileges.**
- **Add and remove the user from groups.**
- **Change the photo/icon.**
- **Reset the password.**

Editing a user

To edit a user, you can right-click the user in the users list, and select Edit User from the floating menu. Or you can click the gear icon under the list and select the same option. Network managed accounts can take short while to load. After an account is loaded, you see the dialog in Figure 3.11.

The basic editing options are straightforward. You can change a user's name and e-mail address directly here by typing in the new information. You also can promote a user to a network administrator by selecting the administrator check box, and you can add a user to a group, as described later in this chapter.

Genius

For more complex user editing, such as changing the account name, you may more easily delete an existing user and create a replacement account from scratch.

3.11 Basic user editing is limited, but very easy to use.

Genius

Although it's not obvious, each account has a unique reference number called a user ID. You can view a user ID by right-clicking an account and selecting Advanced Options from the menu—the User ID appears in a dialog with other specialized features, which are best left unedited. IDs aren't obviously useful, but it's helpful to know they're built into Lion Server. They appear in other places including the Workgroup Manager feature in Server Admin, which is outlined in Chapter 13. The main administrator account ID is always 501.

Resetting the password

Setting a new password for a user is very easy:

1. **Right-click a user.**

2. **Select Reset Password.**

3. **Type a new password, optionally using Password Manager to generate it.**

4. **Repeat the password in the Verify box.**

The password is now reset. You must communicate the new password to a user in some way. E-mail is simple, but not very secure. Some other option, such as a text message, is a more secure solution.

Changing a user's photo to a preset image

It's sometimes useful to modify a user's photo/icon in the users list. You can select from a small number of preset photos. Follow these steps:

1. **Right click a user's name to open the Edit User dialog, as described in the preceding section.**

2. **Right-click the user's current photo or icon at the top left of the dialog, as shown in Figure 3.12.** You also can hover the mouse over the image and left-click the triangle at the bottom right of the photo/icon.

3. **To select a preset image, click any of the images in the floating menu.**

4. **The new image replaces the old image in the list.**

3.12 Using the right-click floating menu to select a new photo or icon.

Creating a custom user image

You also can replace the image with a custom image. Follow these steps to do so:

1. **Repeat the first two steps in the preceding example.**

2. **Select Edit Picture at the top of the floating menu.**

3. **If your Mac has a camera, you can use it to take a photo by clicking the camera icon above the row of buttons.** If it doesn't have a camera, this option does nothing.

4. **The dialog counts 3...2...1...Snap! and keeps the snapped image.**

5. **Use the size slider under the image box to resize the image until it fits inside the rectangular area.**

6. **Select Set to save the image as a photo, or repeat Steps 3-5 to take a new photo.**

Genius

If you zoom in on the image, you can select part of it by dragging inside the box with the mouse. Selecting an area using this trick is easier and quicker than editing a photo with an image editor and saving a cropped version.

Selecting an existing image from disk

To load an image from disk, repeat the first two steps as before. Select Choose, and navigate to an image in your Pictures folder or anywhere else on disk. Select Open at the bottom left of the file selector to load it into the User Picture dialog. You can now zoom, pan, and set or cancel, as explained before.

Genius

You can't select Choose for an image from your iPhoto library. If you try to, you load the iPhoto icon into the image chooser, which is unlikely to be what you want. The trick is not to use Choose at all. Instead, launch iPhoto, and drag and drop any image thumbnail from an event, photo list, or other item in the library onto the User Picture dialog. You can then use the size slider to zoom and pan, and you select Set to set the image. Note that in iPhoto '11 (v9), drag and drop works only with library thumbnails. You can't drag and drop a full-sized photo.

Adding photo effects

You can apply a selection of photo effects to any image selected in the User Picture dialog, whether it was captured live, loaded from disk, or imported directly from the iPhoto library, as follows:

1. **In the User Picture dialog, load or capture an image, or begin with one of the standard images.**

2. **Select the twirl icon to the right of the camera icon in the dialog.**

3. **A small new pop-up window opens, with a grid of preset effects, as shown in Figure 3.13.** You can select an effect from this selection or use the left and right arrows at the bottom of the window to scroll through further effects.

4. **Click an effect to select it and apply it to the image.** You can still pan and zoom large images after applying an effect.

5. If you don't like any of the effects, press Esc to close the window and return to the dialog, or use the left arrow to scroll back to the first selection of effects and click Original.

Controlling access to services

You can enable and disable individual services for each user, as follows:

1. Right-click a user name in the Users list.

2. Select Edit Access to Services.

3. Check or uncheck the various options.

In practice, not all options are available all the time, as shown in Figure 3.14, for reasons that can appear somewhat arbitrary. If you're using managed network accounts, it's easier to use the Profile Manager feature described in Chapter 8 to manage access to services.

3.13 Selecting preset image filters and effects for your photo.

3.14 Managing access to services. When Profile Manager is active, most options here are grayed out.

Setting up Advanced Options

Advanced users can—carefully—use the Advanced Options feature in the floating edit menu to change the directories used by the user, their user ID, and other specialized features. Don't edit these options unless you know exactly what they do, because they can make it impossible for users to log in. Experts can use them to make powerful but obscure changes. If you're not sure what they do, ignore them; you won't be missing any vital features.

Setting a global password policy

To load the global password policy dialog, select the gear icon at the bottom of the Users list and then select Edit Global Password Policy.

This dialog, shown in Figure 3.15, has two features. You can lock out users from the network using the Disable Login option. You also can force users to choose passwords with basic security features, including a regular password update.

It's more secure to supply passwords to users rather than to allow them to set their own passwords. Users often choose memorable names of relatives or pets or memorable dates such as birthdays and anniversaries. Potential hackers typically try these options first. For maximum security, ignore the password option here and create high security updated passwords manually every month or two.

3.15 Setting a global password policy. Use this option to disable network logins, if you need to.

The login control options can lock out users under the specified circumstances. For example, you can use this feature to create short-lived temporary accounts for school or college work, or to lock out login attempts if an account is being hacked and the hacker makes more than a small number of bad password guesses; five is a good maximum. You also can disable an account on a specific date.

Creating and Managing Groups

There are four reasons to create groups:

- **To give each group a shared folder, to simplify file sharing.**
- **To make group members iChat buddies automatically.**
- **To create a shared group wiki.**
- **To use Profile Manager to manage device and network privilege settings for the group as a whole.** This is simpler and more efficient than making these settings for each user individually.

As mentioned earlier, groups can be local—in other words, they're valid on the server Mac and also on the network—or network managed. After you enable Open Directory, all groups become network managed.

Creating a group

To create a group, follow these steps:

1. **Launch Server.App, and select the Groups item at the top left of the window.**
2. **Click the + icon under the groups list.**
3. **Fill in the Full Name field.** The Group Name field is generated automatically.
4. **Click Done.**

Setting up group options

When Lion Server creates a group, it doesn't automatically display the group options for editing, as shown in Figure 3.16.

3.16 Setting up group options.

Follow these steps to select them manually:

1. **In the Groups list, right-click a group and select Edit Group from the floating menu.** Alternatively, select the group and click the pencil icon under the groups list.

2. **To edit the Full Name, type new text into the Full Name box.**

Caution Try to avoid renaming groups. It can confuse some of Lion Server's features. It also can confuse your users.

3. **Click the check box beside Give this group a shared folder, to create a single shared folder for simplified collaboration.**

Genius You can access the shared group folders directly from Finder. The folders appear on the server's main hard disk at <main hard disk>/Groups/<group name>.

4. **Click the check box beside Make group members iChat buddies, to enable automatic buddy updates.** For more about iChat and the iChat server, see Chapter 5.

5. **Click the Create Group Wiki button to log in to the network and access the wiki management page.**

Caution

In spite of the name, this feature doesn't create a group wiki. It simply loads the wiki management page.

6. **Click Done to confirm the changes.** Or continue to the next section to add users.

Adding users to a group

Adding users to a group is perhaps more complex than it should be. An option exists to browse users from a list, but it's not immediately obvious how to find it. For simplified access, follow these steps:

1. **Click the + icon at the bottom of the Group Edit window.**

2. **Type any letter into the box that appears to the left of the icon.** The letter provides an initial starting point for searching the user list.

3. **Select Browse from the floating menu.** A list of users appears in a floating window, shown in Figure 3.17.

4. **Drag users from this list into the Members area in the Group Edit window.**

5. **Click Done when finished to confirm the additions.**

Genius

When you have lots of users, it can take time to scroll through the entire list. You can preselect and filter users by typing text into the search/filter box at the top of the floating user list. The search is inclusive; it returns any item that includes the text you type, so typing "ann" returns "ann," "johann," "annette," and so on.

Genius

You can add groups as well as individual users to a group. This is an easy way to add every member in one group to another. It can be useful way to manage hierarchical teams, but be careful to check that, if you modify group profile settings, they're applied in the correct way and users have the privileges you want them to have.

3.17 The simple way to add users to a group.

Adding a user to a group

You also can add a user to a group from the User Edit dialog by following these steps:

1. **Select Users at the top left of Server.App.**

2. **Click a user in the list.**

3. **Right-click a user or select the gear icon, and then select Edit User.**

4. **Click the + icon under the Groups box.**

5. **Type a letter.** If you know the name of the group you want to put the user in, type its first letter. If you don't, type any letter.

6. **Either select the group directly from the floating menu, or click Browse to view a new window with a list of groups.** Drag and drop the groups you want the user to belong to onto the Groups box, as shown in Figure 3.18.

7. **Click Done to confirm the changes when finished.**

3.18 Using the groups list to add a user to multiple groups.

Genius

The Server Admin application has a sub-application called Workgroup Manager, which offers more advanced management tools for users and groups. To access it, launch Server Admin and select View ➪ Workgroup Manager. This is a complex application with more advanced network management features than Server.App. These features aren't essential on a simple network, and a full introduction to Workgroup Manager is outside the scope of this book. Server Admin also includes a simplified tool for listing user accounts. Select View ➪ Show Users and Groups. Internally, Lion Server treats software processes as users, so you'll see an expanded list of "users" that includes various software services with user IDs lower than 501. This information is useful to experts, but it isn't essential for more basic network management.

How Do I Set Up a Web and E-mail Server?

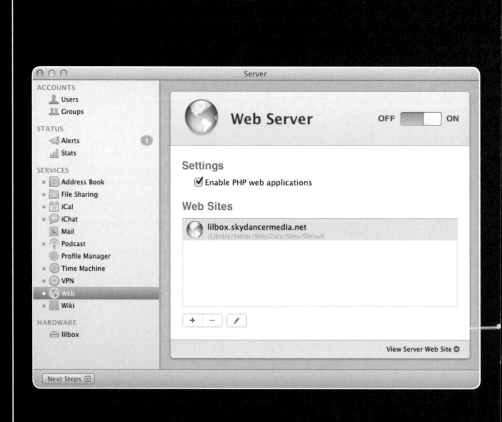

_ion Server includes a web and e-mail server. The web server can support multiple websites, limited only by your hardware's processor power and memory. The e-mail server can create a local e-mail access point that replaces or enhances the e-mail service provided by your current ISP. You also can provide your own web mail service for network users, set up virus filtering and spam removal, and optionally relay e-mail through your ISP's own mail servers.

Understanding Web Server Technology

In the early days of the World Wide Web, web pages were defined by simple, fixed text files. The language used to define the content and layout of a web page is called HTML (Hypertext Markup Language). The first version of HTML was so minimal that almost anyone could design a web page by creating the HTML with a simple text editor. Graphics were added by including simple instructions for displaying static image files, including photos, headers, and logos.

Initially, a web server was a relatively simple file copying service. When a user requested a page, the server copied the file of HTML layout instructions and text—and the graphics files (if any)—to a user's web browser. The browser read the instructions from the file, inserted the graphics as required, and the page appeared on the user's screen.

Figure 4.1 shows how all browsers can still do this. The file created in Text Edit produces the very basic web page shown in Safari.

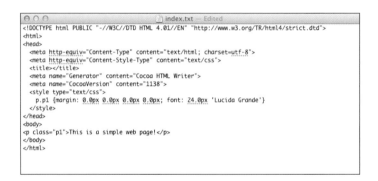

4.1 If you save a Text Edit document with the .html extension, it creates HTML code for you automatically from your text.

It didn't take long for web designers to realize that this approach was very limited. Because a web server is a piece of software that runs on a computer, it can be made to run applications. These applications aren't like the software you use on your desktop; they're more like scripts or small programs that can generate HTML instructions on the fly.

At first, the scripts were extremely basic. They added simple page accessories such as hit counters and dynamic date and time displays. But the key principle—that the web server could store information or read it from elsewhere on the web, process it to order, and generate HTML instructions according to a recipe defined by a web designer—soon made it possible for web designers to create more complex applications.

Many pages today are programmed rather than static, and the user sees a different page at each visit or refresh. This makes it possible to create discussion boards, newspapers and magazines, blogs, search engines, online shops, and other specialized sites where the content changes all the time.

Programmed web pages are created using a variety of techniques. A typical web server doesn't just generate web pages; it also includes a data storage system—known as a *database*—and support for web programming.

Although Lion Server's web server can display static pages, it also supports dynamic web programming. Technically, it includes the following features:

- **A web server based on an application called Apache 2**
- **A database—PostgreSQL**
- **A scripting system—PHP**

You can use the web server in a simple way, to serve static web pages. Experienced web developers also use PHP and PostgreSQL to create more sophisticated designs.

At the most basic level of Lion Server, these features are almost completely hidden. You can treat the web server as a feature that "just works" without worrying about what's happening behind the scenes.

But professional users may need more control. A full introduction to web management would require a much larger book, but some introductory hints about accessing the web server's low-level features are included later in this chapter.

Setting Up Web Server

There are two ways to set up and manage the web server feature in Lion Server.

- **Server App.** You can enable and disable the server, and you can select one or more folders as websites. You also can enable or disable support for PHP.

- **Command Line.** Apache 2 is a very powerful web server with many features, but most of the features are hidden from Server App. For advanced applications, professionals can access them from the command line, using the Terminal application in the /Applications/ Utilities folder, shown in Figure 4.2.

```
Server HD — bash — 126×43
web:IfDefine:_array_id:MACOSXSERVER:IfModule:_array_id:mod_encoding.c:DefaultClientEncoding:_array_index:0 = "UTF-8"
web:IfDefine:_array_id:MACOSXSERVER:IfModule:_array_id:mod_encoding.c:NormalizeUsername:_array_index:0 = "on"
web:IfDefine:_array_id:MACOSXSERVER:IfModule:_array_id:mod_encoding.c:EncodingEngine:_array_index:0 = "on"
web:IfDefine:_array_id:MACOSXSERVER:IfModule:_array_id:mod_ssl.c:SetEnvIf = "User-Agent &quot;.*MSIE.*&quot; nokeepalive ssl-u
nclean-shutdown"
web:IfDefine:_array_id:MACOSXSERVER:IfModule:_array_id:mod_ssl.c:SSLMutex = "file:/var/run/ssl_mutex"
web:IfDefine:_array_id:MACOSXSERVER:IfModule:_array_id:mod_ssl.c:SSLSessionCache = "shmcb:/var/run/ssl_scache(512000)"
web:IfDefine:_array_id:MACOSXSERVER:IfModule:_array_id:mod_ssl.c:AddType:_array_id:application/x-x509-ca-cert:Extensions:_arra
y_index:0 = "crt"
web:IfDefine:_array_id:MACOSXSERVER:IfModule:_array_id:mod_ssl.c:AddType:_array_id:application/x-pkcs7-crl:Extensions:_array_i
ndex:0 = "crl"
web:IfDefine:_array_id:MACOSXSERVER:IfModule:_array_id:mod_ssl.c:SSLSessionCacheTimeout = 300
web:IfDefine:_array_id:MACOSXSERVER:IfModule:_array_id:mod_ssl.c:SSLRandomSeed:_array_index:0 = "startup builtin"
web:IfDefine:_array_id:MACOSXSERVER:IfModule:_array_id:mod_ssl.c:SSLRandomSeed:_array_index:1 = "connect builtin"
web:IfDefine:_array_id:MACOSXSERVER:IfModule:_array_id:mod_ssl.c:SSLPassPhraseDialog = "exec:/etc/apache2/getsslpassphrase"
web:IfDefine:_array_id:MACOSXSERVER:Directory:_array_id:/usr/share/web:Allow = "from all"
web:IfDefine:_array_id:MACOSXSERVER:Directory:_array_id:/usr/share/web:Header:_array_index:0 = "Set Cache-Control no-cache"
web:IfDefine:_array_id:MACOSXSERVER:Directory:_array_id:/usr/share/web:Options:FollowSymlinks = yes
web:IfDefine:_array_id:MACOSXSERVER:Directory:_array_id:/usr/share/web:Options:MultiViews = yes
web:IfDefine:_array_id:MACOSXSERVER:Directory:_array_id:/usr/share/web:Order = "allow,deny"
web:IfDefine:_array_id:MACOSXSERVER:Directory:_array_id:/usr/share/web:AllowOverride = "None"
web:IfDefine:_array_id:WEBSHARING_ON:Include:_array_index:0 = "/private/etc/apache2/extra/httpd-autoindex.conf"
web:IfDefine:_array_id:WEBSHARING_ON:Include:_array_index:1 = "/private/etc/apache2/extra/httpd-userdir.conf"
web:IfDefine:_array_id:WEBSHARING_ON:Include:_array_index:2 = "/private/etc/apache2/extra/httpd-manual.conf"
web:MinSpareServers = 1
web:LockFile:_array_index:0 = "&quot;/private/var/log/apache2/accept.lock&quot;"
web:ServerLimit = 50
web:AccessFileName = ".htaccess"
web:DirectoryMatch:_array_id:".+\\.\\.namedfork":Deny = "from all"
web:DirectoryMatch:_array_id:".+\\.\\.namedfork":Satisfy = "All"
web:DirectoryMatch:_array_id:".+\\.\\.namedfork":Order = "allow,deny"
web:Directory:_array_id:/Library/WebServer/CGI-Executables:Allow = "from all"
web:Directory:_array_id:/Library/WebServer/CGI-Executables:Options:None = yes
web:Directory:_array_id:/Library/WebServer/CGI-Executables:Order = "allow,deny"
web:Directory:_array_id:/Library/WebServer/CGI-Executables:AllowOverride = "None"
web:Timeout = 300
web:ServerRoot = "&quot;/usr&quot;"
web:KeepAliveTimeout = 15
web:NameVirtualHost:_array_index:0 = "*:80"
web:NameVirtualHost:_array_index:1 = "*:443"
web:MaxClients = 50
web:StartServers = 1
lilbox:/ main$
```

4.2 Showing the web server's full list of settings in Terminal. You also can set them using Terminal, if you know what they do.

Note

Command-line control is for experts only. It's useful to know it exists, but it isn't described in detail here. Chapter 13 includes a very basic introduction to managing some of the features of Lion Server from the command line, but expert-level server management takes skills and knowledge that require a much larger book of their own. Adventurous beginners can find information about command-line management using web searches, but a basic understanding of the command-line environment, configuration-file editing, and the low-level OS X file system are essential before attempting this. Note that it's possible *to break Lion Server beyond repair* if you make mistakes at the command line.

Caution

In Snow Leopard Server, the Server Admin application included mid-level web server management options. These have been removed in Lion Server. If you want full control over the web server, you have no option but to use the command line. Unfortunately, Server App has a habit of making its own changes to low-level settings. If you make changes at the command line, any further changes you make in Server App are likely to overwrite them.

Comparing Web Server with commercial hosting

Before you try to set up Web Server, it's worth taking the time to ask if a custom web server is the ideal solution for you.

The appeal is obvious. You have potentially unlimited disk space, and you can update web pages almost instantly, with no upload delays. If you have two web servers on the network, you can use one for quality assurance and testing, perhaps with limited user access, and the other for public viewing. Because there are no restrictions on the content you host, you can experiment with unusual server software or add features that might be restricted for security reasons on a commercial server.

But there are also obvious disadvantages. Most ISPs offer fast download speeds, but very slow upload speeds. While it's possible to run a successful site over a slow broadband uplink, performance will suffer during busy periods, and your hosting will be limited to low-volume applications.

Security and backups are another critical issue. Commercial web hosts offer high-reliability hosting with automatic content backups. They also attempt to maximize security so they can minimize hacker attacks. Securing a web server is a challenging and skilled job, and it's far outside the abilities of anyone who isn't an expert. Even if you have low-value content, it's relatively easy for skilled hackers to hijack a web server and use it invisibly—for example, to relay spam messages.

Because commercial hosting is relatively cheap and secure, it can be worth considering whether the disadvantages of home or office hosting outweigh the fixed overheads.

Web Server is a capable solution for a home server that gives family members access to shared files online. It's perhaps less convincing for professional applications that need high performance and tight security.

Enabling Web Server

Like many of Lion Server's features, Web Server is controlled by a giant virtual toggle switch from Server App. To enable the server, follow these steps:

1. **Launch Server App, if it's not already running.**

2. **Select the Web item from the menu at the left.**

3. **Click the switch at the top right, as shown in Figure 4.3.**

It can take a few moments before the server starts working. Wait until the activity indicator at the bottom right of the pane stops spinning before checking that the server is working.

4.3 Enabling the web server with one of Lion Server's giant toggle switches.

Testing the web server

If you've set up your network correctly (see Chapter 2 for details), you should now be able to view the web server's default page in your web browser.

To check that the server is working, click the View Server Web Site link at the bottom right of the pane. The page shown in Figure 4.4 should appear in your browser. The URL matches the host name and extension—domain, .private or .local—you selected in Chapter 2.

4.4 The web server's default web page. If you see this, everything is working correctly.

Genius

After you see the test page, you should be able to view it from other computers on the network. On local and private networks, use the hostname and the corresponding extension preceded by a dot. On a public network, use the hostname followed the domain name and extension. If you didn't specify a hostname, the standard "www." prefix should work automatically.

Note

You'll notice the default page includes links to services such as mail, a calendar, and a password manager. Mail is described in this chapter. The other options are described in later chapters, but read the next chapter on wikis and blogs before reading those chapters.

Enabling PHP

To enable PHP support, check the Enable PHP web applications box, as shown in Figure 4.5. When this box is checked, PHP code in your web pages runs automatically whenever a page is viewed. You can use it add dynamic web features to your pages.

It's a good idea to leave this feature enabled, even if you don't use PHP. Some web-editing applications assume that PHP is available and may include code automatically. There's no significant performance penalty in using this feature, so it can be left on permanently.

4.5 Enabling PHP features for dynamic web pages.

Replacing the default web page

The web page you've just seen is defined by a set of files at /Library/Server/Web/Data/Sites/ Default. If you use Finder to view this folder, as shown in Figure 4.6, you see the following items:

- **A set of default.html files with two letter extensions.** These files define the contents of the default page and support different languages; for example, default.html.en supports English. The web server selects the correct file from each user's Mac settings.

- **A 'favicon' file.** This is a small graphic file in the .ico format that adds a tiny graphic to the left of the URL in each browser's URL bar. The default file holds the Apple logo.

- **A PNG graphic file called ServerCenter.png.** This holds the main graphic for the page.

- **A small file called info.php.** This is a very small piece of PHP code. By default, it does nothing.

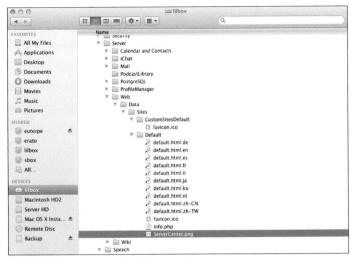

4.6 The files that create the default web page.

If you replace the contents of this folder with your own files, the web server displays them instead of the original default page.

Your replacement page can be as simple or as complex as you want. For this example, we create a very simple replacement by following these steps:

1. **Turn off the web server in Server App.**

2. **Make a copy of the /Default folder in Finder.** Right-click the folder, and select Copy "Default" from the floating menu. Select a different location, right-click again, and select Paste. You may need to authenticate for permission before copying.

Making a copy of the /Default folder is optional but recommended. It creates a safety copy of the original files, so you can reinstall them if you want to.

Note

3. **Drag the contents of the /Default folder to the trash.**

4. **Launch Text Edit.** You can find it in /Applications.

5. **Add some text to the file, and increase the size.** The content doesn't matter.

6. **Save the file to the /Library/Server/Web/Data/Sites/Default folder as "default. html."** Make sure you save it with the .html extension.

7. **Restart the web server.**

8. **Click the link at the bottom right of the page.**

You should see your new page, as shown in Figure 4.7.

4.7 Replacing the default server page with a simple HTML file created in Text Edit.

Genius

If you're used to manually written HTML, you may be wondering where the raw code is hidden. When you save a file as HTML in Text Edit, it creates the HTML code automatically, so you don't need to type it in manually. You can see the original code by selecting Preferences and clicking the Open and Save tab. Check the box beside Ignore rich text commands in HTML files. When you next load an HTML file, Text Edit displays the raw HTML and doesn't try to render it as rich text.

Caution

If you use Lion Server's wiki feature, the default page, which includes your default page if you change it, is replaced by a new set of pages created by Wiki Server 3. Currently, it's difficult for beginners to host custom pages and wiki pages at the same time in Lion Server. More details are provided later in this chapter.

Designing more complex pages

Because the file location of the pages is fixed, you can use any standard web editor to create a more professional page. If you save it to the default folder, it is displayed by the web server.

But note that if you look again at Figure 4.4, the list of links along the bottom of the page includes critical Lion Server features such as webmail.

These features can be accessed only through these web links. If you create a page that doesn't include them, your users won't be able to access them—at all.

This isn't a problem as long as you don't need these features. But if you do want to offer them to network users, you have to add equivalent links to your custom page design.

Adding other websites

In theory, you can host multiple web pages on Lion Server by following these steps:

1. **Click the + (plus) icon at the lower left of the pane.**

2. **The dialog shown in Figure 4.8 should appear.**

3. **Fill in the domain name.** This is the local, private, or public domain name for the site. (You can find more about this option later in this section.)

Note

If Lion Server can't resolve the domain name, it displays a small red warning LED. If it can resolve the name, the LED turns green.

4. **Fill in an IP address.** For a public site, this is the IP address associated with your registered domain name.

5. **Leave the port set to 80.** (Port 80 is the default for all web pages. Don't change it without an exceptionally good reason.)

6. **Leave the CustomSitesDefault content folder unchanged, unless you prefer to host your files in a different location.** (You can find this folder in /Library/Server/Web/Data/Sites/.)

7. **Optionally, you can select one or more groups in the Who Can Access field to limit access to specific users.** By default, your site can be viewed by anyone.

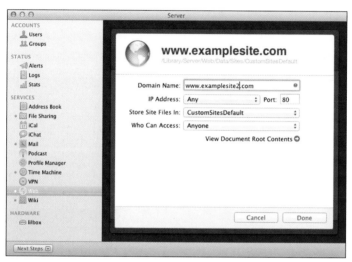

4.8 Adding a website.

In practice, as of Lion Server 10.7.2 this feature doesn't work. Apple has posted a fix for experts at http://support.apple.com/kb/HT4838. But the fix is complex and requires command-line skills, and it's overwritten whenever you restart Lion Server in Server App.

Caution

Making a website visible online is rather more complicated than setting up a web server and preparing files for it. To use Lion Server online, you must set up a NAT service, as described in Chapter 10. But you also must set up *certificates,* special files that identify you and your site to web users. You can use Lion Server on a local network without certificates. But if you try to make your pages visible online without setting up certificate security, visitors see a warning message, and some browsers won't show your site at all. For more information about working with certificates, see Chapter 10.

Unless you're an Apache 2 expert and are comfortable creating and editing configuration files, it's best to assume that this feature doesn't work as advertised and that currently you can host only a single site with Lion Server.

The instructions above are included in case this changes in a future update.

Understanding E-mail Technology

E-mail is less glamorous than the web, but it's used in homes and offices every day. Most users rely on an ISP for their e-mail. The ISP runs a *mail server,* a computer or network application dedicated to sending and receiving e-mail. Where your personal *mail client* application—such as Mac Mail, shown in Figure 4.9, or the mail reader in iOS—manages your personal mail, a mail server manages mail for everyone who accesses it. Users log in to the mail server to send and receive e-mail.

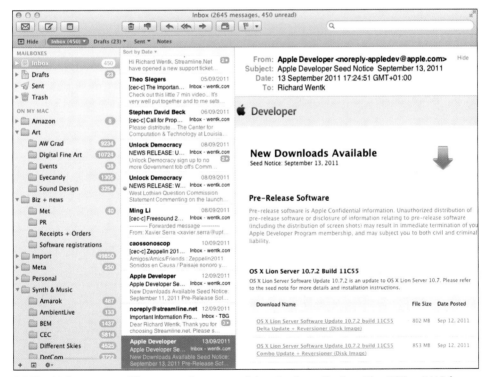

4.9 Mac Mail can access different e-mail servers and download e-mail using either POP or IMAP for each server.

Introducing basic e-mail technology

Lion Server can be set up to provide a mail server, with optional web mail support. To set it up correctly, you should be familiar with these three e-mail technologies:

- **POP (Post Office Protocol).** POP is a simple but popular and reliable e-mail system with limited features. It's sometimes known as POP 3, because the third version is the most widely used.

- **IMAP (Internet Message Access Protocol).** IMAP is widely used by businesses and provides more advanced mail features than POP. It's ideal for network use; for example, IMAP makes it easy for users to manage a single e-mail account from different devices.

- **SMTP (Simple Mail Transfer Protocol).** POP and IMAP are used for receiving mail. SMTP is a common system used to send it.

Some organizations, both public and private, offer web mail as an alternative or complementary service. Under the hood, web mail is very similar to conventional e-mail, but users access it through a web page instead of an e-mail client. The web page has a direct link to a server, and the dynamic HTML that creates the page accesses e-mail through IMAP and SMTP. The details are hidden so users can read and send e-mail as easily as possible. IMAP and SMTP configuration details are built into the web page, and users don't need to set them up manually.

Understanding e-mail issues

E-mail isn't a very secure service. Almost from the earliest days of e-mail, it has been plagued by various security threats and nuisances. These are especially problematic on mixed PC and Mac networks. These issues are included:

- **Spam.** Junk e-mail can clutter inboxes and waste resources. For the last few years, spam has accounted for around 75 percent of all e-mail traffic, as monitored by various security sources. Mail servers include spam filtering as a necessity rather than a luxury.

- **Viruses.** E-mails with viruses and other *malware* (dangerous content) can infect an entire network. Infected computers can be scanned for useful information such as personal and credit card details. They also can be taken over and run remotely to generate and send spam, without the user knowing.

- **Phishing.** Phishing e-mails pretend to be from a secure source—often a major online service such as Google or PayPal, as shown in Figure 4.10—and attempt to manipulate users into logging in to a random website with their username and password.

- **Relaying.** If a mail server is set up to relay messages—receive them and forward them automatically, hackers can use it to disguise the spam they send. This wastes resources, and at worst the server may be blacklisted as a spam source by the rest of the Internet.

Security issues can create catastrophic problems for a network. Losing one Mac to an e-mail problem is bad, but if e-mail isn't protected correctly, problems can spread over an entire network.

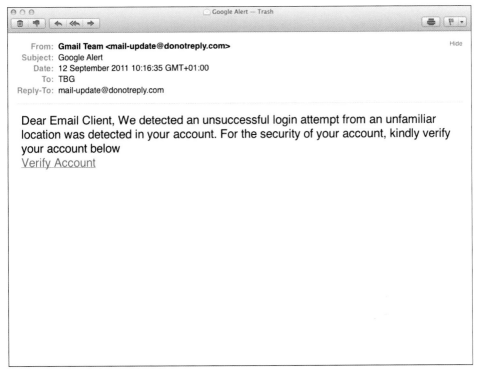

4.10 This e-mail isn't really from Gmail, and the Verify Account link leads to a bogus website that logs the details that users enter, so their accounts can be stolen.

Other more basic and practical issues are involved in running a server. Services may need to be limited to minimize the disk space used and to prevent any one user compromising the performance of the server. These practical issues are included:

- **Maximum message size.** It's often useful to set a large message size so users can receive large attachments, but limit quotas (see the next item) to prevent them from keeping old attachments on the server.

- **User disk quotas.** Quotas limit the amount of disk space each user's mailbox is allowed on the server.

- **Local and Internet e-mail addresses.** When set up correctly, local e-mail addresses, which end in .local, are partially interchangeable with Internet e-mail addresses. But getting the translation process to work correctly can be tricky sometimes.

- **Security and authentication.** Various schemes are used to keep mail access secure and private. Some require certificates; see the note earlier in this chapter. Others rely on hidden network services.

Setting Up Mail Server

Server App includes a simple mail server feature naturally called Mail Server. When running, it provides basic e-mail for network users. Optionally, it also can provide web-mail services.

Mail Server is easy to set up, but can be tricky to use. Integrating user accounts with the mail service and making sure e-mail addresses are compatible with them requires some thought.

Making Mail Server visible to Internet users is more difficult again. This chapter introduces basic setup, explores the security features, and demonstrates how to set up the Mac Mail client so it can use the mail server.

Connecting Mail Server to the Internet is discussed in Chapter 10.

Comparing local e-mail with ISP e-mail

This chapter explains how to set up a private e-mail service on a local network. The server isn't visible on the Internet, and users can send messages only to other network users.

Before you read Chapter 10 and take the extra steps needed to move the server, consider that e-mail can be difficult to administer and keep secure. So it may be easier to off-load e-mail maintenance to an ISP or large web-mail service.

The advantages of using external e-mail are obvious. An ISP is likely to have a protected network with good e-mail security. Some ISPs offer free or cheap e-mail filtering. If your ISP doesn't, various online services can provide the service as an add-on.

If you use commercial web hosting, your domain hosting account almost certainly includes a large number of customizable e-mail addresses that can be distributed among your network users.

A local e-mail server is essential only when you need to keep local e-mail secure and private. In theory, all online e-mail can be intercepted. If it never moves beyond a local network, it's inherently more secure. You also can control e-mail security and set it up to your own specification. Optionally, you also can keep your own e-mail logs for security reasons.

The other advantage is that you can customize local e-mail settings to support very large attachments or large disk quotas—for example, to support e-mail transfer of large media files.

And finally it's not difficult to give every user two addresses—a secure local e-mail account for private messages and a public online account for exchanging messages with the rest of the world.

As a rough guide, for basic home or office, it's likely that ISP e-mail can do all you need. A local server is worth the time only for more specialized applications that require extra flexibility, extra security, or extra-large data volumes.

Enabling Mail Server on a local network

To set up Mail Server on your local network, follow these steps:

1. **Launch Server App, if it's not already running.**

2. **Select the Mail item from the menu at the left, as shown in Figure 4.11.**

3. **Leave the first (domain name) setting unchanged.**

4. **Don't check the box beside Relay outgoing mail through ISP.**

5. **Optionally, check the box for Limit mail… to set a user quota.** The default quota is 200MB per user.

6. **Optionally, enable the Webmail service if you want to give your users access to webmail.**

7. **Click the big toggle switch to On.**

Mail Server takes a few moments to start. Wait until the activity indicator at the bottom right of the pane disappears. Your users can now send and receive e-mail.

Genius

If you click the Edit Filtering Settings… button, you see some default filtering options for removing viruses and spam. It's unlikely you need these on a small local network where users may well know each other. If you connect Mail Server to the Internet, you can use these options to eliminate security threats. The filtering is basic, but it should cover all issues—except for phishing, which can only be solved by educating users.

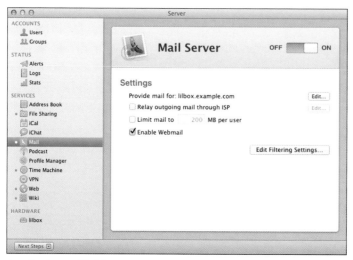

4.11 Setting up Mail Server.

Using Webmail

The Webmail service is the simplest way to access local mail. It uses the user account system described in Chapter 3 to read and set e-mail addresses. Unfortunately, this feature doesn't work correctly, so some manual adjustment may be necessary before you can use the service as intended.

Logging in to Webmail

The default server page and the wiki Home Page described in Chapter 5 both include a link to the Webmail service. If you've changed the default web server page and this link isn't visible, you can access the service directly from http://[hostname]/webmail.

To login, type your user name and password into the boxes and select Login, as shown in Figure 4.12.

Genius

You can use the http:// [hostname]/webmail address to access Webmail from any mobile device, including an iPhone. Although the iPhone has a tiny screen, you can access all the Webmail features from Safari. To zoom in and make your messages less tiny and more readable, use the standard iPhone pinch gesture.

Getting started with Webmail

After you login, you see the page shown in Figure 4.13. If you've used any webmail service, you should find that most of the features are familiar. A list of mailboxes appears at the left. If you have more than one e-mail account, you can create multiple boxes here to receive messages from all of them.

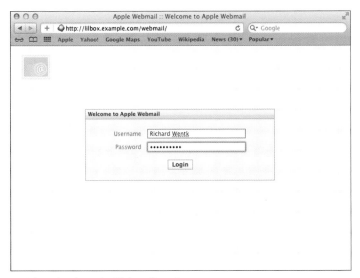

4.12 Logging in to the Webmail service.

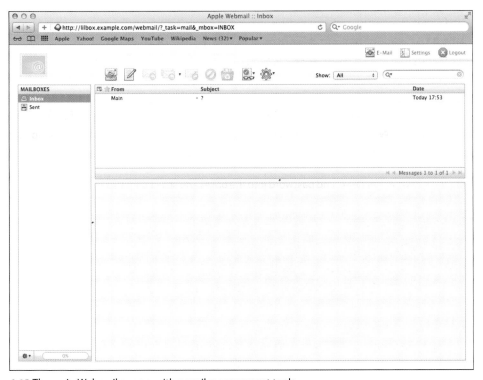

4.13 The main Webmail screen, with e-mail management tools.

You can create mail, read mail you've received, trash old messages, and so on using the icons across the top of the window. Table 4.1 lists the function of each icon, from left to right.

Table 4.1 Webmail icons

Icon	Function
Check mail	Checks the server, and downloads mail. In practice, mail arrives in your inbox almost instantly, so you don't often need to check it manually.
Create e-mail	Opens an e-mail editor, with a Send button at the bottom left.
Reply	Creates a reply to the currently selected e-mail.
Reply to all	Creates a reply to a bulk or list e-mail, and includes every recipient. The tiny triangle to the right of this icon selects All or List reply options.
Forward	Forwards the e-mail to another recipient.
Trash	Deletes the e-mail.
Mark as Junk	The green recycling box icon flags the e-mail as spam.
Tag and flag	The star and glasses icon includes a menu with four tagging options: read, unread, flagged, and unflagged.
Actions	The gear icon includes special features. Use this option to print, download, and resend messages. You also can use a Show source option to view the raw unformatted text of the message.

Checking your Identity

Before you can use the service, check your Identity—the user setting that defines your e-mail address. By default, Webmail creates an address based on your *display name*—your full name and surname. It should create an address based on your *account* name—the combined name Lion Server generates from your display name automatically when you create your user account in Server App.

The technical problem is that the display name usually includes a space. The account name doesn't. E-mail addresses can't include spaces, so you must repair this manually before you can send e-mail.

To check and repair your Identity, follow these steps:

1. **Select the Settings icon near the top right of the page.**

2. **Click the Identities tab.**

3. **Click your address under the Identities column at the left, as shown in Figure 4.14.**

4. **Check the E-Mail field; if there's a space, remove it.**

5. **Click Save to save the changes.**

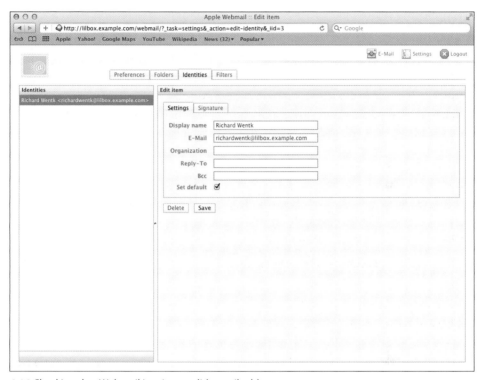

4.14 Checking that Webmail is using a valid e-mail address.

 Caution The e-mail address *must* match your account name. Don't try to customize it. If you do, the mail server doesn't recognize your customized address and recipients can't reply to you.

Sending mail

To send a message, click the Create E-mail icon. You see the e-mail editor shown in Figure 4.15. Table 4.2 lists the icons.

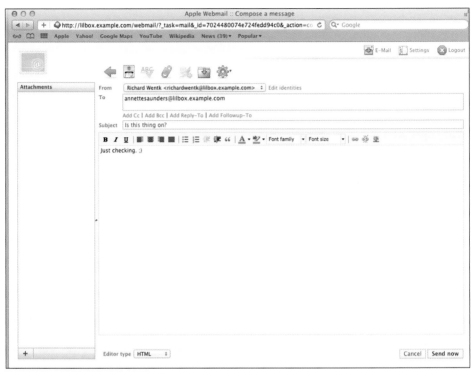

4.15 Working with the Webmail editor.

Table 4.2 E-Mail Editor Icons

Icon	Function
Message list	The green arrow returns you to the message list. You also can access the list by selecting the E-Mail icon near the top right of the page.
Send now	Send the e-mail. You also can click the Send now button at the bottom right of the page.
Check spelling	The ABC/check icon does nothing. (If you're viewing the editor in Safari on a Mac, Safari uses your Mac's spell-check settings. Misspelled words are underlined automatically.)
Attachment	Use the paperclip icon to add an attachment to the file. Attachments are listed in the column at the left of the page.
Insert signature	If you have signature text defined in Settings, this icon appends it to a message.
Action	The gear icon displays a selection of extra options: Return receipt, Delivery status notification, Priority, and Save location. These special features are rarely used, but they can be useful on a network when you need to check that a message has been delivered and read.

When you click Send now, your message is passed to the mail server service. Recipients can read it using Webmail, after they login. They also can use a standard e-mail client.

Receiving mail

As soon as a user logs in, Webmail lists his messages. If new messages have arrived, they're tagged with a small star icon, which shows they're unread, as shown in Figure 4.16.

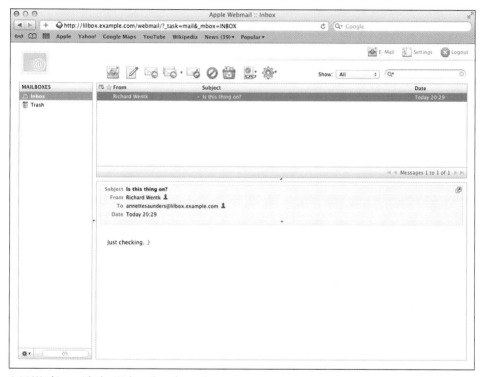

4.16 Working with the Webmail reader and manager.

The mail reader page has at least one strange quirk. As of version 10.7.2, you can't delete messages until you enable the Trash folder, and you have to enable the folder manually.

To enable the folder, follow these steps:

1. **Select Settings near the top right of the page.**

2. **Select Special Folders from the Section column at the left.**

3. **Select the Trash item from the Trash menu.**

4. **Optionally, you can enable the other special folders: Drafts, Sent, and Junk.**

5. **Click Save.** When you return to the E-Mail page, the new folders are listed at the left, and you can now delete e-mails, tag them as junk, and so on.

Using Mac Mail and other clients

The server can be temperamental when used with a client and must be set up carefully.

Most Internet mail servers use alternative server names, such as mail.[hostname], pop.[hostname], and so on.

When you set up Mail Server using Server App, you can't use these aliases. It's important that the mail server names you use in your client software match the server name you defined in Server App. It's also critical that all user e-mail addresses and accounts include the same matching server name.

This example illustrates the settings that work for Mac Mail. When Mac Mail runs for the first time, it goes through a set of dialogs that create a user account. To create a working account, follow these steps:

1. **Launch Mac Mail.** It's in /Applications.

2. **In the first dialog, enter your name.** This name is for display only; it appears next to your e-mail address in messages, but it isn't used while sending and receiving.

3. **Enter your e-mail address.** This address *must* match the e-mail address in your user account. (Refer to Chapter 3.) The domain name or local host name after the @ sign *must* match the domain/host name in the Mail Server settings.

4. **Enter your e-mail password.** This password *must* match the one used by your user account, as shown in Figure 4.17. Click Continue.

5. **Mac Mail is likely to complain that Mail Server's certificate is invalid.** For local e-mail, ignore this warning. (For more about installing valid certificates, see Chapter 10.)

6. **The next dialog defines the settings for incoming e-mail.** Begin by filling in the Description field. This is for your benefit; it appears as the connection/account name in Mac Mail, but it has no other use.

4.17 Setting up Mac Mail to work with Mail Server.

7. **Set the Incoming Mail Server name.** This name *must* match the host/domain name set up for Mail Server in Server App. (See earlier in this chapter for details.)

8. **Set the User Name.** This is the e-mail address used to login to the server. Enter the same address you used in Step 3, as shown in Figure 4.18.

Caution

By default, Mac Mail gets this wrong. It inserts the account name with no domain/ host name. You need to change this to show the full e-mail address.

9. **Click Continue to show the incoming server settings.** Select Password. Leave the Secure Sockets Layer option unchecked.

10. **Click Continue again to show the outgoing server settings, shown in Figure 4.19.**

11. **Fill in the Description field.** Again, this is for display only.

12. **Set the Outgoing Mail Server.** Use the host/domain name you set up for Mail Server.

13. **Check the Use Authentication box.** Fill in the same user name and password you used in Steps 3 and 8.

4.18 Setting up incoming server settings.

4.19 Setting up outgoing server settings.

14. **Click past the certificate warning if it appears again.**

15. **Click Create to go online and check your e-mail.** You can now exchange e-mail with other users on the network, who can use Webmail or their e-mail clients.

Exploring Mail in Server Admin

The Mail control panels in Server Admin, shown in Figure 4.20, include extra setup and management options that aren't included in Server App. To view this page, launch Server Admin and click the Mail item in the list at the left.

Most options are intended for expert system administrators, but it can be worth exploring them briefly. You can leave the default settings unchanged. The one significant exception is the item labeled Refuse messages larger than…, shown in the figure. You can set this to a larger number to support larger attachments.

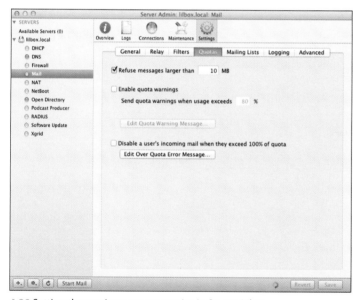

4.20 Setting the maximum message size in Server Admin.

How Do I Enhance Collaboration with Wikis, Blogs, and Chat?

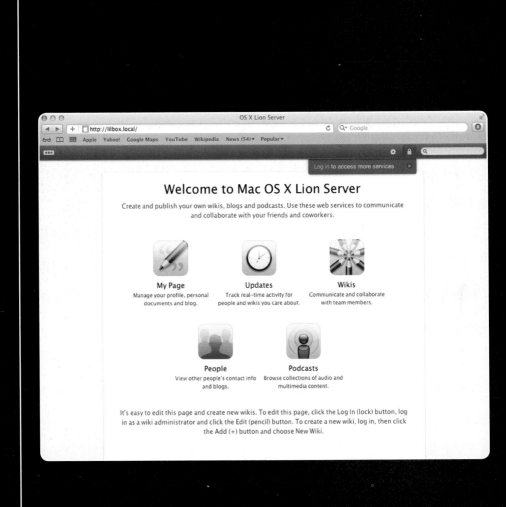

Lion Server includes wiki, blog, and chat features that make it easier for users to share important information and updates as they happen. Wikis make it possible for groups to share information about projects in a collaborative environment. Blogs are ideal for posting updates and personal information. Chat can replace phone calls, video calls, and text messages. For short communications, it also can replace e-mail. Combining these features creates a powerful and productive environment for project collaboration and for sharing personal updates.

Understanding Wiki Server 3

Traditionally, web pages are *read only:* Viewers can't change them. Understandably, individuals and organizations want total control over the content of their pages, so they don't allow editing by outsiders. And web design can be challenging, so it's often left to professionals.

Lion Server's Wiki Server 3 provides a simplified page design system that doesn't need professional skills. Pages can be created and edited by individuals or by groups, who can work together to share comments and information about projects, share files, check schedules and events, and access related content such as podcasts and video files.

Because Wiki Server 3 is web-based, pages can be viewed in any compatible browser on any platform. Some of Lion Server's features are available only to Mac and iOS users. But Wiki Server 3 can be accessed from almost any computer with a working browser.

Genius Wikis and blogs live on a special website created by Lion Server. But Lion Server can manage more than one site at a time. The wiki and blog features use web technology, but they're independent of any other web pages you put up on your server. You can give your users access to both, either, or neither.

Note The Wiki Server Home Page isn't just for wikis; it's the main web portal to many key user features in Lion Server, including web mail, Lion Server's calendar, and the profile manager. For more details see Chapters 4, 6, and 8.

Understanding blogs

Figure 5.1 shows a new default blog post made in Wiki Server 3 and viewed with Safari. Blogs are simple web pages with three unusual features:

- **Blogs are easy to create.** Blog software hides the complexity of full-fat web design behind simplified page design tools. The tools limit what can be done on a blog page, but they make it easy to create web pages—so easy that anyone can do it.

- **Blogs are arranged in date order, like a diary.** Blogs were invented as online diaries, but date ordered posts are also useful for other applications such as project updates.

Blogs may include a section for comments added by readers. The blog software automatically keeps track of comments as they appear and adds them to the page. Everyone can view existing comments, and some users can be allowed to add comments.

5.1 Lion Server's default empty blog post lists the information you can include on a blog page.

Caution Lion Server's blog feature is perhaps best described as understated. If you're used to other blogging platforms, you may find it rather minimal. It's also important to understand that the blog feature is *disabled by default*, and every user has to enable it for himself. It isn't difficult to do this, but the blog option is hidden, so it's easy to miss it. For details, see later in this chapter.

Understanding wikis

Like blogs, wikis—the default Lion Server wiki page is shown in Figure 5.2—use a similar simplified editing system. Unlike blogs, wikis can be updated by many different users who share full responsibility for the content.

The Wikipedia (www.wikipedia.org) online encyclopedia is one the best known wikis, and it demonstrates how wikis work in practice. Each article can be edited by any reader at any time. A minority of edits are controversial or unwelcome. The majority aren't, so the value and accuracy of the content remains relatively high.

But a wiki doesn't have to be an encyclopedia. The wiki format is ideal for collaborative project papers and specifications, for shared community notes, and even for recipes and family updates.

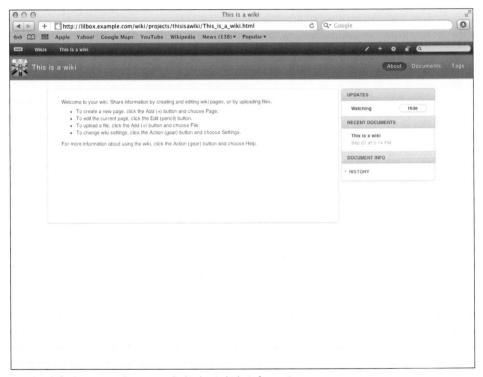

5.2 The default empty wiki page includes basic help information.

Genius

Wiki is Hawaiian for "quick." The word was chosen by creator Ward Cunningham because he wanted the technology to be "the simplest online database that could possibly work."

Working with Wiki Server 3

Wiki Server 3 includes both blog and wiki tools, and also includes links to the calendar and schedule features in Lion Server. The result is more than the sum of its parts. The individual elements are:

- **A Home Page.** This is the main entry point to Wiki Server 3, with large icons that link to the other features. Wiki Server 3 includes a smaller floating version of this page for quick access from any content.

- **Personal pages.** Known as My Page, these are for projects or individuals. Home pages are relatively static and are often used to display summary information about an individual, group, or project.

- **Wiki pages.** These are ideal for collaborative articles and for content that evolves as a project develops.

- **Uploaded files.** Also known as Documents, Wiki Server includes a general web-based file sharing feature that can be used to share documents, media content, and other useful files.

- **Blogs.** These timed and dated series of pages are often used for updates, comments, and news.

- **Podcasts.** These video and audio files are usually created with Lion Server's Podcast Producer feature. (For more details, see Chapter 7.)

In addition to the basic features, Wiki Server 3 also includes an update/watch option that lists recent activity. This feature condenses changes into a list that looks similar to an online message board.

Caution Wiki Server 3 is web-based, and content can be viewed and edited on most compatible browsers on most platforms. For example, it's just as easy to log in and make changes from a Windows PC running Google Chrome as it is from a Mac running Safari. However, Wiki Server 3's support for the iPhone and iPad is limited. While it's possible to view all wiki content, it isn't possible to edit it.

Genius You can find some examples of wiki applications on the Learn about Wikis ➪ Ways to use Wiki Server 3 page in Wiki Help, which is accessed from the help menu item under the gear icon at the top of the wiki page. The online help is comprehensive and worth exploring.

Comparing Lion Server and Wordpress

Wordpress (www.wordpress.org) is a popular free software suite that runs on almost any web server and provides a powerful and sophisticated blogging environment, with an impressive selection of plug-ins and add-ons, many of which are also free. Because of its popularity and relative ease of use, Wordpress has become an informal industry standard.

Lion Server's blog features are less sophisticated than those built into Wordpress. For example, it's very difficult for non-experts to customize the look and layout of pages created by Lion Server or to add extra features.

However, it's important to understand that Wordpress and Lion Server are designed to do two different jobs.

In Lion Server, the emphasis is on collaboration. Visual style isn't an obvious priority. But it's easy to use calendars for scheduling and to share files and media content.

Wordpress is aimed more at writers and online publishers who need to create a strong visual impression and who need good tools for managing comments that may include spam.

Lion Server's features work best in a small relatively closed environment where users are trusted to collaborate and where content is more important than looks and image. Wordpress is a better solution for internet-wide publishing, publicity, and self-promotion.

It's possible to install Wordpress on Lion Server and use it as an alternative blogging platform, but the process isn't completely straightforward and beginners may find it challenging. For more information, see Appendix A.

Using Wiki Server 3

The wiki feature in Lion Server is disabled by default. Enabling it is a very simple process, described here. After it's running, network users can log in and begin to create and update content.

Enabling Wiki Server

To enable Wiki Server, follow these steps:

1. **Launch Server App, if it's not already running.**
2. **Select the Wiki item from the menu at the left.**
3. **Click the switch at the top right, as shown in Figure 5.3.**

5.3 Enabling Wiki Server with one giant virtual switch.

Selecting wiki creators

By default, all users are allowed to create wikis. Optionally, you can use the menu near the top of the pane to limit access to a smaller subset of users, as follows:

1. **Click the menu, and select the option labeled only some users.**

2. **Click the + (plus) icon at the bottom-left corner of the sheet that appears, as shown in Figure 5.4.**

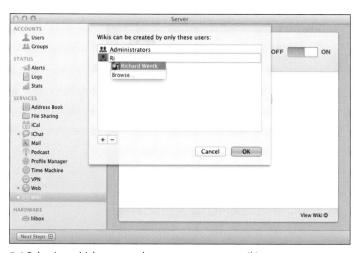

5.4 Selecting which users and groups can create a wiki.

3. **If you know the name of the person or group you want to add, type the first couple of letters.** The name appears in the menu. Select the name to add the person or group.

4. **If you need to browse the user list, type any letter and select Browse from the menu.** You can then drag multiple groups and names into the window. Click OK when you're finished.

Note Users with network administration privileges are allowed to read and edit everyone's wikis, documents, and blogs. So if you're a network administrator, you have unlimited access to all the content on the server and can change it at will.

Viewing the Home Page

When you enable it, Wiki Server creates a set of web pages for you. This is an automatic process, and it takes a few moments. Check the status of the activity indicator at the bottom right of the Server pane to see when it's finished.

When the activity indicator disappears, click the View Wiki link above it. You should see the main server Home Page shown in Figure 5.5. This page displays the main collaborative features built into Wiki Server and includes a link to Lion Server's webmail (see Chapter 4) and to the Profile Manager (see Chapter 8).

Genius If you make Lion Server's web server accessible to the Internet, the wiki pages become visible too. You can fix this by using two separate servers—one for Internet traffic and one for local wiki access. Because wiki pages are web pages, there's no other way to split web traffic and wiki traffic.

Working with the tool bar

Every page displayed by Wiki Server 3 includes a toolbar at the top of the page, which you can see in many of the figures in this chapter. The list of visible icons depends on the context, but you can typically find some or all of the following:

- **Home.** This icon looks like a film strip and links to the small floating Home Page, with a similar selection of links: Home, My Page, Updates, Wikis, and People. Click each item to select it.

- **Content.** This appears as one or more words that link to relevant content. The format is known as a breadcrumb trail; each section is followed by one or more sub-links. For example, when you select People, a list that appears where you can select a person from the names that appear to right of People. If you select that person's blog, Blog appears to the right of his name. And so on.

- **Edit.** This icon looks like a pen and is visible only on pages with editable wiki or blog content. Click it to load Wiki Server 3's simplified web editor, described in more detail later in the chapter.

- **Add.** Select the + (plus) icon to add new content, which may include a new page, new section, new blog post, or new files, depending on the context.

- **Action.** Click the gear icon for help. In certain contexts, it also shows a link to a page called Settings, which displays extra features.

- **Login.** Select the padlock to log in and log out.

5.5 The Wiki Server entry page—a portal to all of Lion Server's collaborative features.

Working with My Page, blogs, and files

The My Page feature provides a profile page—also known as the About page—for every active Wiki Server user. You can provide information about yourself on this page and create a cache of documents and files for other users to download. Optionally, you can create and update a personal blog.

Genius

Think of My Page as your personal space on the server, with information about you, a selection of useful files that other users can download, and information about personal updates and projects.

Logging in

Before you can use any of the features of Wiki Server, you must log in with your network account. (For more information about creating and managing network accounts, see Chapter 3.)

To log in, follow these steps:

1. **Open a web browser on any computer on the network.** All the popular web browsers are compatible. Navigate to the server's wiki login page at http://[hostname]/wiki.

2. **Click the padlock icon in the toolbar near the top right of the page.**

3. **Enter your account name and password, as shown in Figure 5.6.**

4. **Click the Log In button.** The locked padlock is replaced by an open padlock when you log in successfully. The rest of the screen remains the same.

5. **Optionally, check the Remember Me box to tell your browser to remember your password.** This is not a secure option! Anyone who knows your username and has access to your computer can log in without knowing your password.

6. **To log out when finished, click the open padlock.**

Note

Webmail—marked e-mail at the bottom of the wiki page—has its own separate login. Logging into your wiki account doesn't give you access to webmail, and vice versa. Guests can select the Wikis and People links without logging in at all, although some wikis can be hidden from guests, for security and privacy.

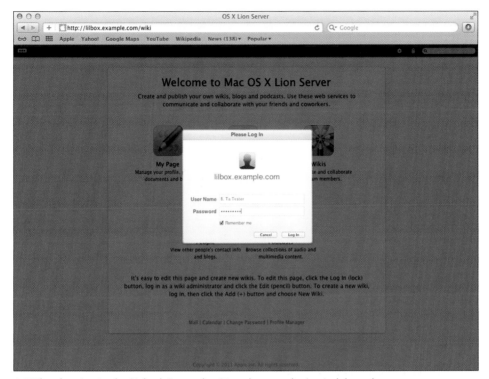

5.6 When logging in, don't check Remember Me unless you don't mind that other users can access your account from your computer!

Caution Wiki Server users aren't logged out automatically when a Mac or PC shuts down. Most browsers include a feature that restores open pages after a shut down, and this bypasses Lion Server's login security. If a user doesn't log out manually, the next person who uses that computer can access the previous user's account. It's important to tell users that *they must log out manually when they finish.*

Getting started with My Page

My Page appears on the list of features in Wiki Server 3 that you see before you log in (refer to Figure 5.5). To access My Page, log in and click the My Page icon. You see the page shown in Figure 5.7.

My Page is a simple feature with plenty of options. In outline, it's your personal page on the server. It offers three kinds of content that you can share with other network users. Use it to share personal and project information and files.

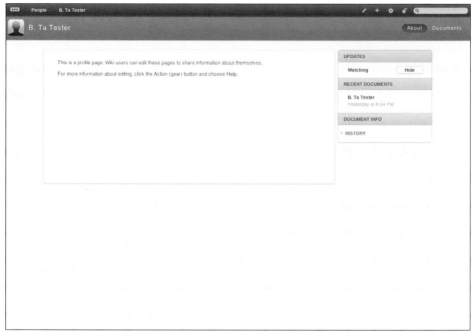

5.7 Viewing an empty My Page.

You can view coworkers' and family members' pages to keep track of what they're doing and to access files they want to share.

The rest of this section introduces details of editing, organization, and navigation. But before going further, it's useful to learn the functions of the content links that appear at the top right of each My Page. If you can remember these links, you'll understand how the content is organized.

These links are available:

- **About.** Use this to show personal or project data. When a user clicks your name in any of the other pages generated by Wiki Server 3, this is the page she sees. You can add contact details, interests, areas of responsibility, and other personal information to this page.

- **Documents.** Use this to share documents and files. Files are uploaded to the web server ready to be downloaded by other users. Files can include freeform documents, such as pages of text and graphics. They also can include other media, including audio and video files, PDF documents, and so on.

● **A blog option.** Use this for diary-like updates and progress reports. (This feature is disabled by default in Lion Server, and only appears when users enable it.)

Genius

Uploading files to the web server can waste space. For local network users, it's more efficient to embed file links into blog posts or profile pages, and give users direct access to the files from their own copy of Finder. For details, see Chapter 6.

My Page also includes a sidebar at the right with three navigation and maintenance features:

● **Updates.** When "Watching" is visible, edits you make are listed for other users when they access their Updates link from the main Wiki Server menu. Click the "Hide" button—the text next to it changes to "Not watching"—to keep your edits hidden.

● **Recent documents.** This is a list of recent files uploaded to your documents area.

● **Document info.** In spite of the name, this has nothing to do with the documents area. Instead, it shows a history of edits and versions to the main page. Select each version to view it. You can select Show Changes to highlight edits, as shown in Figure 5.8.

5.8 Exploring the navigation and maintenance sidebar.

Using the Editor

One of the key features of Wiki Server 3 is the Post Editor, which is used for My Page, wiki entries, and blog posts.

The editor hides the complexity of the HTML (Hypertext Markup Language) used in professional web design behind simplified tools that work rather like a standard text editor.

When you click the pencil icon, a new toolbar appears with a set of editing icons, which are described over the next few pages. You also have Cancel or Save buttons at the far right, as shown in Figure 5.9. As you'd expect, Save makes your changes permanent, while Cancel reverts to the original document.

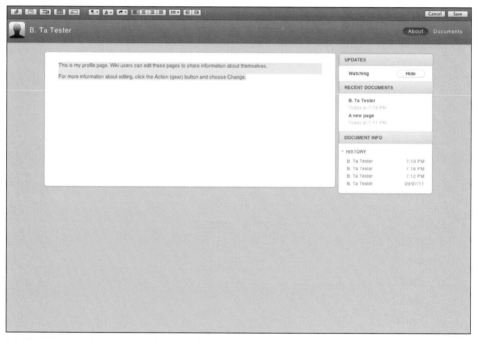

5.9 The Editor toolbar appears when you click the pencil icon.

The first group of icons manages embedded and attached files, and the icons are listed from left to right in Table 5.1. Figure 5.10 shows an edited page with two embedded items—a small piece of HTML and an audio file.

Genius

The icons aren't very clear or easy to understand. But if you hover your mouse over them, you see a tooltip for each one.

Table 5.1 Editor Options—Embedded and Attached Files

Option	Description
Attachment	This uploads an attachment and adds it to the page, creating a clickable download link. Use this option as an alternative to the Documents feature to embed files directly into a page.
Image	This uploads an image file and inserts it into the page. The file is scaled automatically to fit the page.
Audio or movie	This uploads an audio or video file and inserts it into the page embedded in a player.
Table	This inserts a simple table. Click the gray sidebars to add and remove rows, or add a header.
HTML snippet	Use this option to insert a block of raw HTML code. It appears inside a frame that has limited dimensions, so you can't use this feature to create complex effects.

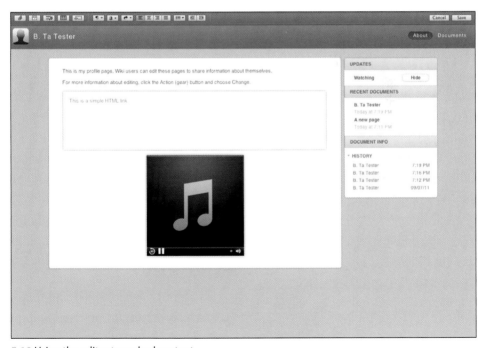

5.10 Using the editor to embed content.

Caution

As of version 10.7.2, the Table button appears intermittently.

Genius

All embedded items display a clickable delete button at the top left when you hover over them with the mouse. Deleting an item removes it from the server but doesn't affect the original source.

Table 5.2 shows the text- and link-editing options. You can apply a small number of preset styles to text, create and delete links in the text, manage justification, and create both numbered and bulleted lists.

Table 5.2 Editor Options—Text Styles and Links

Function	Description
Paragraph Styles	Sets one of a small selection of standard text styles, including three levels of headers, monospace, block quote, and standard paragraph.
Text Styles	Applies a small selection of preset colors, underlines, and highlights to the selected text.
Link Options	Creates links to various pages. Recent pages are shown for quick linking. Also includes an unlink option.
Justification	Four buttons that apply left, center, right and full-width justification to selected text.
List Options	Three buttons that create bulleted or numbered lists and control the indentation level of list items.
Indentation Options	Two buttons that add and remove a single tabbed indentation.

These are limited options, and there's no way to customize or extend them. But they're adequate for basic document creation. You can improve the look of documents further with the media embedding features. Figure 5.11 shows a simple example of styled text.

Genius

If you've used other blogging or web design tools, you may be wondering how to hotlink online files into your content. You can't. Wiki Server 3's editor is designed to make this impossible; all content is stored on the local server. However, you can always download content from a web page online and upload it to the server manually. (As with all web content, it's important to make sure you have copyright permission before you do this.)

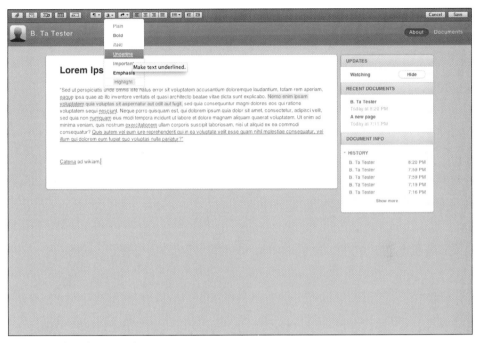

5.11 Using the editor to style text.

Caution
Because the editor is web-based, the usual right-click floating options available in many editors aren't available, and cut and paste are absent. For complex documents, you can save time by preparing the text in a word processor.

Creating a blog

Although you could use the History feature to create a diary-like blog, Wiki Server 3 includes a more powerful blog feature that supports comments and other basic blog features. To access it, select the Action (gear) icon and click Settings and then Services, as shown in Figure 5.12. Check the Services: Blog check box, and click Save at the bottom right to enable the blog editor.

The page reloads, and you see that a new Blog item has appeared in the list at the left. Select Blog, and you see the screen in Figure 5.13.

These options control who can read your blog and who can add comments to it. With the suggested settings shown in the figure, only you can edit your blog and add new entries, but everyone can read it. Only users with a login account can leave comments.

5.12 Enabling the blog feature.

5.13 Controlling blog settings.

Alternatively, you can give logged in users no access by default, but override this by typing one or more groups or individuals into the empty field at the top of the dialog to give them exclusive access.

The Comment Moderation field gives you the option to preview comments before they're published. If you're working with trusted family or colleagues, you can leave this option set to None, and comments appear immediately.

In less trustworthy environments, you may find it useful to check comments before allowing them to appear.

Don't forget to click Save to save the settings!

Note

Blogs are enabled individually for each user. Unless users enable the blog feature manually, they can't use it.

Genius

If the blog appears on the Internet, it's likely to attract link spam—comments that look like inane or vaguely relevant chit-chat, but which are really an excuse for the poster to embed a link to their website, which increases their search engine rankings. In theory, it's possible to filter link spam automatically. Unfortunately, Wiki Server 3 doesn't have this feature. So if your blog is visible online, it's useful to moderate comments manually—or at least to check comments regularly to make sure you're not being spammed.

Making a blog post

After blogging is enabled, a New Blog Post in My Blog option appears in the menu under the + (plus) icon on your main page.

Select this option to create a new post. Fill in a title; the title appears at the top of the post and is shown in summary listings of updates and new content elsewhere in Wiki Server 3.

You can then use the standard editor to add your words, images, and other content to the post, as shown in Figure 5.14.

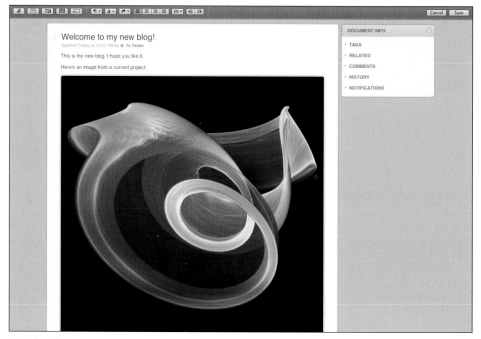

5.14 Creating a post.

Using Document Info

Blog posts have a unique sidebar at the right, labeled Document Info. This adds further optional features and search options, shown in full form in Figure 5.15. To add one of these options, click the disclosure triangle and then select the + (plus) icon.

From top to bottom, the sidebar includes the following:

- **Tags.** Tags are keywords. Adding tags makes it easier to find relevant posts when users search your blog. For example, on a family blog, you can tag all vacation posts with a "vacation" tag. Adding tags can be a chore, but the more tags you add, the easier it is to find content.

- **Related.** Use this feature to show other blog posts with more loosely related content. As with tags, this is a manual feature, but this feature includes a search tool that you can use to look for relevant keywords.

You can add multiple tags by typing Return after each one.

Genius

114

Genius

Wiki Server 3 adds an automated search option for each tag, selected with a button. Click the tag button to reveal a list of posts that share that tag. Tagging can be tedious, but it makes a big difference to the usability of your blog and helps organize content that would otherwise be difficult to find.

Note

The comment field is designed for small and short comments, not for long and extended replies. It's a limited facility. Extended debates and conversations are best left to other media, such as e-mail.

- **Comments.** Select this to reveal comments and to access a comment editor.
- **History.** This summarizes the new posts and edits on the blog.
- **Notifications.** You can opt to receive an e-mail when the document is updated; this is useful only when you're reading someone else's blog, when you allow others to edit your blog, or when a new comment is added.

Adding a comment

You can add comments to your own blog or to any other blog for which you have commenting privileges, as set by each user in his personal blog settings.

To add a comment, follow these steps, as shown in Figure 5.16:

1. **Select a user's Blog link to view her blog.**

2. **Click a post title to open it.**

3. **If the Comments field isn't expanded in the Document Info sidebar, click it to expand it.**

5.15 Using Document Info.

115

4. **Click the + (plus) icon to add a comment.**

5. **Click the check mark to save the comment, or click the X to cancel.**

Working with wikis

As mentioned earlier, wikis can be edited and created by everyone—or at least, everyone you've given wiki privileges to in Server App. All qualified users can created a wiki and edit an existing wiki.

Creating a wiki

To create a wiki, follow these steps:

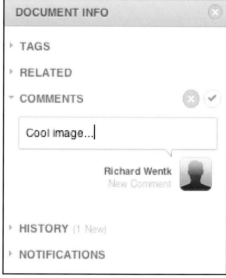

1. **Click the + (plus) icon in the top right of the toolbar.**

5.16 Adding a comment.

2. **Select New Wiki from the menu.**

3. **Enter a Name and Description for the new Wiki in the dialog that appears.** Optionally, you can upload an image file to customize the wiki icon. Click Next.

4. **Set the wiki access privileges, as shown in Figure 5.17.** By default, only you can read and edit the wiki, so you'll find it useful to change the settings to those in the figure.

5. **Click the Create button at the lower right.**

6. **Click the Go to Wiki link to view the new welcome page for the wiki.**

Note

To delete a wiki, click the gear icon and select the Delete Wiki… option. Only network administrators and the creator of a wiki are allowed to delete it.

Editing a wiki

Editing a wiki is just like editing a blog. Wiki Server 3 uses the same editor, and you can add the same kinds of content and apply the same text styles. The key difference is that there's no right-sidebar option for viewing comments because wikis don't support comments.

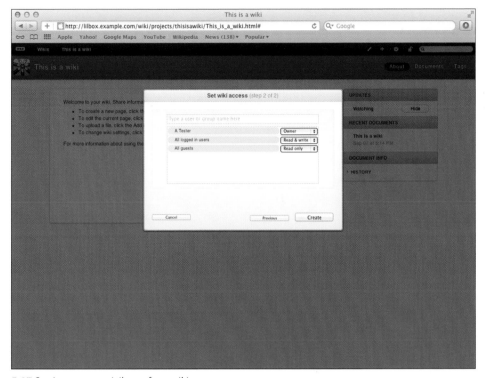

5.17 Setting access privileges for a wiki.

Changing wiki settings

Wiki owners (and network administrators) can change wiki settings at any time, to add or remove access for groups or individuals users.

To change the settings, click the gear icon and select Settings. You see the dialog shown in Figure 5.18, with four tabs at the left:

- **General.** Use this to change the name, description, and icon.

- **Permissions.** This repeats the permission dialog shown in Figure 5.17, with extra blog features.

- **Services.** You can enable a separate blog for each wiki and add an optional calendar for event scheduling. The calendar is visible to everyone who can view the wiki. (For more information about using a calendar, see Chapter 6.)

- **About Page.** You can create an optional About Page, which includes introductory text.

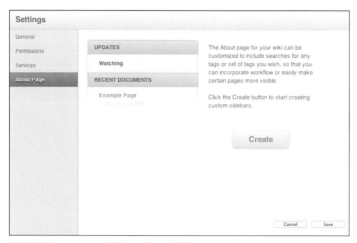

5.18 Setting access privileges for a wiki.

Using the wiki

Coming to grips with the organization of pages, blogs, wikis, people, and updates in Wiki Server 3 can be challenging. The features aren't complex, but the relationships between them are perhaps not as obvious as they could be.

A useful timesaver is to understand that a set of wiki pages is very similar to a set of user pages, but with shared editing.

In practice, there's lots of overlap between the features of an individual's user space and a wiki. Both support an About page, document sharing, and an optional blog. The calendar feature is exclusive to a wiki. The other difference is that editing duties are shared between all wiki users.

But under the hood, both are collections of web pages with similar features. Instead of attempting to master wikis as if they were unrelated, you can take what you know about user pages and apply it to wikis almost unchanged.

Working with people, tags, and updates

As blogs and wikis develop, it becomes harder to find useful information by random browsing. Wiki Server 3 includes three features that help you find information quickly:

- **People.** A list of active contributors
- **Updates.** A table that shows recent activity
- **Tags.** A list of tags, which works rather like an index

You can access People and Updates from the Home Page. The Tags feature is harder to find, but it's easy to work with after you know where it is.

Viewing People

To view a list of contributors, select the People icon on the Wiki Server 3 Home Page. Figure 5.19 shows a typical list of contributors. You can do two things on this page:

- **Click the name of each user to view their About page.** From there, you can easily navigate to her documents and blog.

- **Turn updates on and off for each user.** Click the buttons at the right of his name. When Hide Updates is showing, new content isn't listed by the Updates feature.

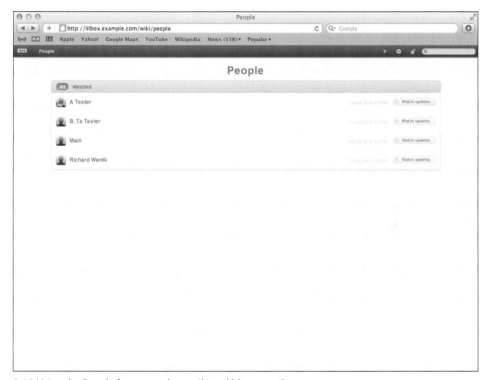

5.19 Using the People feature to show wiki and blog contributors.

Caution

The People feature does *not* show a list of all network users. Nor does it show a list of blog viewers. It does show a list of everyone who has created content on Wiki Server 3. Users who haven't added content don't appear in this list.

Using Updates

To view new content, select Updates on the Home Page. Figure 5.20 shows a typical list. You can use the options in the mini-toolbar above the listings to select different types of content. The All and Unread options take precedence over the Showing options:

- **All.** Shows everything

- **Unread.** Shows new content you haven't read

- **Showing.** A view selector with four options:

    - **Show Favorites.** Displays pages you view regularly

    - **Show My Pages.** Displays your own content

    - **Show Hot Pages.** Displays pages you've marked as Hot

    - **Show Everything.** Shows everything, as you'd expect

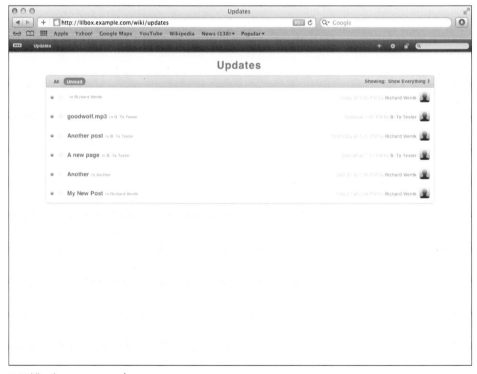

5.20 Viewing content updates.

Note

The Updates feature doesn't just show posts; it also shows uploaded media files, images, documents, and all other types of uploadable content.

Genius

To mark a blog post as a favorite, click the star to the left of the title. To mark a blog post as hot, click the gear icon and select Mark as Hot.

Caution

Tag searches are inclusive. You can click multiple tags to narrow your searches further. To remove a tag from the search list, click it again.

Searching with and without tags

The content search feature isn't immediately obvious. To access it, select any post with any tag. Click any tag. Then select the Search option near the top left of the main toolbar.

You see a long list—and it may be very long indeed—of all content on the server. You also see a new search dialog at the top right, as shown in Figure 5.21.

You can now select tags to filter content, sort in various orders, and even show deleted documents.

Getting Started with iChat Server

5.21 Using the search feature.

Wikis and blogs are ideal for written content, images, tables, and media files. But it's often useful for individuals to collaborate more directly. Lion Server also includes iChat Server, which provides text chat, live video, instant messaging, and live file sharing.

iChat Server uses a technology called Jabber, which is used by some Internet chat servers. The iChat client—the software that users use to connect to iChat sessions, shown in Figure 5.22—also is compatible with popular instant messaging formats such as AOL Instant Messenger, Yahoo! Messenger, Google Talk, and Apple's older chat rooms at me.com and Mac.com.

When you set up iChat Server, you create your own local version of these services. Network users can log in to your server and use the local chat facilities. On local and private networks, this is a secure option, because chat traffic is private and never reaches the Internet. But you also can make your chat public—for example, to support free online technical support chat.

5.22 Lion Server is bundled with the iChat client, which supports a selection of compatible chat and IM services.

> **Caution** Text chat uses almost no network resources at all. Audio chat is moderately intensive, and when there are many simultaneous conversations, other network traffic slows down. Video chat can be very demanding. If you plan to offer video chat to more than a handful of people, make sure your network uses gigabit Ethernet as a minimum and expect some slowdowns in network performance.

Enabling iChat Server

iChat Server is enabling in Server App, with another example of the familiar giant toggle switch. To enable it, follow these steps:

1. **Launch Server App, if it's not already running.**

2. **Select the iChat item from the menu at the left.**

3. **Click the switch at the top right, as shown in Figure 5.23.**

There are only two options:

- **Archive all chat messages.** This saves message traffic to /Library/Server/iChat/Data/ message_archives. This file can get very big, so don't enable this feature unless you need it.

- **Enable server-to-server federation.** If your server is connected to the Internet, this connects your iChat server with other compatible online servers, including Google Chat. (This feature requires a working NAT service and correct Firewall settings. For details, see Chapters 10 and 12.) Leave the option unchecked for secure local chat. Click Edit to select a list of servers to which to connect.

5.23 Enabling iChat Server with a giant virtual switch.

Using iChat Server

Before a user can connect to the server, you must create a network account for him, as described in Chapter 3. To use the local server, every user must set up her iChat client software by hand.

To connect to the server, follow these steps:

1. **Launch the iChat client.** You can find it in the Applications folder.

2. **Select Accounts.** Click the Account Information tab if it isn't already visible. Click the + (plus) icon to create a new account.

3. **Type a description.** This is for your use only; this field isn't used by the software.

4. **Type an account name.** The first part of this name *must* match the Account Name field created for the user in the Users feature in Server App. The second part is the full host name and domain, if there is one, as shown in Figure 5.24.

5. **Click the Server Settings tab.**

6. **Uncheck the Automatically find server and port box.**

7. **Type the server name—the full name used after the @ symbol in Step 4—into the Server field.**

8. **Make sure the port number is 5222.**

9. **Click the Account Information tab again. Click Enable this account.** The iChat client should log in to the server.

You should now be able to use all the video and text chat features of iChat on your local network. Where users share a group, they appear in iChat's buddy list automatically.

5.24 Setting up the iChat client to work with the iChat server.

Caution

The account name is *not* the user's e-mail address. It's also *not* the user's full name. Because the Users feature in Server App doesn't show the Account Name after it has been created, this can lead to confusion. Be sure to write down the account names for each user as you create them. Alternatively, use a scheme that makes it easy to guess the account name afterward.

The computer name *must* include the host name and any domain. For a non-public network, .private and .local work. On a public network, use the standard hostname. domain.three-letter-extension—for example lilbox.example.com.

Genius

If you select Bonjour from the Accounts menu and check the Enable Bonjour instant messaging box, you can bypass much of the setup process. Bonjour chat accounts are valid only on your network and not on the Internet. But for local chat, this is a simpler and quicker option than setting up an account manually. The Bonjour name matches your login name.

How Can I Share Files, Calendars, and Contacts?

Data sharing is a key feature in Lion Server. It helps improve productivity at work and can be very useful at home. Although data-sharing features may not be as obviously appealing as setting a custom web server or private e-mail system, don't overlook them; they can be at least as powerful when you need to get things done. This chapter introduces file sharing, calendar sharing, and address book sharing, and it explains how to set them up in your server.

Getting Started with Data Sharing

Data sharing is one of the key benefits of Lion Server. These features are available:

- **File sharing.** You can share files locally and remotely, with other Macs, with Windows and Linux PCs, and with portable devices.

- **Calendar sharing.** You can share one or more calendars, which can appear in iCal and in compatible applications, including Lion Server's own Wiki (see Chapter 5).

- **Contact sharing.** You can share one or more address books that appear in Address Book.

With OS X Lion, you can share data from your server and via iCloud. Both approaches have their benefits. This chapter includes a section about iCloud near the end, so you can work out which technology matches your needs most closely.

Introducing File Sharing

File sharing allows you to view files on one computer from another. Optionally, you also may be able to edit the files "in place" remotely as if they were on a local disk.

Note

View means *browse in a file manager*. The point of file sharing is to make disks and directories appear in file manager applications on other computers on the network. For Mac users, this includes Finder.

Lion Server's file-sharing features are based on those built into OS X Lion, shown in Figure 6.1. They also include extra options that aren't available in Lion.

Understanding file sharing

From the user's point of view, there are two ways to use file sharing:

- **Shares.** A share is a specific disk or folder set up for shared access. Access can be limited to specific users on the network, or it can be left open. Different users may have different access privileges; for example, some users may be able to edit shared files, while others may only be able to read them. Shares are also known as *share points*.

- **Open.** Open access connects to a computer disk on the network and makes it possible to browse it in a file manager (for example, Finder on the Mac, Windows Explorer on Windows, and so on). Open access is less controlled than a share, and it gives network users access to most of the remote computer's disk system.

6.1 Lion's file-sharing settings are directly connected to Lion Server's settings on the same machine.

Shares are typically used as drop boxes for specific limited collaboration. A team working on a project can leave files in a share, edit them, or copy them to some other location when they're finished. The key point about shares is that usually only one directory is visible; the rest of the file system is hidden.

Open access is more generous. Network users can treat remote disks on networked computers as if they were local. They can change the directory structure, use the remote disk for manual project backups, and generally treat the file system as their own—although depending on the settings of the remote computer, they may still need to supply a username and password.

Genius

Open access is particularly useful when you're adding a Mac to the network for your own private use. If you need to share files, it's much easier to access them directly on a remote disk in Finder than it is to copy them to a shared folder on one computer and copy them from the shared folder on another. In a family setting, you may want to make some disks open and restrict access to directories on other disks.

Technically, both types of file sharing are set up the same way. Lion Server creates a number of shares by default, but you can remove items from this list or add your own. If you define an entire disk as a share, you've created a disk with open access.

Note File sharing in this context is unrelated to the file sharing of pirated music, video, and other content online. That file sharing is a different process, it uses different tools, and it's outside the scope of this book.

Genius Don't forget that Wiki Server, described in Chapter 5, includes web-based file sharing for individuals and wikis. The file sharing in this chapter is file-based, and independent of the web-based wiki interface. Files shared by the wiki system are buried inside Lion Server's own file store. While it's possible to nominate the wiki-specific folders as shares that can appear in Finder on the network, it's simpler to keep the two options separate.

Enabling file sharing

File Sharing is one of the services listed in Server.app. It must be enabled before you can use it. Follow these steps:

1. **Launch Server.app from /Applications, if it isn't running already.**

2. **Select the File Sharing item from the list at the left.**

3. **If File Sharing isn't already running, click the switch at the top right, as shown in Figure 6.2.**

6.2 Enabling File Sharing in Server.app. "Music" has been added to the list of shared folders.

Caution The file-sharing options in Server.app and System Preferences affect the same set of internal settings. If you're using Lion Server, don't make changes to file sharing in System Preferences. It's less confusing to set up and manage sharing from one location.

Understanding shares

When you create a share, you start by selecting a folder or disk as the *shared point*. As explained above, you can select a single folder and leave the rest of the disk hidden from other network users, or you can select a disk to create an open share.

By default, Lion Server creates the shares shown in Figure 6.3, as follows:

- **Groups.** This share exists is a default share point for workgroups, which are described in Chapter 3. Users in a group can always access the shared folder for that group.

- **[User's] Public Folder.** Every user also has his own public folder on the network. He can copy files to this folder to make them visible to other network users. Depending on how access privileges are set up, other users also may be able to edit these files.

- **Public.** This is a generic public drop-box for the server as a whole. Other Macs on the network have their own corresponding Public shares.

6.3 Lion Server's default list of shares.

- **Users.** This is a standard /Users folder on the server. Network users can open this folder to view the user directories of every user on the shared Mac. But unless they have administrator privileges, they can't read the files in each user's directory—with the exception of a single folder called Public, which includes a public folder called Drop Box that can be used as a default personal share.

When a share is *guest accessible,* network users can access it by using a special guest account, which doesn't require a password.

When a share isn't guest accessible, network users must enter a username and password. The username defines the access privileges they're given for that share. The share is invisible to guest users.

Understanding file sharing technology

Before going further, it's useful to understand a little about file-sharing technologies.

File sharing is a simple idea in theory, but it's unexpectedly complex in practice. Historically, many different manufacturers created their own unique and largely incompatible network technologies.

The key point about network technologies is that if you don't set them up properly, users can't see your shares. (In the extreme case, if you don't select any of the technologies for a share, it never appears on the network.)

Three technologies survive in Lion Server. They have different properties, they're used for different applications, and they're summarized in Table 6.1.

Table 6.1 File-sharing technologies

Acronym	Meaning	Function
AFP	Apple Filing Protocol	Connects Macs to Macs. It originally was invented by Apple in MacOS, but it's compatible with OS X. It's now something of a legacy technology, but it's occasionally used in external Network Attached Storage (NAS) products to make them compatible with Macs.
SMB	Server Message Block	Known as Samba (and never as Server Message Block), SMB connects computers of all types. This is now the default technology for file sharing on LANs that include more than one type of computer, and it can be used to share files between Macs.
WebDAV	Web Distributed Authoring and Versioning	A relatively recent web-based file sharing technology, WebDAV often is used to share files with mobile devices. OS X and iOS do not include software that can read WebDAV shares, but third-party applications do.

Different technologies are accessed in different ways. AFP shares are integrated, to some extent, with Finder. SMB shares aren't; Finder often needs to be told to connect to an SMB share. If you don't connect manually, the share remains hidden.

WebDAV shares aren't visible in Finder at all. They may be visible on other kinds of computers on the network. And they should be visible on mobile devices running WebDAV-compatible software.

Genius

SMB (Samba) is an open-source project. Snow Leopard's Samba support used original open-source code and wasn't outstandingly reliable. Samba shares either didn't appear in Finder, or they didn't work reliably. Apple rewrote the Samba support in Lion and Lion Server, and it's much improved now. Usually it just works, as it should.

Creating a new share

To create a share, follow these steps:

1. **Launch Server.app from /Applications, if it isn't running.**

2. **Select the File Sharing item from the list at the left.**

3. **Click the + (plus) icon at the lower left of the pane.**

4. **Select a disk and a folder in the directory display, as shown in Figure 6.4.**

5. **Click Choose to confirm your selection.**

6. **Wait a few moments while File Sharing sets up your share point.**

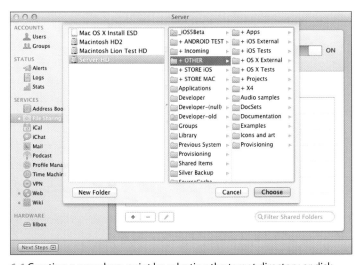

6.4 Creating a new share point by selecting the target directory or disk.

The share is set up with default settings. It's added to the list of shares, but if you want to customize the technologies the share supports, you must do some further setting up, as shown in Figure 6.5.

Follow these steps:

1. **Select the share from the list of share points.**

2. **Click the pencil icon toward the bottom of the pane.**

3. **Set up access control by adding or removing users from the access list.**

4. **Set up technology support by checking the boxes under the Settings header.**

5. **Click Done to confirm your changes.**

6.5 Customizing a share's settings.

Setting up access control

Access control lists how users can access files. Each share has its own separate list of users, and you can set different access privileges for each user.

These are the four access options:

- **Read & Write.** This gives a user full access. She can read the file, copy it, and edit it.

- **Read only.** A user can read the file, but he can't edit it. If he copies it, he can't edit the copy.

- **Write only.** A user can update or overwrite the file, usually by saving it from an application. She can't read it, so she can't load it into an editor. (This option is rarely used.)

- **No access.** As the name suggests, the user can see the file in a directory listing, but he can't open it, copy it, write to it, or edit it.

To change access control for a user who's already listed, click the menu to the far right of the user's name. Select a new access option from the menu, as shown in Figure 6.6.

6.6 Customizing access control for a user.

Genius

Users can include individuals or groups. It's quicker to set up access for a group—and add exceptions for specific users if you need them—than to list every individual on the server and set up access for each in turn.

Adding and removing users

Before going further, it's important to understand that the users who appear here are created under the Users and Groups items at the top of the list on the left in Server.app. For more information about using that section, see Chapter 3.

To remove an existing user from a share, select his name in the Access list and click the - (minus) icon.

To add a user, follow these steps:

1. **Click the + (plus) icon under the access list.**

2. **If you know the user's name, type it into the box.**

3. **If you don't know the user's name, type any letter into the box and select the name from the list that appears, as shown in Figure 6.7.**

4. **You also can select a Browse option to open a separate window with a list of all users.**

5. **After the user appears in the list, you can set up her access privileges using the menu at the right, as described in the preceding section.** Click Done to apply the changes.

6.7 Adding a new user.

Genius

The default access for unlisted users is the setting for Everyone Else at the bottom of the list. You can't delete the Everyone Else pseudo-user.

Note that typically you add groups first and then add individual users if you need to overwrite the settings for the group they're in. (For speed and efficiency, it's a good idea to plan your access list so it contains as few entries as possible.)

Changing share settings

Each share has five settings that select the technology supported by the share and set up guest access for it.

The settings, as shown in Figure 6.8, are as follows:

- **Share with Mac clients (AFP).** This makes the share visible to Macs on the network and to other computers that have AFP support built in. When you enable this option, the share appears in Finder on other Macs on the network.

- **Share with Windows clients (SMB).** This makes the share visible to other computers, including Macs, Windows PCs, and Linux PCs. (However, see the note in the next section for more information about sharing with Windows PCs.)

- **Share with iOS devices (WebDAV).** This enables web-based sharing for iOS devices. With the right software, iOS devices can read and/or edit files in the share. (To find compatible software, search for WebDAV in the App Store. To set up a connection, enter your server URL or IP address and personal login details.)

- **Allow guest users to access this share.** When checked, all network users can access the share with a default password-free guest account. Access privileges for the guest account are set by the Everyone Else option.

- **Make available for home directories over AFP/SMB.** This option sets up automatic access for home directories. (Note that because of a bug in Lion Server, you won't be able to use fast user switching if you select this option for a user share.)

6.8 Managing share settings.

Genius Some of the settings mention *clients*. This is just a complicated way to say "access software." For example, *Windows client* means "a piece of software running on a Windows PC that can access this share."

Accessing shares

On a Mac, you can access shares in two ways:

- **Direct access.** AFP shares should usually appear in Finder, in the Shared list at the left of Finder. If you're logged in as an administrator on your server, you should have full read access on the remote Mac, but you won't have read/write access unless you also have an account on the remote Mac.

- **Connect to Server.** You can use the Connect to Server feature built into Finder, as shown in Figure 6.9, to access SMB and AFP shares that don't appear in Finder automatically and to read files on Windows and Linux computers that are running a Samba server. (Windows does this by default when you set up disks and folders for sharing.) Select Go ⇨ Connect to Server.

6.9 Using Finder's Connect to Server feature to select a server.

You can connect to a server using its IP address or local network name, prefixing both with smb:// as shown in the Figure. (The IP address is usually more reliable, if you know it. It can be difficult to get domain lookups working reliably on a mixed network.)

After you select a server, you see a list of shares, as shown in Figure 6.10. You can select any share from the list. You are then asked to log in as a guest or to supply a username and password that define access privileges in the usual way.

6.10 Using Finder's Connect to Server feature to select a server.

Connect to Server works with most computers and with server-based external storage, including NAS boxes. Login options and security features aren't standardized. You can usually log in with a guest account to access files, but—depending on local security settings—you may not be able to edit them.

Setting up shares for access from a Windows PC

When you set up an SMB share, it's automatically compatible with Windows PCs - almost.

Windows PCs include a workgroup feature that groups related computers together whenever you access the network with a file browser. To access shares on a Windows PC, you must make your Mac part of the target workgroup.

Windows networks use a system called WINS (Windows Internet Name Service) to find each other. Lion Server includes a WINS option, and you can use it to set a Mac's workgroup affiliation, as shown in Figure 6.11.

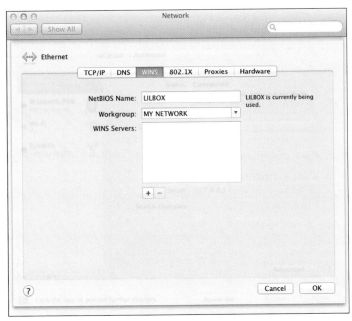

6.11 Setting a Windows workgroup for the server.

In Windows networks, the default workgroup is called WORKGROUP. Many Windows networks keep this workgroup name. If this is true for you, you don't need to change anything; your Lion Server Mac should appear as a computer in the Microsoft Windows Network list in Windows Explorer.

Other networks define custom workgroups. To make your Mac appear in a different workgroup, you need to make changes to the WINS settings.

Caution The process described in this section isn't entirely reliable, and you may need to repeat the steps several times before it works. You may even need to restart your Mac *and* the PC that's trying to connect to it. Name and workgroup changes can take a while to become active on a Windows network. Technically, both the name and the workgroup are broadcast at a set interval, which defaults to around 15 minutes. Changes won't register before then unless you force an update by powering down and powering up again.

To change the workgroup name and computer name, follow these steps:

1. **Select from the menu at the top left, and click System Preferences.**
2. **Select the Network item.**
3. **Select Ethernet from the list at the left.**

Note These steps assume your server is connected to the network over Ethernet (cable). If you're connected over WiFi, select WiFi instead. The WINS options for both are identical.

4. **Click the Advanced button at the lower right.**
5. **Click the WINS tab near the top of the pane.**
6. **Type the new computer name into the NetBIOS name field.**
7. **Type the new workgroup name into the Workgroup field.**
8. **Click OK to confirm the changes.**
9. **Click Apply on the main network dialog.** This is a critical step, but it's easy to forget it and wonder why your changes have been lost.

You should now be able to view the directories on the server from Windows Explorer, as shown in Figure 6.12

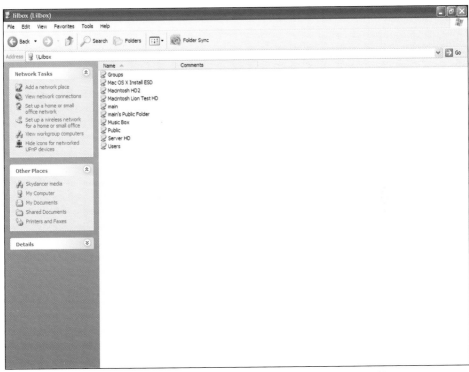

6.12 Viewing a Mac's disk system from a Windows XP PC

 Caution Windows PCs are likely to prompt you for a username and password the first time you access a share. The name determines access privileges on the remote Mac. Administrator accounts have full open sharing. User accounts are limited to shares.

Getting Started with Address Book Server

Many home and small business users treat Address Book as a contacts list that just works.

By default, Address Book stores contacts in a file on your Mac. But Address Book can link to lists of contacts from other sources. You can access these sources by selecting Preferences from the main Address Book menu and then selecting Accounts.

141

There are two default accounts, shown in Figure 6.13: On My Mac (local) and iCloud. As you'd expect, the On My Mac account manages local contacts, and the iCloud account pulls contacts from the user's default iCloud account. (If users don't have an iCloud account, this option doesn't appear.)

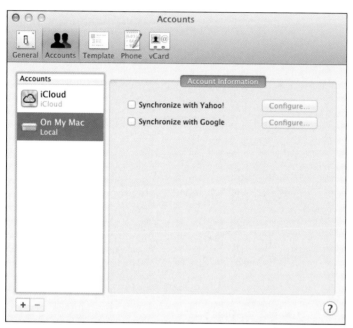

6.13 The two default accounts set up for Address Book.

 Genius If you select the On My Mac account, you'll see options to synchronize your Google and Yahoo! contacts with Address Book. To use these options, enter a Google or Yahoo! username or password.

But Address Book is more powerful than it looks. You can add further accounts and use them to access contacts on external servers.

Click the + (plus) icon at the bottom left to add a custom account. You'll see the sheet shown in Figure 6.14. Other kinds of sources are listed when you click the Account type menu, as follows:

- **A CardDAV account.** You can select a server compatible with CardDAV (Card Distributed Authoring and Versioning), described in more detail next.

- **A Microsoft Exchange Server account.** This is compatible with Microsoft Exchange systems, including Hotmail.

- **An LDAP (Lightweight Directory Access Protocol) server.** You can use this feature to display contacts stored in Lion Server's own list of network users.

- **An iCloud user account.** This option pulls contacts from a user's iCloud account. There's more about iCloud synchronization at the end of this chapter.

- **A Yahoo! user account.** This option pulls contacts from a user's Yahoo! account.

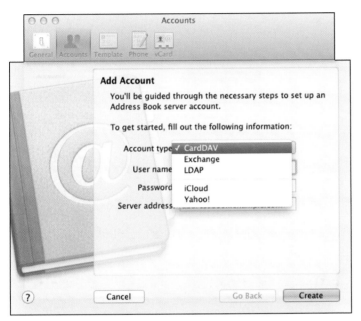

6.14 Selecting an account type.

Setting up Address Book Server

As you may have guessed by now, the Address Book Server feature built into Lion Server adds a CardDAV server to the network. You can select this server in preferences in Address Book and use it as a single source of contacts.

Like other services in Lion Server, Address Book Server is enabled with a giant toggle switch, as shown in Figure 6.15.

If you have Open Directory set up for network user control, as described in Chapter 3, you can include the networked users in the Address Book by checking the Include directory contacts in search box.

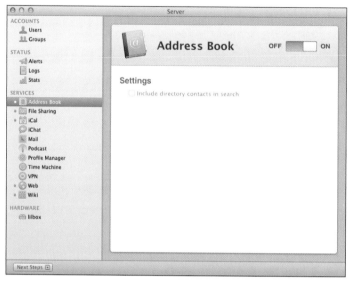

6.15 Enabling Address Book Server.

Using Address Book Server

CardDAV is a contact-specific relative of WebDAV. Like WebDAV, it's web-based, which means it can be used with compatible client software on other platforms. (You also can access the server directly via a web page for testing, as described later in this section.)

Contact information is shared among everyone who uses the server with the same username and password. Because contact information is inclusive (Address Book displays all contacts from every account it's logged in to), everyone can read the shared address book.

Genius

When you add another account to Address Book, technically you're *binding* it to a server.

To set up the server in this way, follow these steps:

1. **Launch Server.app, if it isn't running already.**

2. **Create a new user account that will be used for shared address book management. (For detailed instructions, see Chapter 3.)**

3. **Enable Address Book server, as described in the preceding section.**

4. **Launch Address Book, and select Preferences from the main menu.**

5. **Click Accounts.**

6. **Click the + (plus) icon at the bottom left to show the Add Account dialog, shown in Figure 6.16.**

7. **Select the CardDAV Account type.**

8. **Enter a username and password.** The username is the account name created in Step 2. It is *not* the e-mail address or the user's full (display) name.

9. **Enter the server name.** Use the server's host name, as set up in Chapter 2. Do *not* use the computer name or prefix the name with "addressbook."

10. **Click the Create button at the bottom right.**

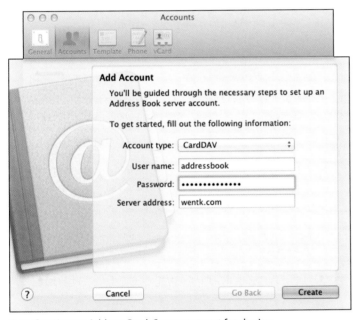

6.16 Creating an Address Book Server account for sharing.

The process is simple, but it's not completely robust. As of Lion Server 10.7.2, Lion Server sometimes complains that it can't find valid usernames. If this happens, click the Create button again.

You can check that an account name is valid by opening Safari and typing http://[server name or IP address]:8800. For example, if the server's local IP address is 192.168.0.99, type http://192.168.0.99:8800. Enter the account name and password you created.

This step also confirms that the server name you entered in Step 9 is correct. If you can't get the server name to work, DNS may not be set properly. As a temporary fix, you can type in your server's IP address followed by :8800 to check that the server is actually working.

This connects you to port 8800, which is the web-based interface for the CardDAV server. You can then use the login form that appears to test that you're entering a valid username and password. A successful login displays the web page shown in Figure 6.17.

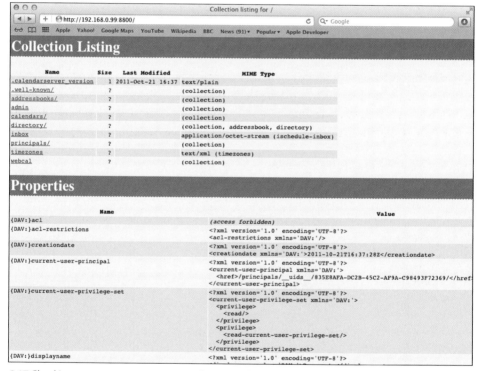

6.17 Checking server name, username, and password by logging in to the CardDAV server from a web browser.

Genius

You can't do much on the CardDAV web page, but experts can check the internal settings of the CardDAV server.

Alternatives to Address Book Server

You may think setting up a single user account for shared access is a crude solution—and you'd be right. If you need finer control over a company address book, you have three choices. You can try to create special groups to split contact access and contact management. This isn't a simple process, but advanced users can try to work through the user-suggested details at https://discussions.apple.com/thread/2140884?start=0&tstart=0. The other alternative is to use a different contacts server. Address Book Server (www. addressbookserver.com) is a popular choice, and that addresses many of Lion Server's address book management issues. Advanced users may want to consider the free open-source alternatives described at http://www.ronregev.com/misc/pim_server_tutorial/. Finally, for simple sharing, you can create a shared iCloud account, described later in this chapter.

To confirm that the server is working in Address Book, open the Address Book client and click the red "leather" tab at the top of a left page to view the server list, shown in Figure 6.18. You see the server listed under the server name you gave when setting it up. Note also that you can filter contacts to show *only* those on the server, by selecting the All [servername] option.

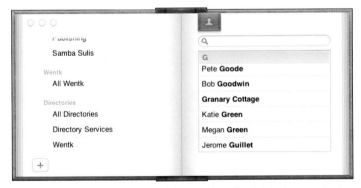

6.18 Confirm that the server is visible in Address Book. In this example, the server is called Wentk, short for the wentk.com server name.

Getting Started with iCal Server

iCal is Apple's calendar management client. In the same way that Address Book Server works with Address Book, iCal Server works with iCal to support shared calendars. Unlike Address Book Server, iCal Server has some extra features and options, introduced in this section.

Genius

iCal Server is on port 8008. As with Address Book Server, you can log in from a web browser by typing http://[server domain or IP address]:8008, followed by a user-name and password. As with Address Book server, you see a page full of settings and other diagnostic information; you can't use this option to edit or view calendar data.

Enabling iCal Server

To enable iCal Server, launch Server.app, select the iCal option from the list at the left, and click the giant toggle switch at the top right of the page, as shown in Figure 6.19.

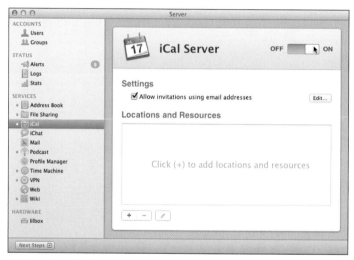

6.19 Enabling iCal Server

Setting up iCal Server options

When you enable iCal Server, you see that it includes unique options not included in other server applications. If you're not already familiar with iCal and calendar management software, it may not be obvious what they do.

- **E-mail invitations.** iCal Server can send out e-mail messages from a standard address to let recipients know when the calendar has been updated. Users can reply to these mes-sages to accept invitations.

- **Locations and Resources.** These extra "users" are described later in this section.

Setting up e-mail invitations

To enable e-mail invitations, follow these steps:

1. **Use Server.app's Users feature to create a user called calendar.invitations (or some other useful name).**

2. **Select iCal Server from the list at the left, and enable it.**

3. **Check the box beside Allow invitations using email address.**

4. **Click the Edit button.**

5. **Enter the calendar.invitations@... e-mail address on the server, as shown in Figure 6.20.**

6.20 Setting the e-mail address that will send and receive invitations.

6. **Click Next.**

7. **Set up the incoming mail server options, as shown in Figure 6.21.** Enter the e-mail address for the user account name and password you created in Step 1. Port numbers are set automatically from the mail server type and the SSL (Secure Sockets Layer) option.

8. **Click the Next button.**

Note

If you check the SSL box to set up secure e-mail, you must have a valid SSL certificate installed, as described in Chapter 10.

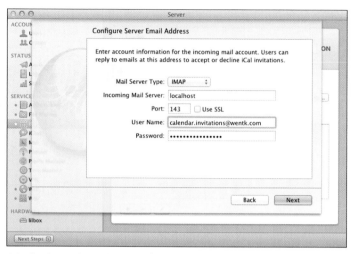

6.21 Setting up incoming e-mail.

Genius

You can use an external e-mail account here, on an external server or a service such as Google or Yahoo!. To use this option, enter the login details for the external service and make sure SSL is checked.

9. **Set up outgoing e-mail options.** Enter the options as shown in Figure 6.22, replacing the user e-mail address and password you created in Step 1. Select CRAM-MD5 authentication, and don't check SSL.

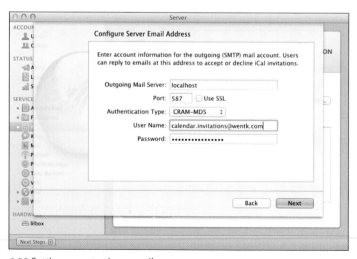

6.22 Setting up outgoing e-mail.

10. **Click Next, and then click Finish.**

Caution These instructions *should* work, but iCal e-mails are notoriously dependent on other settings. At the very least, you must have a working e-mail service running on the server (as described in Chapter 4), and iCal users must have valid e-mail addresses on the server. If the Firewall service (described in Chapter 12) is running, it must be open to allow e-mail traffic. Even then, you may find that this feature doesn't work as advertised, especially if you're trying to integrate it with external e-mail systems.

Setting up locations, resources, and delegates

If you're not familiar with the Locations and Resources features of iCal Server, it's not obvious what they do. From the context, it's tempting to assume they refer to obscure technical jargon. In fact, they're much simpler, but to set them up, you need to know what a delegate is. Here's your "decoder ring":

- **Locations.** As the name suggests, these are physical locations you can book for an event, such as a meeting room.

- **Resources.** These are physical resources you can book, such as a projector.

- **Delegate.** With the possible exception of Apple's Siri voice recognition system, most physical locations and resources don't have the intelligence to manage their own schedules. A delegate is the person responsible for managing the resource or location, who receives an e-mail or some other notification when the resource or location is booked.

In practice, both locations and resources are optional "users" who can appear on a calendar with bookable times and dates.

To set up a resource or location, follow these steps:

1. **Click the + (plus) icon at the lower left of the iCal Server pane.**

2. **Select either Location or Resource from the top menu, as shown in Figure 6.23.**

3. **Give the resource or location a name.** This is for display only, although it appears in associated calendars.

4. **In the next menu, select Automatically if you want iCal Server to add bookings to the calendar without checking them, or select With Delegate Approval if you want to delegate the bookings to a designated human.**

5. **Add a delegate's username in the Delegate field.** You can type in the name or browse it from a list.

6.23 Setting up a location or resource.

Using iCal Server

Because iCal Server uses the web-based CalDAV system, it's (somewhat) compatible with calendar clients such as Microsoft Outlook. Most Mac users will use it in one of two ways:

⦿ **As part of a Wiki.** Wiki Server 3 includes a calendar feature for each Wiki. This is the simplest and most reliable way to use iCal Server.

⦿ **Via the Mac iCal client.** You can select iCal Server as a calendar server manually.

Adding a calendar to a wiki

When iCal is running, it can be added as a wiki service. A calendar can then be included with each wiki, and wiki users can view it—and modify it, if they're allowed to.

To add a calendar to a wiki, follow these steps:

1. **Follow the steps in Chapter 5 to enable Wiki Server 3 and to create a new wiki.**

2. **Click the Action (gear) icon near the top right of the page.**

3. **Select Settings.**

4. **Select Services from the list at the left, as shown in Figure 6.24.**

5. **Check the Calendar option.**

6. **Click Save.**

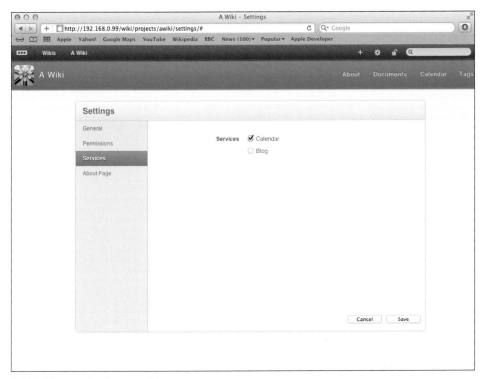

6.24 Adding a calendar to a wiki.

Note Permissions for the calendar are the same as those for the wiki as a whole: Typically, only wiki members are allowed to change the calendar. The calendar isn't clever enough to manage individual users, but you can create multiple calendars by clicking the + (plus) icon at the lower left, which can be a time-consuming but effective way to give every user a unique calendar of her own.

To use your new calendar, click the new Calendar option from the menu near the top right. You can view the day display, shown in Figure 6.25, or the week or month display. To add an event, drag the mouse in the calendar area and fill in your event settings.

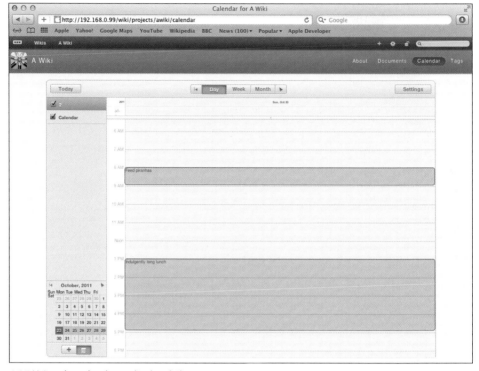

6.25 Using the calendar to display daily events.

Using iCal Server with iCal

Like Address Book, iCal uses an account-based system to access one or more calendar servers, and it automatically merges data from all accounts. Also like Address Book, you can find the Add Account feature in the Accounts tab in iCal Preferences.

Unlike Address Book, iCal doesn't support any external accounts by default. Events on a user's own Mac just work, and this personal account can't be edited.

But you can add external accounts of the following types, as shown in Figure 6.26:

- **CalDAV.** You can select a CalDAV-compatible server. In practice, this usually means the iCal Server built into Lion Server.

- **Microsoft Exchange Server account.** This is compatible with Microsoft Exchange systems, including Outlook.

- **iCloud user account.** This option pulls calendar information from a user's iCloud account.

- **MobileMe user account.** This option pulls calendar information from a MobileMe account.

- **Google user account.** This option pulls calendar information from a Google Calendar account.

- **Yahoo! user account.** This option pulls calendar information from a Yahoo! account.

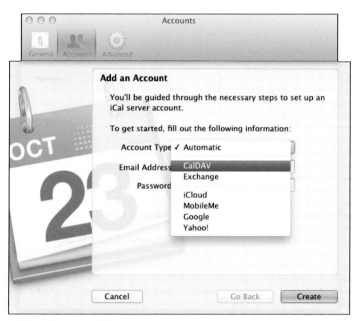

6.26 Adding a new iCal account.

Genius

The Automatic option polls each type of account in turn, trying your e-mail address and password as a login option. It's usually better to set up accounts manually so you know which service you're connecting to!

Caution

Apple no longer supports MobileMe, so don't choose this option. This is an unfortunate event, because MobileMe was an effective way to share calendars and address books across multiple users.

After the calendar account is set up, you can begin to use its collaborative features. The specific benefit of an iCal Server account is that it supports delegation. To nominate another user as a delegate for your account, follow these steps:

1. **Set up an iCal Server account in iCal Preferences, using the preceding set of steps.**

2. **Select the account from the list at the left, as shown in Figure 6.27.**

6.27 Checking which users have set you as a delegate for their accounts.

3. **Click Edit at the bottom right of the pane.**

4. **Click the + (plus) icon at the lower right to open the Manage Account Access dialog.**

5. **Type a username, or browse to select a user.**

6. **Optionally, check the Allow Write box to give them write access to your calendar, as shown in Figure 6.28.**

7. **Click Done at the bottom right.**

Because it's not completely clear why there are two similar dialogs here, it's important to understand that the first dialog shows the users who have nominated you as a delegate for *their* calendars. You can view this dialog, but you can't edit it.

The second dialog shows the other users you are nominating as a delegate for *your* calendar. These users can view your calendar. If you check the Allow Write box, they also can change it.

6.28 Setting up delegates for your account.

Sharing with iCloud

Apple's new iCloud service attracted lots of interest when it was launched in 2011. At first sight, it seems to overlap with some of Lion Server's features.

In fact, it does—and also doesn't. iCloud is set up for personal sharing between devices, rather than sharing between individuals. The key benefit is instant (or nearly instant) synchronization of data, contacts, and other details between Macs and portable iDevices. Figure 6.29 shows the supported services.

In practice, this means that data often *passes through* iCloud rather than being permanently stored there. Edits are saved and copied, but iCloud isn't an external data store like a virtual version of Time Machine; it's more of a holding pen for data changes. iCloud checks that all related files on all devices registered to an account are identical. After they are, it resets itself.

Note The data distribution model applies to contact information, address books, and other basic features. The Photo Stream feature is more complex, but a full discussion is outside the scope of this book.

6.29 Supported services in iCloud.

By default, iCloud supports device sharing only for a single user account. However, users can create multiple accounts, as long as they have separate Apple IDs or e-mail addresses.

This makes it possible for families and small businesses to share calendars and addresses using iCloud. Because both iCal and Address Book support iCloud accounts, it's very easy indeed to set up a shared account, add it to the accounts list in both clients, and enable contact and calendar sharing across multiple Macs and iDevices.

Genius

Simple iCloud sharing lacks the individual user permissions of a full business solution, but it can be an accessible option for smaller organizations. Given that the sharing features in Lion Server can be temperamental and difficult to set up, it's certainly worth exploring as a straightforward alternative for simple group sharing.

How Can I Create and Share Podcasts?

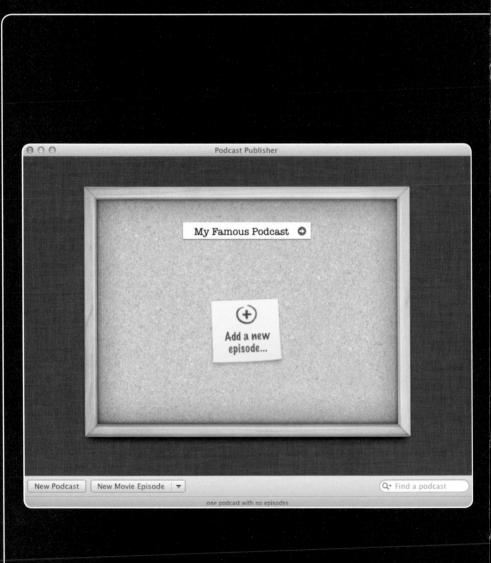

Lion Server includes two separate but related podcast factories that can automate the creation and distribution of podcasts. Podcast tools are distributed throughout various parts of Lion Server. The "factories" are easy to customize, and after you set them up, you can use them to distribute original footage with just a couple of mouse clicks. This chapter introduces the podcast tools and illustrates how they work together to manage the podcast production process.

Introducing Podcast Creation

A podcast is a media clip intended for online distribution. Podcasts are stored on a host server—typically, a web server or iTunes. When a new *episode* of the podcast is produced, users receive a notification by e-mail or as part of an RSS (Really Simple Syndication) feed. Then they can listen to or view the content.

A key aim of podcast production is simplicity. You can record a presentation using a simple webcam or screen grabber and auto-create chapters and sections. If you don't use an external video editor, only minimal "top and tail" editing of clip start and end points is available, as shown in Figure 7.1.

7.1 Working with simple "top and tail" editing in Podcast Publisher.

This simplified editing process is ideal for lectures and presentations. The editing tools support picture-in-picture effects that combine video of a presenter with a Keynote presentation. Podcast branding, with stock introductory and credit footage, is also supported.

If you're used to more complex editors, such as iMovie shown in Figure 7.2, it's important to understand that these minimal editing options can't compete with the features of a dedicated editor. Instead, they're designed to make it easy to create and distribute content with as little effort as possible.

However, if you want to create more complex productions, you can still use tools such as iMovie and Final Cut Pro to create video content. Then you can import it into the podcast production process.

7.2 The full-fat editing options of iMovie aren't built into the podcast tools.

Genius

Although podcasts often are assumed to be audio or video clips, they can contain a mix of audio, video, PDF, and mobi (e-book) content.

A key concept is a *workflow*—a programmed series of events that captures, creates, encodes, and distributes a podcast. Using the steps defined in the workflow, Lion Server automates the time-consuming encoding and distribution process. After you've recorded or uploaded a video, Lion Server does the rest. And if you're set up for iTunes distribution, the workflow can create an iTunes-compatible podcast and send out iTunes-compatible notifications.

Note

Snow Leopard server included media streaming features, which were ideal for local network and remote web viewing of podcasts. Unfortunately, this feature has been removed in Lion Server. You can still upload podcast files to various destinations, but you can't stream them over the network to network users. Minimal web-based streaming is included, but you can't modify the default settings, and it lacks the sophistication and professional flexibility of the previous streaming features.

Genius

OS X Lion includes a file conversion feature that can convert video files created on other systems, such as Windows-compatible .AVIs, into Mac-compatible .MOV files. To use it, right-click the file in Finder, select Encode Selected Video Files, and choose the 1080p option. There are many (far too many) different video file types in use, and this feature isn't compatible with all of them. But it's compatible with the most common types, and it's an easy way to create footage you can import into the podcast process. You can add support for other file formats by installing a free add-on called Perian from http://perian.org.

Getting Started with Podcast Creation

Before you can begin working with podcasts, you must familiarize yourself with the podcast components built into Lion Server:

- **Podcast Capture.** Shown in Figure 7.3, this capture tool is built into Lion and Lion Server. It was also bundled with previous versions of OS X. Podcast Capture can record video and audio from a camcorder, microphone, or your Mac's screen, import a file, or combine live video with presentation content. It passes your recordings to Podcast Producer, which is the behind-the-scenes podcast server.

7.3 Podcast Capture is the original podcast recording front-end.

- **Podcast Publisher.** Shown in Figure 7.4, Podcast Publisher is an improved and updated capture and distribution supplied with OS X Lion. It can record from a camcorder or webcam or from your Mac's screen. You can apply top and tail editing, and then distribute to iTunes, to e-mail, or the desktop with one click. You also can send the recording to Podcast Producer.

7.4 Podcast Publisher is the updated recording tool supplied with OS X Lion.

- **Podcast Producer.** Shown in Figure 7.5, the main element in Lion Server, Podcast Producer manages, processes, assembles, converts, and distributes the raw video and audio captured by Podcast Capture and Podcast Publisher.

- **Podcast Composer.** Shown in Figure 7.6, this is a *workflow editor*. It defines the steps Producer follows as it converts a captured video into a distributed podcast. You can create multiple workflows for different distribution targets and applications.

Caution

Even with Xgrid, podcast production may need plenty of processor power and memory. Although you can run Podcast Producer on the same Mac as you run a web and e-mail server, it's better to use separate hardware for both. Otherwise, the web server may become unresponsive when podcasts are being prepared.

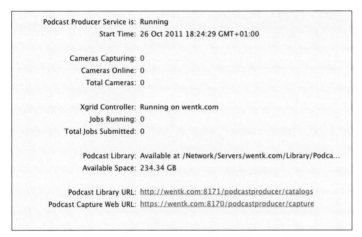

Podcast Producer Service is: Running
Start Time: 26 Oct 2011 18:24:29 GMT+01:00

Cameras Capturing: 0
Cameras Online: 0
Total Cameras: 0

Xgrid Controller: Running on wentk.com
Jobs Running: 0
Total Jobs Submitted: 0

Podcast Library: Available at /Network/Servers/wentk.com/Library/Podca...
Available Space: 234.34 GB

Podcast Library URL: http://wentk.com:8171/podcastproducer/catalogs
Podcast Capture Web URL: https://wentk.com:8170/podcastproducer/capture

7.5 Podcast Producer is the core element of the podcast production process.

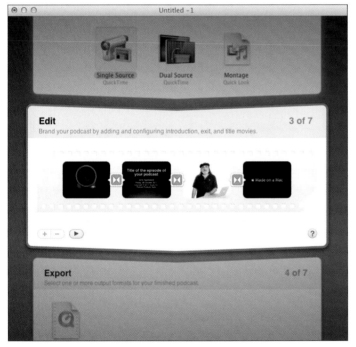

7.6 You can create preset workflows in Podcast Composer.

- **Xgrid.** Shown in Figure 7.7, Xgrid is a distributed processing tool that spreads Podcast Producer's workload across Macs on the network. With Xgrid, podcast creation is shared among many computers that work in parallel. This can dramatically decrease the time Podcast Producer takes to prepare, convert, and distribute a podcast.

Which tools should you use? If you're creating simple podcasts as a single user or adding podcasts to the wiki server introduced in Chapter 5, use Podcast Publisher and the Podcast service in Server.app.

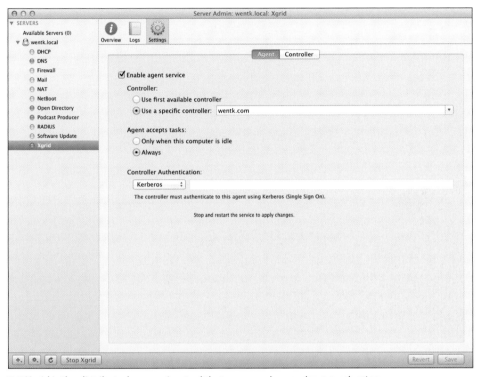

7.7 Xgrid is the distributed processing tool that can speed up podcast production.

If you're running a more complex "podcast factory" and need to create and distribute podcasts from multiple authors, use Podcast Producer and Podcast Capture.

In practice, it's useful to set up Podcast Producer in both situations, because it's a more powerful tool and better at processing and distribution. So this chapter starts with the more complex option and then introduces Podcast Publisher and the Podcast service.

Note Another advantage of Podcast Producer and Podcast Capture is that you can use both without installing a valid public SSL (Secure Sockets Layer, or online security) certificate. Podcast Publisher complains about the default security that's set up automatically in Lion Server. Occasionally, it refuses to work at all. For more information about setting up your server with a valid certificate, see Chapter 10.

Setting Up Podcast Producer

To make Lion Server's podcast features work for you, you must set them up in a specific order, as follows:

1. **Set up Podcast Producer.** An Assistant is built into Podcast Producer. If you use it, it creates useful default settings for Podcast Producer, and it sets up Xgrid automatically.

2. **Use Podcast Composer to define one or more workflows.**

3. **Set up a web server.** For public distribution via the web or iTunes, the server must be visible on the Internet. (See Chapter 10 for details.) For distribution on a local network, you can simply enable the web server in Server.app.

4. **Use Podcast Capture or Podcast Publisher to create a podcast episode.**

5. **Send the episode to Podcast Producer for conversion and distribution.**

Configuring Podcast Producer

Podcast Producer is a complex piece of software, with many options. It relies on the following services:

- **Open Directory.** This feature is used to create a network user account for the podcast service. This account is for internal use; it isn't used as a personal user account.

- **File sharing.** Podcast Producer creates a library folder on the server that's used for uploading, processing, and distributing files.

- **An Xgrid controller.** Xgrid uses a *controller* to send work to *agents* on the network. The controller distributes jobs, and the agents (Macs on the network) do the work. The controller collects their outputs and assembles the contribution from each agent to create a set of final output files.

Experienced administrators can set up Podcast Producer manually. But this requires advanced skills and knowledge, and it's easier to use the Assistant feature shown in Figure 7.8. It creates the correct settings and launches the required services automatically.

To use the Assistant, follow these steps:

1. **Launch Server Admin, if it isn't running already.**

2. **Select your server at the top of the list on the left side of the window.**

3. **Click Settings.**

4. **Select the Services tab.**

5. **Check the boxes for all services, as shown in Figure 7.9.**

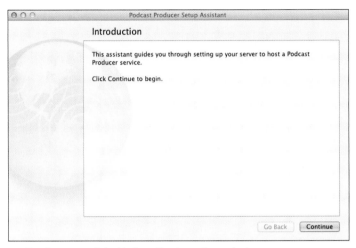

7.8 The first page of the Podcast Producer Setup Assistant.

7.9 Making sure all services are visible and editable in Server Admin.

Note Checking the boxes in the Services tab of the Server Admin Settings doesn't enable the services; it makes them visible and ready for editing.

6. **Select Podcast Producer from the list at the left.**

7. **Click the Overview icon at the top of the window.**

8. **Click the Configure Podcast Producer… button at the lower right.**

9. **Click Continue.**

10. **Leave the Express Setup option selected, as shown in Figure 7.10, and click Continue.**

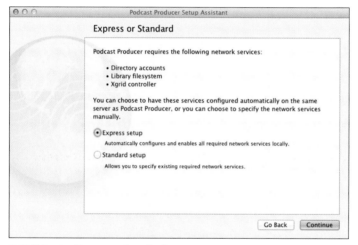

7.10 Selecting Express or Standard setup.

Genius You can use the Standard option to select a user for the podcast creation process, set up a podcast library location manually and set it up as an NFS share (see Chapter 6), and select an existing Xgrid controller if you have one. Express setup automatically sets up useful defaults for these options.

11. **Click through the pages until you see the dialog shown in Figure 7.11.**

12. **Enter the directory administrator credentials you created in Chapter 3.** This step gives the Assistant permission to add a user account that will be used for podcast management.

13. **Wait patiently.** The setup process can take a few minutes.

Genius

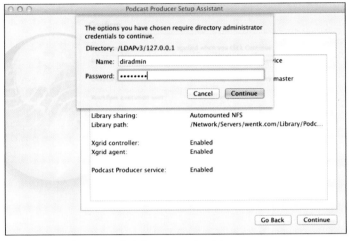

7.11 Entering directory administrator credentials.

14. **When the Summary page appears, as shown in Figure 7.12, you're ready to create podcasts.**

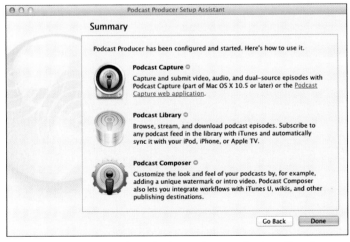

7.12 The Summary page shows further podcast applications. You also can run them directly from /Applications.

Exploring the podcast system

After you reach the summary page shown in Figure 7.12, you can do three things:

- **Create a podcast using Podcast Capture.**
- **Explore the Podcast Library.**
- **Create a workflow using Podcast Composer.**

The links on the last page of the Assistant give you quick access to these features. Clearly, it isn't convenient to run the Assistant every time you want to use them, but you don't need to, because you also can access them from other locations.

Podcast Capture and Podcast Publisher are conventional applications. You can run them from /Applications/Utilities.

Podcast Capture also is available as a web application. You can find a link to the web app in the Podcast Composer overview pane, shown in Figure 7.13. This pane also includes a clickable link to the Podcast Library, which is displayed in a web browser.

Introducing the Podcast Library

To podcast viewers, the Podcast Library appears as a web page. If your web server is online, Internet users can access your podcasts from the web page URL, which takes the form feed //[web server IP address or URL]: 8171/podcastproducer/catalogs.

Each podcast is part of a *feed* that sorts and filters the podcasts in the library according to useful criteria.

Genius

Technically, a feed is a subscription tool, built around a technology called RSS (Really Simple Syndication). Some browsers (Safari and Firefox) have built in support for RSS, and you can use them to subscribe to a feed simply by accessing the library and selecting one or more of the criteria listed next. Other browsers (Internet Explorer and Google Chrome) either require external plug-ins to support RSS or don't support RSS; if you don't use Safari or Firefox to view the library, you may not see a list of feeds at all.

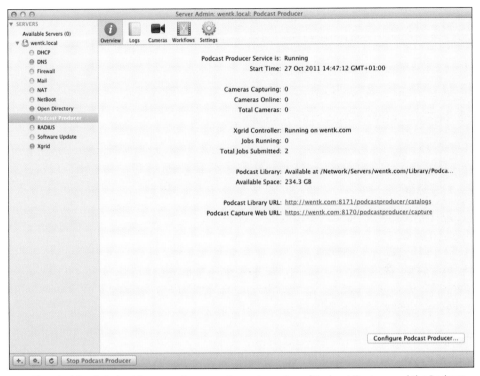

7.13 The two blue links in this pane take you to the web version of Podcast Capture and the Podcast Library.

These feed selection options are available:

- **Keywords.** You can filter podcast titles to select those with one or more keywords.

- **History.** This arranges podcasts in broad date order, with subcategories that includes Today, Yesterday, Last Seven Days, This Month, and This Year.

- **Custom.** This option displays podcasts with customized additional criteria. By default, there are no customized criteria, so this option does nothing.

- **User.** This displays podcasts listed by their author's names.

- **Workflow.** This displays podcasts grouped into the workflows used to create them. You can use this option to select podcasts created from screen recordings, single camera recordings, dual source recordings, or some other custom workflow criterion.

Figure 7.14 shows the Podcast Library in Safari.

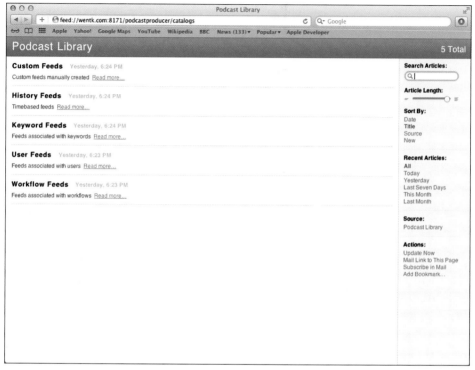

7.14 Viewing the Podcast Library in Safari.

On the right side of the page are further search and sort options, as follows:

- **Article Length.** This doesn't select podcasts by length; it alters the displayed list to make it larger or smaller in the browser window.

- **Sort By.** You can sort by data, title, or source, or you can choose to see a list of the most recent podcasts by selecting New.

- **Recent Articles.** This list is similar to the History feed, but shows last month's podcasts instead of this year's.

- **Source.** This is a quick reminder of the feed details.

- **Actions.** Use this option to refresh the podcast lists, mail links to the page, subscribe via e-mail, or create a browser bookmark.

Working with the Podcast Library

The Podcast Library is stored on disk in a folder called /Library/PodcastProducer/ Shared. Although there's a /Podcasts folder, you can't access this folder even if you have network administrator privileges. The contents of the folder can be changed only from your Mac's superuser/root account.

However, even if you log in as root, don't try to edit, move, or delete anything in the folder. The podcast management system is built around a database, which runs invisibly behind the scenes. If you try to move or delete podcast files manually, the contents of the database may become corrupted.

This means there's no easy way to delete podcasts after they're created. You can't delete them with Finder, and you won't find a delete feature anywhere in the Podcast Library or in Podcast Producer.

Only very experienced users can delete podcasts safely, because deleting a podcast is a complex process, which requires manual database access and command-line editing. Unfortunately, it's impossible to give simple instructions, but adventurous users can do a web search for "podcast producer delete" to find useful summaries of the process.

Creating a podcast with Podcast Capture

Whether you use the Mac version of Podcast Capture or the web app, the recording process is very simple.

Genius

The web-app version of Podcast Capture runs on Windows and Linux PCs as well as Macs. It doesn't support screen recording, but you should be able to make recordings with a webcam and, if you're fairly lucky, with an attached camcorder. You can use it to import files created using a video editor.

To create a podcast, follow these steps:

1. **Launch Podcast Composer.**

2. **Click the login button.**

3. **Select a server.** If you only have a single server, this field defaults to it.

4. **Enter a valid network username and password, as shown in Figure 7.15.** This name can be any network user. Optionally, you can check the box beside remember this password in my keychain, so that you don't have to enter the password again.

5. **Select a podcast type.** These are the default options:

   - **Video.** Single camera live video

   - **Dual.** A combination of screen capture and single camera video

   - **Screen.** Live screen capture (Mac application only)

7.15 Logging in to record a podcast.

   - **Audio.** Audio only from an attached microphone, webcam, or camcorder

   - **Existing file.** Video imported from an existing file (This option simply loads a file; it doesn't support further recording.)

6. **Click the recording button to begin recording.**

7. **After the countdown, improvise your podcast or speak from a prepared script.** If you are using the Dual option, you can use Keynote or some other presentation tool to display associated content while you speak.

8. **Click the recording button again when you're finished.**

9. **Click Start Over to redo the podcast, or click Publish if you are satisfied with the recording, as shown in Figure 7.16.**

10. **If you're publishing, enter an Episode Title and a Description.** These extra details appear in the Podcast Library after the podcast is created.

11. **Click Submit to send the recording to Podcast Producer.** Podcast Producer

7.16 Getting ready to publish a recording.

automatically converts into the formats selected in the default workflow and uploads the resulting files to the Podcast Library for distribution.

Genius

If you're deft with the recording button and a naturally gifted performer, you can pause/restart the podcast multiple times to create a deliberate jerky jump-cut effect as you speak. There's no undo option, so if you make a mistake, you have to redo the entire recording. But if you get it right, it can look impressively spontaneous, without the stiffness of a straight talking-head shot. You can, of course, also create the same effect with manual editing in iMovie or Final Cut Pro. But it's more challenging—and more satisfying—to perform it live.

12. **Wait...** Depending on the length of the recording, it can take from a few minutes to a few hours to process and upload the podcast to the Podcast Library.

13. **Check that the podcast is visible in the Podcast Library.** Open the web page, as described earlier in this chapter, and select User Feeds. You should see your username. Click Read more... to see your new podcast, as shown in Figure 7.17. In this example, you see that iPhone/iPod, AppleTV, and Audio versions appear automatically, because they're part of the default workflow.

7.17 Finding a new user podcast in the Library.

14. **View or listen to a version by clicking it.** The content appears in Safari in a QuickTime player.

Genius

While the podcast is being processed, you can check its status in the Overview pane of Podcast Producer in Server Admin. The key element is the number of Jobs Running on the Xgrid Controller, as shown in Figure 7.18. (You also can view this statistic in the equivalent page of the Xgrid controller.) While there is at least one job, podcasts are working their way through the system. Note that Podcast Producer can work on multiple podcasts from multiple users simultaneously, so the jobs count may become quite high at busy times.

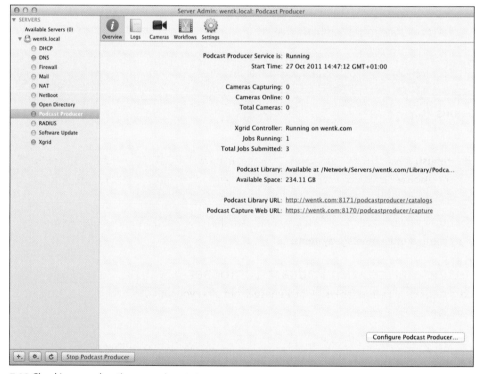

7.18 Checking a podcast's processing status.

Understanding Podcast Composer

When you view your podcast, you'll see that a short branding "trailer" video, an animated title sequence, and a short credits video have been added automatically. You'll also see that various versions are created by Podcast Producer.

You can control these options and many others in Podcast Composer, as shown in Figure 7.19. You can define the following elements in your workflow:

- **The workflow name, author, and description.** These are for display only. They don't affect content processing.

- **A podcast source.** You can select a single source from a camera, desktop recorder, or microphone; a combined camera and desktop recorder; a document such as a PDF, PowerPoint, or Keynote presentation; and so on.

- **A "branding" video added as an introduction sequence, a preset title animation, and a credits playout video.** These elements bookend your content and give it a professional-looking beginning and end.

- **Export options.** You can define target platforms for the podcast, including mobile devices, Apple TV, and desktop video.

Genius

For experts, the export options are compression, codec, and pixel dimension presets that define the file size, quality, and image size of the output. You can select multiple export options to create content for multiple targets simultaneously.

- **Publish destinations.** The exported content is always copied to the Podcast Library. But you also can send copies to other destinations, including standard Mac folders, other servers, and the Apple Wiki system introduced in Chapter 5.

- **Notifications.** This option sends a notification that a new podcast is ready by e-mail, chat, and other message systems.

Getting started with Podcast Composer

Podcast Composer's interface is slightly unusual, but after you understand how it works, it's easy to use. Remember these three key points:

- **Top to bottom, the workflow steps are fixed.** You can edit each step, but you can't change the sequence of steps. Click a step to select it for editing. You can scroll only one step at a time in either direction.

- **Editable items are displayed with a clickable info (i) icon.** The icon appears only when you hover the mouse over the item. Click the icon to display a floating inspector with options.

- **You can add and remove elements from a workflow step with the standard OS X + (plus) and - (minus) icons.**

Caution   As of version 10.7.2, there are no online help articles for Podcast Composer.

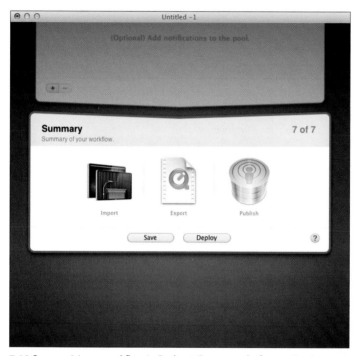

7.19 Summarizing a workflow in Podcast Composer before saving it or deploying it to Podcast Producer.

Creating a workflow

To create a new workflow, select File ⇨ New from the main menu. This creates a new sequence of steps with useful defaults. Then you can edit each step in turn. Many of the options are self-explanatory. These are some of the less obvious options:

- **Import source.** The automatic chapter generation option creates chapter markers in the content whenever there's an obvious scene change. Viewers can use this feature for quicker navigation. Automatic transitions animate the scene changes.

- **Edit.** You have a maximum of four slots for bookend/branding/credit videos. Click the info icon to select one of the preset videos or to import your own. Double-click the blue arrow icons to select a transition effect between the videos, as shown in Figure 7.20.

● **Export.** Unless you're sure that your audience watches your content only on portable devices, it can be useful to add all possible output options. This increases audience reach, at the cost of extra processing time when preparing each podcast.

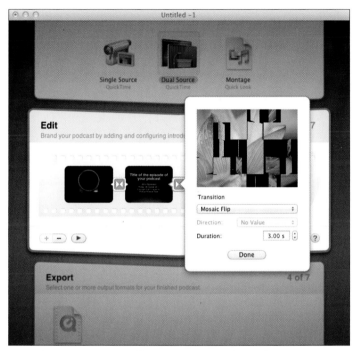

7.20 Selecting a transition effect to animate the change between supporting video content and your podcast.

● **Publish.** Some of the options are very specialized: Few users will have Final Cut Server installed or be in need of an FTP (File Transfer Protocol) feature to copy podcasts to a remote location. But you may find it useful to create a custom folder for podcasts. The Apple Wiki option is enabled by default in the standard workflow, and it makes podcasts available for users of Wiki Server 3.

● **Notify.** E-mail and iChat are the most useful options, and they need username and server credentials. iTunes U is for academic organizations. The iTunes option sends notifications to subscribed iTunes users.

● **Summary.** Save saves the workflow as a file to a location of your choice. Use this option if you want to create another version of your workflow with minor changes; you can reopen your saved file later. Deploy installs the workflow in Podcast Producer. Users can select it in Podcast Capture and Podcast Publisher. Once deployed, it's automatically added as a workflow option in these applications.

Working with Podcast and Podcast Publisher

Although you don't need to set up Podcast Producer to use Podcast and Podcast Publisher, you'll find both tools are easier to use and more productive if you do. And if you take the time to work through the earlier sections in this chapter, you'll have a better understanding of the podcast process and the way the different tools work together.

Podcast Publisher is a newer and slightly more advanced recording tool than Podcast Capture. In some situations, it can be more productive and easier to use.

Setting up the Podcast Service

Before you can use Podcast Publisher, you must set up the Podcast service in Server.app. To do this, enable the service using the giant toggle switch and add an administrator account—a user with a network account who will have podcasting privileges.

Note Counterintuitively, the Podcast service runs somewhat independently of Podcast Producer. You *must* set up the Podcast service if you want to use Podcast Publisher, even if Podcast Producer is already running.

To set up the Podcast service, follow these steps:

1. **Launch Server.app, if it isn't already running.**

2. **Select Podcast from the list of items at the left.**

3. **Click the big toggle switch to turn on the service.**

4. **Click the + (plus) icon at the lower left.**

5. **Select at least one user from the list that appears to add the user to the Administrators list, shown in Figure 7.21.** Users in this list are allowed to record and publish podcasts.

6. **Optionally, use the Podcast library feeds are viewable by... menu to limit podcast distribution.** By default, all users can view podcasts, but you can restrict viewing privileges to network users with valid accounts (authenticated users) or to podcast creators.

7.21 Setting up the Podcast service.

Using Podcast Publisher

After the Podcast service is running, you can launch Podcast Publisher from /Applications/Utilities and record your first podcast.

The process is very similar to using Podcast Capture, with a few key differences:

- **There's no desktop recording.** You can record only from a camera or microphone. Unsurprisingly, there's also no combined desktop and camera recording.

- **Podcasts are automatically serialized.** Podcasts have a generic name that applies to a series of podcasts with multiple episodes. You can add a new episode by selecting New Movie Episode or New Audio Episode on the main ("corkboard") page.

- **You can top and tail video and audio.** Grab the gold left and right clip markers to remove unwanted material at the start and end of a recording.

- **You can overwrite podcasts.** Click a podcast on the corkboard to select it for re-recording.

- **Podcast Publisher publishes to a different library, as shown in Figure 7.22.** It publishes to Wiki Server, and the podcasts appear using the wiki interface described in Chapter 5. This library doesn't overlap with the Podcast Producer library. Content is completely independent.

- **You can delete podcasts from the wiki library.** Click the cross-in-a-circle icon to the left of a podcast to delete it.

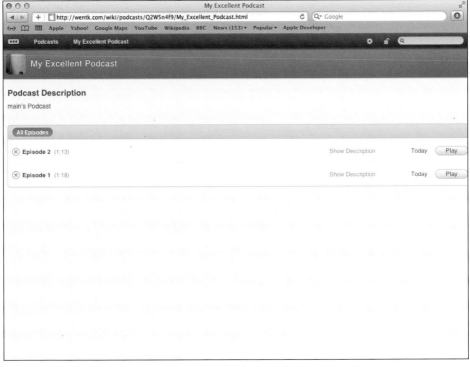

7.22 The separate Podcast Publisher library, used with the Podcast service in Server.app.

- **You can send content to Podcast Producer by selecting the Remote Workflow share option.** Then you can apply one of the workflows you created with Podcast Composer. Or you can select one of the defaults. Content sent to Remote Workflow *does* appear in the Podcast Producer library, but *not* in the wiki library.

- **You can Announce podcasts.** Click the Announce button after sharing to create an e-mail message.

Note

To get Remote Workflow working correctly you must specify your server name and provide a valid user account. Use one of the Administrator accounts you set up for the Podcast service in Server.app.

How Do I Manage Profiles and Devices?

Setting up devices can be tough for users when they're not experts on networking technology. Some settings need expert skills, and it would be useful to package settings and distribute them from a central location, instead of expecting users to make sense of them from a list of instructions. Profile Manager in Lion Server automates the creation and distribution of settings. It also includes feature restrictions that limit what users can do with their devices and security options that can lock or wipe devices if they're lost or stolen.

Understanding Profiles

When you bought your Mac or iOS device, you likely had to set up Mail, the calendar, your contacts list, and other features manually. Experienced users find the setup process simple. Less-experienced users can struggle with it. If they make a mistake, they may not be able to get the most from their device.

With the Profile Manager feature in Lion Server, you can set up your users' devices automatically with useful defaults: profiles. When Profile Manager is working, settings are packaged into profiles that can be downloaded and installed over the network.

Note   Apple runs an Enterprise Program for apps that are used in-house in businesses and other organizations and that aren't made available to the public through iTunes or the App Store. Profile Manager can distribute these apps for you over your network, so users don't have to install them by hand.

Profile Manager also supports device security. You can lock a device remotely, so it can't be used without a passcode. You can wipe the passcode to reset it, if a user forgets it. You also can wipe all the data and settings, to protect sensitive information if a device is stolen or lost.

Note   iCloud offers similar security options. You can lock an iPhone remotely, force it to play a sound or display a message, or wipe it. The critical difference is that iCloud allows a user to manage his or her own device. Lion Server allows a network administrator to secure multiple devices.

Getting Started with Profile Manager

Profile Manager is enabled in Server.app, with the usual large toggle switch. Figure 8.1 shows the few settings.

In fact, Profile Manager is a complex service with many options and features. Three components are available in addition to the simple front end you can see in Server.app:

- **An administration tool.** You can use this to set up and customize profiles for individual users and for groups, to manage devices, and to perform distribution and security tasks.

- **A user portal.** Users connect to the portal to enroll devices (to set them up so they can be used with Profile Manager) and to download and install profiles.

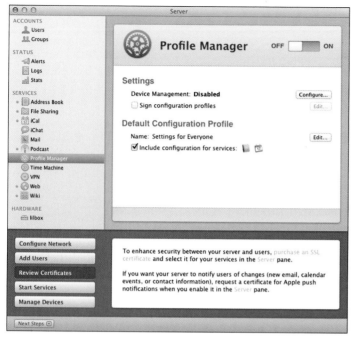

8.1 This view of Profile Manager in Server.app is deceptively simple.

- **A device management server.** After a device is enrolled, you can use this tool to update its profile automatically. The user doesn't need to do anything; she can see and use an updated profile after installation. You also can use this tool to access the remote security features on enrolled devices.

All components, except for the minimal interface in Server.app, are managed via a web interface, as shown in Figure 8.2. You can use the web interface to set up devices, work with users and groups, edit and change profiles, and perform security tasks.

Caution

You may see (null)(null) entries in the user list because some users were created and deleted with Workgroup Manager, which is part of the Server Admin tools. In theory, Workgroup Manager should be completely compatible with other parts of Lion Server. In practice, this is a bug; it doesn't delete users as completely as it should. Workgroup Manager is introduced briefly in Chapter 13. Until this bug is fixed, I recommend you create and delete users in Server.app.

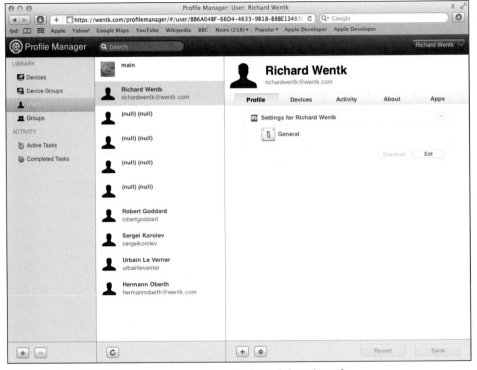

8.2 The bulk of Profile Manager is managed through this web-based interface.

Setting Up Profile Manager

Setting up the Profile Manager service isn't difficult, but you need to know about a couple of complications.

The first is that you must install a security certificate before you start. The certificate proves to users that your server isn't an impostor server that will try to hijack their devices. See Chapter 11 for information about getting and installing a certificate.

The second is that Profile Manager automatically includes settings for the services that are enabled in Server.app. Typically, you should set up Lion Server with the services you want and then set up Profile Manager last, before you hand your server over to live users.

However, you should create the users and groups you'll be using before launching Profile Manager. As of version 10.7.2, groups and users may not update correctly if they're changed while Profile Manager is running. Occasionally, you may even need to restart the server before Profile Manager notices that the user list has changed.

Enabling Profile Manager

Although Profile Manager has the traditional Lion Server giant toggle switch, don't flick it yet. Begin by clicking the Configure button under the toggle to run the Configuration Assistant, as shown in Figure 8.3. (Don't forget to install your security certificate before you do this.)

Note If you can't see the Configure button, click the toggle, wait until the busy indicator stops spinning at the bottom left, click the toggle again, and wait again.

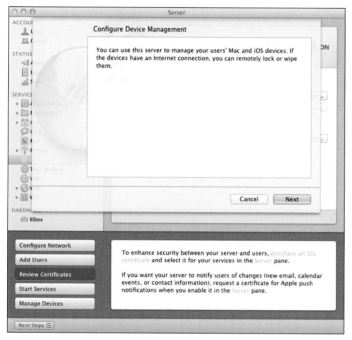

8.3 Running the Configuration Assistant.

The Assistant isn't complex; it checks that a valid certificate exists and tells you to install one if it doesn't find one. If everything is set up properly, you'll see the report in Figure 8.4, which confirms that you can enable Profile Manager and begin to use it.

Caution Note that you can run the Configuration Assistant only once. After you run it, the Configure button disappears.

8.4 Getting a clean bill of health from the Configuration Assistant.

You should now do two things:

1. **In Server.app, enable all the services you'll be using.** As you do this, you'll see service icons appear to the right of the Include configuration for services check box.

2. **Click the big toggle switch.**

After a minute or two, Profile Manager completes its internal setup. You can now access the web interface and start using its features.

Optionally, you can change the name of the default profile. Click the Edit box to the right of the Name field; it defaults to Settings for Everyone. The name change is for display only; it has no effect on the operation of Profile Manager.

Genius

Even though Profile Manager operates through a web interface, you don't need to enable Web Server for it. The two services run independently.

Introducing the Profile Manager web interface

To access the web interface, click the Open Profile Manager link at the bottom right of the page. You also can click the Profile Manager link on the default Lion Server web page and on the Wiki Server 3 login page.

Note Only Network Administrators can access the Profile Manager. If you're logged in with a standard user account and you click the Profile Manager link, you'll be asked to login again.

The interface, shown in Figure 8.5, has three elements:

- **A Library.** This includes users, groups, and devices. An Activity list under the Library displays information about active Profile Manager actions and events.

- **A list area.** This displays lists of the items selected in the Library.

- **A detail area.** This displays details for each individual selected item.

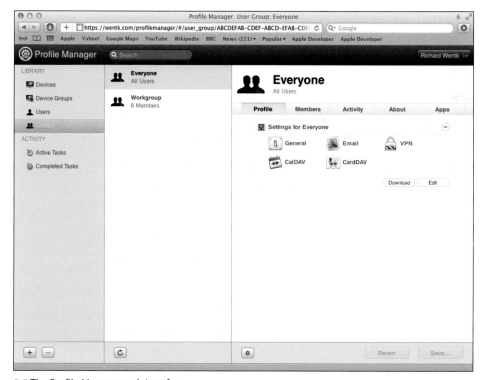

8.5 The Profile Manager web interface.

Using Profile Manager

As an administrator, you can use the web interface to do three things:

- **Add devices and create device groups.**

- **Create profiles for users, groups, devices, and device groups.** Optionally, you can install profiles automatically without user intervention. And you can assign devices to users.

- **Wipe or lock a device, or remove its passcode.**

Note

You can't create users or groups in Profile Manager. The web interface reads user and group information from the Mac's local contacts and Open Directory list.

Managing devices

To add a single device, follow these steps:

1. **Click Devices in the Library.**

2. **Click the + (plus) icon at the lower left of the page.**

3. **Select Add Placeholder.**

4. **Enter a name for the device.** This is for display only.

5. **Enter a serial number for the device, as shown in Figure 8.6.**

6. **Click Add.**

The device is added to the library.

The Serial Number menu includes three options:

- **UDID (Unique Device IDentifier).** This is an Apple-specific ID built into iOS devices.

- **IMEI (International Mobile Equipment Identity).** This identity is built into all mobile devices.

- **MEID (Mobile Equipment Identifier).** This is similar to an IMEI, but it uses hexadecimal (base sixteen) digits to create a shorter number.

You can find an iOS device's IMEI number by opening the Preferences app and selecting General ⇨ About. But using the UDID number is easier, because you can copy it from iTunes and paste it into the serial number field without retyping it, as follows:

1. **Connect your device to a PC or Mac.**

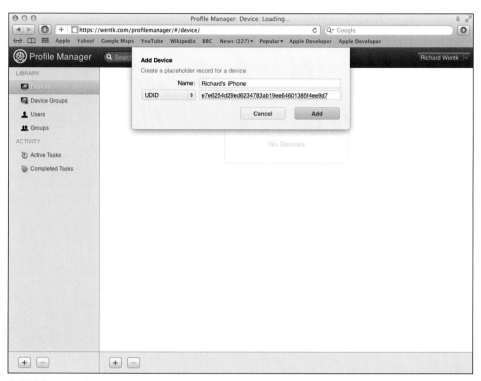

8.6 Adding a device.

2. **If iTunes doesn't launch automatically, launch it manually.**

3. **Click the connected Device under the Devices header at the left.**

4. **Click the Summary tab near the top of the page.**

5. **Click the Serial Number field in the box in the middle of the page, as shown in Figure 8.7.**

6. **Select Edit ⇨ Copy from the iTunes menu.**

Now you can right-click the serial number field in Profile Manager and select Paste to insert the UDID.

195

Caution

Apple will move away from using UDIDs over the next few years. It's not clear yet whether UDIDs will be replaced with an alternative Apple-specific ID or whether users will be forced to use IMEIs.

8.7 Finding a UDID, and copying it from iTunes.

Creating device groups

Use device groups to collect devices that require related settings. You can update or install a profile on all the devices in a group with a single operation.

To create a group, select Device Groups from the list at the left and click the + (plus) icon. Give your group a useful name—the name field at the top right of the window is highlighted for editing—and click anywhere in the white area below to finish.

To add one or more devices to a group, click the Members tab near the top of the page, click the + (plus) icon at the bottom of the device group, select Add Devices, and click the Add button to the right of the device(s) you want to add, as shown in Figure 8.8. Click Done when you're finished, and click Save to confirm all changes.

You can remove devices by clicking the X at the right of the window next to each device.

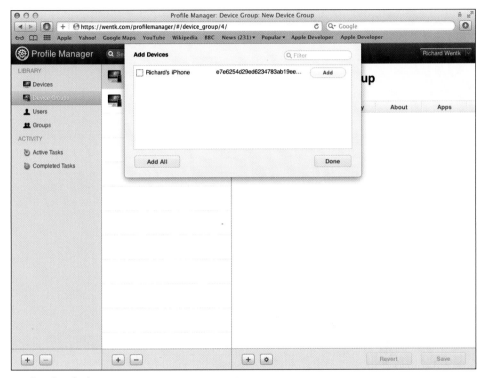

8.8 Creating device groups.

Assigning devices to users

By default, users have no device. After you've defined some devices, you can change this as follows:

1. **Select Users from the Library.**

2. **Select a user from the list in the middle of the page.**

3. **Click the Devices tab under the user's name at the top of the page.**

4. **Click the + (plus) icon at the bottom of the page, and select Add Devices.**

5. **Click Add next to the device you want to assign to the user.**

6. **Click Done after assigning the device.** The device appears under the user's name, as shown in Figure 8.9.

7. **When you have finished assigning devices, click Save at the bottom right of the screen to confirm the changes.**

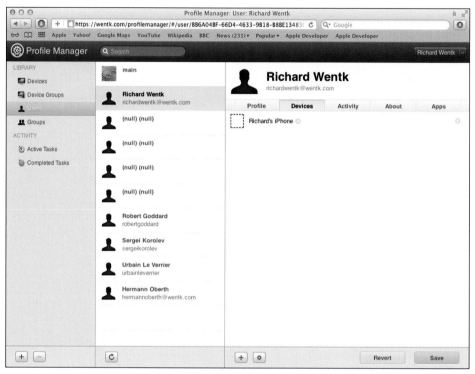

8.9 Assigning a device to a user.

Note

You can click the arrow to the right of a device to open its device page or click the X at the far right of the window to remove it from the user's collection.

Creating profiles

Profiles are complex; think of them as downloadable preferences. A complete profile can include the settings you would usually define in System Preferences on a Mac or in Settings on an iOS device. It also can include extra options that aren't usually user-configurable.

Figure 8.10 shows a Settings page in Profile Manager, which you use to define the contents of a profile. Each setting is called a *payload*.

Before going further it's important to understand that you can define profiles for groups, for users, for device groups, and for individual devices. The later options in this list override the earlier ones, so you can create a generic group profile, assign it to the devices used by that group, but make a single change to the profile of a single device in the group.

Users can install profiles manually by selecting them from a list. You also can set up Profile Manager to install them automatically and invisibly.

To define a profile for a user, select the user from the list in the middle of the pane, click the Profile tab, and click Edit. By default, only the General item in each profile is set up. As you add more items, more icons are added to the settings that appear in this pane.

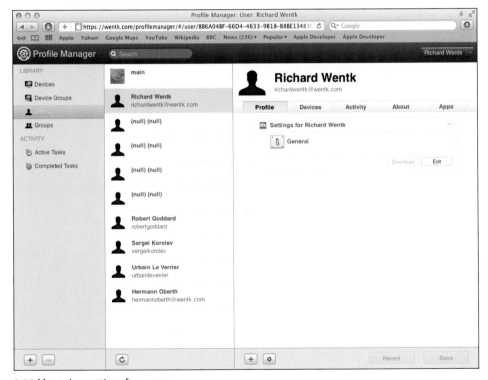

8.10 Managing settings for a user.

Understanding payloads

The complete list of payloads is long. Each payload defines the settings for one feature, such as a security passcode, or for one application, such as e-mail.

A complete explanation of all the possible settings and options for every payload would fill a few chapters in this book, and it wouldn't be helpful, because if you've set up a Mac or iOS device, you'll already know which settings to use for many of the options.

Payloads are collected into three groups. The first group has settings that apply to iOS devices and Macs:

- **General.** This payload is always included. It defines the distribution option for the profile—manual download or automatic updated via push technology. It also defines whether a user can remove a profile.

- **Passcode.** Passcodes are used to lock devices to prevent unauthorized access. This option, shown in Figure 8.11, defines settings for passcode security, including auto-lock options, minimum passcode complexity, and the maximum time a passcode can be used before it's replaced.

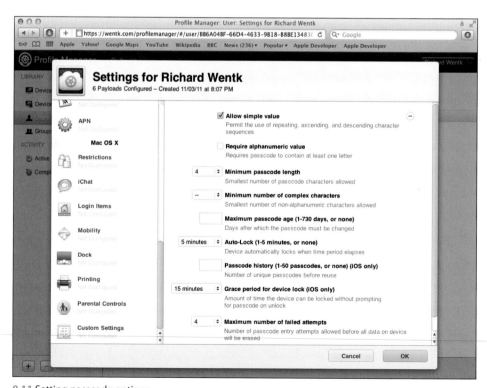

8.11 Setting passcode options.

- **Email.** This is a standard e-mail client configuration page. Use it to select POP (Post Office Protocol) or IMAP (Internet Message Access Protocol) email. If you're using Lion Server as your e-mail server, fill in the details listed in Chapter 4.

- **Exchange.** This includes client settings for access to a Microsoft Exchange server.

- **LDAP.** This includes client settings for access to an LDAP (Lightweight Directory Access Protocol) account. If you've set up network accounts for users, enter the login details for each user here.

- **CardDAV.** This includes client settings for an Address Book server. See Chapter 6 for details.

- **CalDAV.** This includes client settings for a Calendar server. See Chapter 6.

- **Network.** This includes WiFi access settings. For Macs, you also can specify secure network access. (Lion Server doesn't include simple support for this feature, so ignore it unless you're setting up network access for a different server.)

- **VPN (Virtual Private Network) settings.** An example is shown in Figure 8.12. For more information about setting up this feature to work with Lion Server's VPN, see Chapter 11.

8.12 Setting VPN options.

- **Certificate.** You can specify one or more security certificates to support network features and applications. See Chapter 10 for more information about certificates. although to use this feature correctly, you may need to include other software-specific supporting certificates generated for your network.

- **SCEP (Simple Certificate Enrollment Protocol).** SCEP makes it easier for users to obtain security certificates. Lion Server doesn't support SCEP, so you can ignore this option unless your users will use an external server with SCEP support.

- **Web Clips.** This feature places web links on a device's desktop. The links appear as micro-apps with their own icons. You can create web clips manually on any iOS device by loading a page into Safari, tapping the Share icon, and selecting Add to Home Screen. With this option, you can predefine web clips for a device's desktop, adding a custom label and custom icon.

- **Security and Privacy.** Enabling this option sends diagnostic data to Apple. (It's usually best left turned off, because the data can take up network bandwidth.)

The next group of payloads is specific to iOS devices:

- **Restrictions.** Use this feature to enable and disable core iOS features, including the Siri voice recognition system, iCloud support, app installation, and so on. Figure 8.13 shows one example. Note that the Applications settings can block access to YouTube, iTunes, and Safari, and the Media Content settings can limit media access to certain types and regions.

- **Subscribed Calendars.** Use this option to give users access to a calendar server, either an external server or one built into Lion Server. See Chapter 6 for details.

- **APN.** Access Point Name settings define access to advanced cell/mobile carrier features. (If you don't know what these settings do, don't change them.)

The final group of payloads defines settings for Macs:

- **Restrictions.** This feature is the Mac OS X equivalent of the iOS restrictions. You can define which Mac features are enabled, which applications can be run, which Dashboard widgets are supported, and which media sources the user can view, although for OS X Media restrictions are defined by the hardware they're played on rather than by content or region.

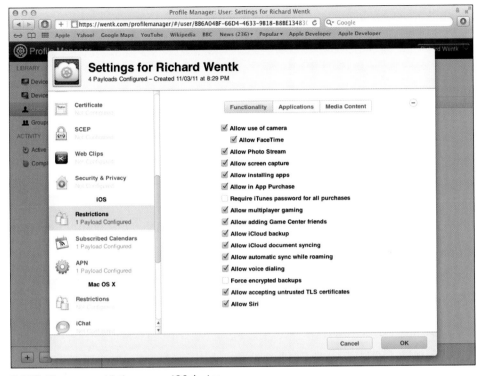

8.13 Setting user restrictions on an iOS device.

- ● **iChat.** Use this option to set up access to an iChat server. For details of Lion Server's own iChat service, see Chapter 3.

- ● **Login Items.** This option defines the applications, files and folders, and hard disks available after login.

- ● **Mobility.** This option defines a mobile account with a home folder that can be accessed over the network from any location. It also defines sync options, shown in Figure 8.14, that merge information on the local Mac with the equivalent data stored on the network server.

- ● **Dock.** These settings for the Dock include size, behavior, and visible applications.

- ● **Printing.** This option defines a list of printers that can be used on the network, with default print settings.

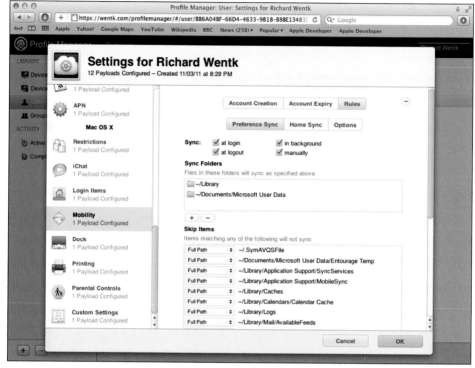

8.14 Setting up sync options. This option is most useful for experienced Mac and network administrators.

- **Parental Controls.** This option is a minimal set of controls that can remove profane words from Dictionary searches, and allow or deny access to specific websites, as shown in Figure 8.15. You also can limit the amount of time users spend with their computers and enforce curfews.

Genius

In spite of the name, you also can use parental controls to manage employee time—for example, to limit access to external game servers or entertainment websites. (It's best to let employees know that the name of the feature doesn't imply anything about your relationship with them.)

- **Custom Settings.** This advanced option can be used to set application preferences that aren't included in the other settings. To use it, you must know what a preference domain is and how to set key value pairs. For details, refer to a guide for OS X/Cocoa programming.

204

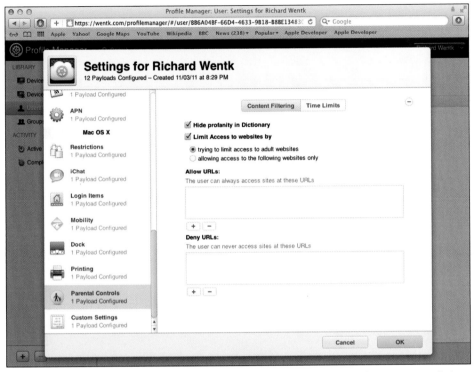

8.15 Setting up parental control options, which also can be used by network administrators to limit employee access to the Internet.

Creating profiles

A profile is simply one or more payloads. To create a profile, work through the list defining the settings and options you need. If you don't need an option, leave it unchanged and it won't be included in the profile.

Note that some payloads include multiple options. Look for + (plus) and - (minus) buttons at the top left of the pane to add or remove payloads, as required.

Distributing profiles automatically

After you have completed your profile, click the Save button at the lower right of the page.

Users can now choose to download it manually, as described later in this chapter. It also can be distributed automatically, via push notifications. Use the General payload steps described in the previous section to define which distribution method applies. When you edit the contents of a profile set up for automatic distribution, the updated profile is uploaded to devices automatically.

To use automatic distribution, you must enable the push notifications feature in Server.app. Follow these steps:

1. **Launch Server.app, if it isn't already running.**

2. **Log in to the server, and click the server name under the Hardware tab at the bottom left of the pane.**

3. **Click the Settings tab near the top of the window.**

4. **Click the Enable Apple push notifications check box, as shown in Figure 8.16.**

5. **Follow the instructions to obtain a push notification certificate.** You need a valid Apple ID. You can use the one associated with your iTunes account.

6. **The certificate downloads and installs automatically.** After installation, push notification services start running automatically.

 Caution Don't use a developer Apple ID when asking for a push notification certificate. Developers must go through a different and more complex process to obtain their certificates. If you have only a developer ID, create another one.

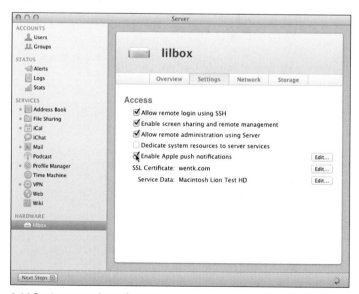

8.16 Setting up push notifications.

Working with the User Portal

Users can access the portal through their browser by adding /mydevices to the server's URL. For example, if the server URL is example.com, the user portal is example.com/mydevices.

Users are asked to log in with their network accounts before they can access the service.

After they are logged in, they see the page shown in Figure 8.17.

The simple interface includes two options on this page:

- **Devices.** Users can use this option to enroll a device in Profile Manager. (As an administrator, this saves you work because you don't have to enroll devices and assign them to users manually.)

- **Profiles.** Profiles you create appear in a list. User can download them and install them.

When a user enrolls a device, his System Preferences application is replaced by Device Enrollment, which includes a profile manager, as shown in Figure 8.18. The Profile Manager lists the profiles the user can select and installs them automatically. The usual access to System Preferences is now hidden from the user. The figure shows the Mac version of the process: The iOS equivalent is recognizably similar.

8.17 Accessing the user portal to enroll devices and download profiles.

Caution

Don't install Device Enrollment on your server, or you'll be forced to use Profile Manager to manage the server's preferences, which would not be a good thing.

After System Preferences has been hidden and overridden, users can use the second part of the User Portal to select and download profiles, as shown in Figure 8.19.

8.18 Replacing System Preferences with Device Enrollment.

The Settings for Everyone is the default profile and always appears here (unless you changed the name to something else in Server.app.) If you create groups, users, device groups, or user profiles that include the user's account or the user's devices, those profiles are added to the list on this page.

The Trust Profile includes a security certificate that authenticates the profiles and prevents outside impersonation. If your server has a self-signed certificate instead of a full authenticated certificate created and signed by a Certificate Authority, users are asked to confirm that the self-signed certificate is valid.

Users can click View Contents to see the contents of a profile, although this simply shows a list of icons that represent each payload. Users can't see the settings included in each payload.

8.19 Viewing the available profiles in a user account and their contents.

Securing devices

You can lock, wipe, or reset the passcodes of devices assigned to users or user groups. To use the security features, follow these steps:

1. **Open the Profile Manager web interface; log in if necessary.**

2. **Click Users or Groups from the list in the Library at the left.**

3. **Select a user or group.**

4. **Click the Profile tab from the list at the top right, if it isn't selected already.**

5. **Click the Action (gear) icon near the bottom of the pane.**

6. **Select one of the security options from the menu, as shown in Figure 8.20.**

The Profile Manager sends the appropriate message to the device, and it will be locked, wiped, or have its passcode removed.

Note
To make the security features work correctly, push notifications must be enabled in Server.app. Macs must have a check mark beside Wake for network access in their Energy Saver preferences.

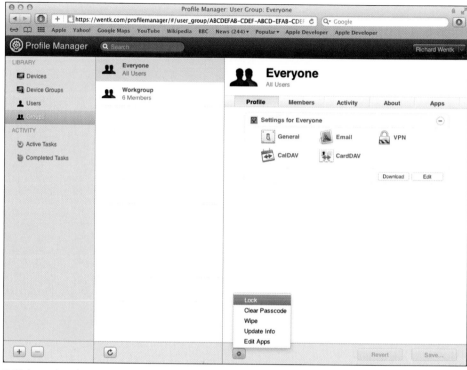

8.20 Accessing the security options in Profile Manager.

Genius

If you're already managing user devices, consider using the iCloud version of this feature. You'll need the iCloud account details of each user. The advantage of using iCloud is that it includes a Find My Device feature that displays the device location on a map. Location sensing is accurate to a few tens of feet, so this feature can't pick out a thief from a crowd. But it can be a useful memory jogger for users who aren't sure whether their phone is at home, in a bar, or somewhere else.

How Do I Keep Data Safe and Secure?

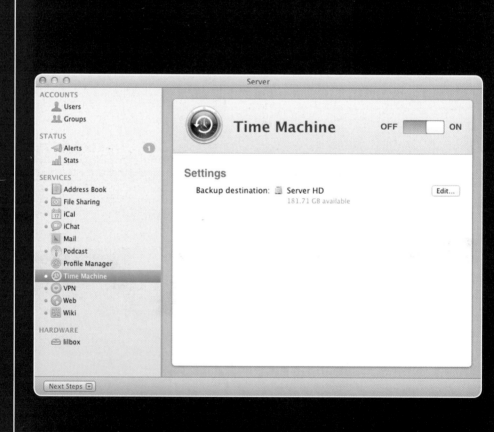

Lion includes Time Machine for local backups. Lion Server has Time Machine Server, which can provide backup services for every Mac on the network. But it's important to understand that Time Machine Server may not always be the best backup solution. This chapter looks at Time Machine Server and some possible alternatives, and it explains how to maximize data security while minimizing costs and inconvenience.

Getting Started with Backups

Backups seem simple in theory, but they can be complex in practice. Apple's Time Machine technology promises set-and-forget backups for Macs. Time Machine Server offers an extended service for remote backups stored on a server.

Both options can work well for some applications, but are less suitable for others. Backups can be critical; losing personal data is heartbreaking, but losing commercial data can literally destroy a small business. So it's important to consider backups in detail.

Understanding backup essentials

Although all backup solutions create safety copies, they do not create them in the same way or with the same security and flexibility. Consider these key issues:

- **Reliability.** How likely is it that a backup will be damaged or corrupted? If it's corrupted, how much of your data will be lost? For example, a single disk drive is less reliable than a commercial RAID (Redundant Array of Independent Disks) system, which keeps at least two copies automatically.

- **Convenience and speed.** How easy and quick is it to recover data? It's cheap and easy to keep backups on a slow external USB drive. But if it takes days to recover the data from the drive, which is possible with today's larger capacity hard disks, the convenience factor is low.

- **Data volume.** How much data will need to be backed up? How large will the backup disks need to be?

- **Physical security.** A local disk backup is worthless if your house or office is flooded or burns down. For maximum safety, copies of critical data should be kept in at least two physical locations.

- **Software security.** Not all solutions store all data. Some backup solutions can retrieve user data, but they can't reinstall OS X for you.

- **Network overhead.** For networked solutions, how much extra traffic will be added to the network? Will it have a noticeable effect on other services?

- **Cost.** Some backup solutions require a regular subscription. This may seem unattractive, but it can be cheaper than buying specialized backup hardware and software.

Most solutions trade off cost against the other factors. But it's important to think about which features matter to you before you create your backup system for Lion Server.

Understanding backup types

In theory, you can use a generic set-and-forget solution such as Time Machine to manage your backups. In practice, Time Machine has some limitations, especially when used to back up a server. And you may choose to perform certain types of backup manually.

There are three different types of backups:

- **System backups.** These create a complete bootable version of your system disk. Optionally, they may include all the other drives in your Mac.

- **Data backups.** These restore the data on one or more drives, but they don't try to reinstall OS X. For example, it's often useful to clone a hard disk to create a physical copy you can keep offsite.

- **Project backups.** These are relatively small backups of the files used in a project. They may include multiple versions of the project, as shown in Figure 9.1. Project backups are often created manually.

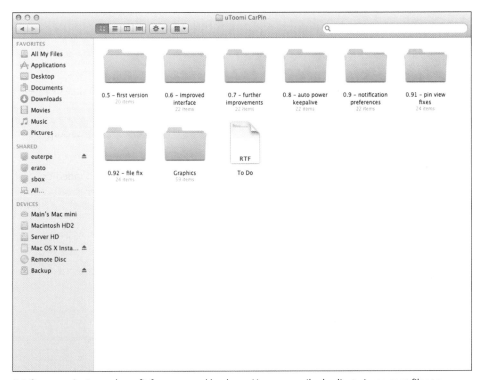

9.1 Some projects can benefit from manual backups. You can easily duplicate important files to multiple physical locations and keep independent multiple versions.

Genius

Choosing a backup solution is one area of network management where some initial thought can save you a fortune later—literally.

For more information about handling these different kinds of backups, see the section later in this chapter.

Looking at backup hardware

The quality, performance, and speed of backup solutions depend on the hardware used. Apple is keen to sell its Time Capsule products, but many alternative solutions are available:

- **Slow external disk drive.** USB 2 and Firewire drives are very cheap and have large capacities. But the limited speed means they're not suitable for volumes of more than 1TB or so, unless you're not in a hurry.

- **Fast external drive.** External drives with Thunderbolt connectivity are becoming more common. Although relatively expensive, performance is vastly faster than that of USB 2 and Firewire, making them suitable for volumes of between 1TB and 4TB. They also can provide very fast backup of smaller volumes.

- **Hybrid drives.** Several manufacturers make hybrid external drives that connect over USB or Thunderbolt but include multiple physical drives that support RAID for maximum reliability.

- **NAS (Network Attached Storage) device.** Available from various manufacturers in a variety of configurations that often include RAID options, NAS boxes connect to your network over Ethernet. Unfortunately, many drives are relatively slow; they may be slower than directly connected USB 2 drives. NAS boxes can be good for manual project backups, but they are less ideal for more demanding applications.

- **SAN (Storage Area Network) device.** Unlike a NAS box, a SAN box uses fast network technologies such as iSCSI to create a remote disk drive that can be at least as fast as an internal drive. SAN solutions are expensive, but they're recommended for high-performance commercial applications.

216

● **Apple's Time Capsule.** Available with storage up to 3TB, Time Capsule hardware includes AirPort technology for WiFi backups. Time Capsule can be convenient, but it's likely to be slow and isn't ideal for fast recovery after data loss.

9.2 Apple's Time Capsule is a good choice for low volume home or small office applications, but it's not for high-performance commercial use.

Caution
As of version 10.7.2, Lion and Lion Server appear to have connectivity issues with certain NAS drives. Search online for the latest information before buying one of these solutions.

Genius
Apple hardware is currently limited to slow USB 2 and Firewire connections and fast Thunderbolt connections. It's likely that at some point in 2012 and later you'll be able to buy adaptors that connect the Thunderbolt ports on recent Macs to faster USB 3 drives. You won't get the speed of a full Thunderbolt connection, but you will get much better performance than from a USB 2 drive. When it becomes available, this will be a good and affordable solution.

Looking at remote storage

In addition to local backup hardware, you also can use online storage options for backups. Some broadband ISPs offer this service for free; others offer a subscription service for a solution such as Crashplan (www.crashplan.com).

You can set up an automated backup system that copies some or all of your files to another server. If you lose the files, you can download them again. This is sometimes known as "cloud" storage because the storage isn't localized and you can access it from anywhere.

The best commercial solutions can monitor your data for corruption and inform you when there's a problem.

Remote storage is inherently secure and is (usually) inherently reliable. But it relies on access to very fast broadband connections, and backing up large volumes of data regularly can strain your network. It also can become expensive.

9.3 Crashplan is one of many remote backup solutions.

Can iCloud be used for backups?

iCloud is a new service Apple introduced for OS X Lion and iOS 5. Although iCloud has some features in common with a remote backup service iCloud isn't optimized for Mac backups, and has some issues that can affect iOS backups.

You can enable iCloud backup for iOS devices in iTunes by selecting the device and clicking the "Back up to iCloud" option in the Backup sub-pane. But be aware that iCloud storage is limited. The basic free service offers 5GB, which is a very small amount. At the time of this writing, the maximum available is 100GB, for an annual subscription of $100. This isn't generous compared to the terabyte capacities of physical drives, but it is large enough for small-scale project storage. Some users report that if a device requires more than 5GB of storage, you are automatically billed for the extra on a monthly basis.

iCloud also has no links to Time Machine, and no support—yet—for Mac backups. It also won't backup your iTunes music files, unless you subscribe to Apple's Match service, with a further entry price of $25.Generally, unclear pricing and limited storage make iCloud less appealing than other backup options.

Working with Backups in Practice

After you have an installation of Lion Server with a number of users and their associated data, which can include e-mails, web pages, media files, and other critical information, it's *critical* that you back it up. If you don't, you can lose more than your installation of Lion Server; you can lose web pages, address books, e-mails, and any other content created by your users.

Creating system backups

Time Machine, shown in Figure 9.4, can create system backups for Lion Server. A system backup is a complete snapshot of your system, and it includes all installed software, settings, and user information.

Time Machine can be a simple, free, low-maintenance solution for system backups. But be aware that if you need to recover your server quickly, you should invest in a fast disk system to support it. A Thunderbolt disk or SAN unit is ideal, because these can restore your server in less than an hour.

If recovery time isn't critical, you can use slower USB 2.0 or Firewire 400/800 drives, providing you understand that a full system restore can take anywhere from a couple of hours to more than a day.

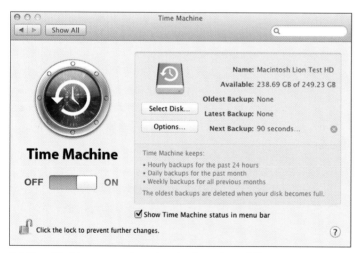

9.4 Time Machine can create system backups, but a full system restore can take a long time.

Caution

Time Capsule products should be treated as slower drives, and wireless backups should be treated as an even slower option.

To restore your installation from Time Machine, follow these steps:

1. **Restart your Mac, and press and hold (command)-R.** This launches the Recovery Console, which was introduced in Chapter 1.

2. **Select the Restore from Time Machine Backup option.**

3. **Select your Time Machine disk as the backup source.** If you have multiple versions of OS X installed, be sure you select the correct one!

4. **Select the most recent backup from the list.** If your most recent copy of Lion Server was obviously damaged or corrupted, you may need to restore from an older backup.

5. **Select a destination disk.** This is usually the disk or partition on which you installed Lion Server.

6. **Click Restore.** And then wait. When the restore operation is completed, Lion Server boots from the restored disk automatically.

Creating data backups

Time Machine can't create multiple physical copies; this makes it difficult to keep a spare copy of your system disk at a safe remote location.

Unfortunately, you can't simply drag the folder created by Time Machine to another disk. The files are locked by Time Machine, and you can't use Finder to copy them. The backups also contain hidden files, which you can't access at all in Finder.

However, you can use Disk Utility to clone your Time Machine drive. You also can use the same technique to clone other hard disks in your server, as shown in Figure 9.5, which demonstrates how to clone one of the internal drives in a Mac Mini Server to the other drive.

Cloning a Time Machine drive

To clone a Time Machine drive using Disk Utility, follow these steps:

1. **Stop Time Machine.** You won't be able to copy any data unless you do this.

2. **Launch Disk Utility.**

3. **Click the Restore tab.**

4. **Select the Time Machine source volume by clicking it from the list at the left.**

5. **Select a destination volume by dragging it from the list at the left and dropping it on the Destination field.**

6. **Click Restore.**

7. **When the cloning process finishes, remove the spare disk and restart Time Machine.**

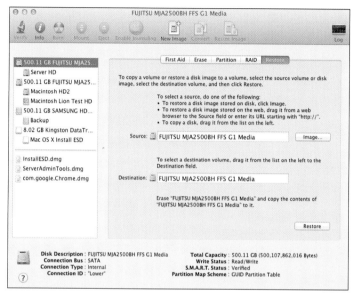

9.5 Disk Utility can be used for data backups. In this example, one Mac Mini Server drive is being copied to another identical drive.

Genius

If your Time Machine disk crashes, you can simply stop Time Machine and swap in the spare drive with the copy of your backup. When you restart Time Machine, it carries on as normal, reading and writing backup information to the spare drive.

Cloning another data drive

To clone any other disk drive in your Mac, repeat the steps listed previously, but don't stop and restart Time Machine. To replace a disk, simply swap in the copy physically, either inside your Mac or by connecting it via USB, Firewire, or Thunderbolt.

Caution

The Disk Utility Restore option user interface is best described as quirky. You must select the Source by clicking in the list of volumes at the left and the Destination by dragging an item from the list of volumes at the left. You may find that this isn't entirely intuitive.

Caution

Disk cloning works best when you clone entire disk volumes (drives). Cloning partitions is a more complex process. Time Machine works best with a single stand-alone drive, and it's worth investing in a couple. If you create a partition for Time Machine on the system drive, you'll lose your backups *and* your system if that drive crashes. For more complex backups—including backups of your Lion Server boot disk and data—Carbon Copy Cloner is a free (donationware) utility available from www.bombich.com.

Creating project backups

Project backups are particularly useful for creative applications where you may need to produce multiple versions of one or more output files. For example, designers often sketch a number of versions of a logo, with supporting files for each version. One design is usually chosen after client discussions, and the designer must be able to load that one sketch to produce a finished file.

Time Machine's sequential backup system isn't suitable for this kind of work. Unfortunately, neither is Lion's new auto-versioning system. Fortunately, auto-versioning isn't fully implemented yet, and it remains an optional feature in many creative applications.

This means it's still possible (for now) to manage project backups the traditional way, saving versions as you go and copying them to a backup device with drag-and-drop in Finder.

Genius

Dropbox (www.dropbox.com) is a popular solution for remote backup and file sharing. The first 2GB of storage are free.

Be aware of these two issues:

- **Remote copies are safer than local copies.** As with all backups, copies on a device in a remote location are more secure than those on a USB or other local drive connected directly to your Mac.

- **Occasionally, hidden files can't be copied in Finder.** This is a problem only for applications that access the hidden UNIX-based file system that underpins OS X. Fortunately most applications don't do this.

As long as you're aware of these issues and remember to create copies as you work, manual backups can be a practical way to manage project files and keep them safe.

Note that advanced users can force Finder to display hidden files by using a utility like Zettaboom's The Big Reveal, as shown in Figure 9.6. You can't edit most of these files without super-user access, which is introduced in Chapter 13. In fact, you can't even read some of them, and it's a very bad idea indeed to try to delete them. But you can use this option to see how the hidden file system is organized.

Understanding RAID

RAID links physical disk drives to create a combined system with improved performance. Depending on the configuration, you can improve disk speeds by splitting data across two or more drives (RAID 0) at the expense of reliability; if either drive fails, all data is lost.

You can improve security by making automatic copies of the same data across two or more drives (RAID 5). If either drive fails, the data is still safe, but the disk system works more slowly. RAID 5 can include *hot-swapping* and auto-repair: You can replace a failed disk with a new one while the system is still running, and it automatically makes a new copy of the data on the old drive.

RAID 10 combines the features of RAID 0 and RAID 5, but it requires at least four physical drives.

RAID is built into certain NAS and SAN boxes, and it's available on a small number of cheap external drive enclosures that support multiple physical disks.

OS X also supports software RAID in Disk Utility. If you have two identical drives, you can set them up as a single volume in Disk Utility for *striping* (improved speed) or *mirroring* (improved security). Performance isn't as good as for hardware RAID, and if you use external drives with this version of RAID, you must be extremely careful to avoid power loss and unplugged cables.

RAID can be an excellent choice for robust network backups. Because reliability is so important for a network server, it's well worth investing in a basic RAID 5 system for backups. For high-performance systems, you can improve reliability and performance with a RAID 10 system built into a Mac Pro.

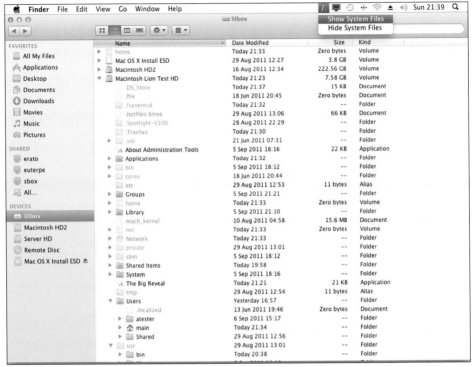

9.6 Using a utility to view hidden system files in Finder. You can't usually copy them in Finder, but you can see where they are.

Using Time Machine Server

Lion Server includes an additional backup option that can provide backup services for all Macs on a network. Time Machine Server is a virtual disk drive that network users can specify when they run Time Machine on their own Macs.

Although Time Machine Server is very easy to use, it can be a demanding application, especially on networks with ten or more users.

You must understand these two key issues:

- **Disk capacity.** The server Mac must have enough disk space to back up every disk on every Mac on the network.

- **Network bandwidth.** If there are many Macs with many large files that are updated regularly, Time Machine's hourly backups can create lots of network traffic. If file sizes are extreme—as they may be for video or 3D animation, Time Machine can't complete its hourly cycle.

Because of the limitations, Time Machine Server can work well on a simple home network with a handful of Macs whose disks are only partially filled or in a small business office that doesn't produce much data.

But it may not be ideal in busy creative offices with large collections of media files. If you run a media studio, be prepared to invest in expensive network disk storage and fast network connections. Otherwise, Time Machine Server may not be able to give you the results you expect.

It's also worth considering that running Time Machine on individual Macs equipped with a fast local disk drive may be more efficient than attempting to centralize backups over your network. For some applications, online or cloud storage may be a practical alternative.

Setting up Time Machine Server

Time Machine server is very easy to use. To set it up, follow these steps:

1. **Launch Server App, if it isn't already running.**

2. **Select Time Machine from the list of services at the left.**

3. **Click Edit to select a target disk drive, as shown in Figure 9.7.**

4. **Select a drive, and click Use for Backup.**

5. **Click the giant toggle switch to On.**

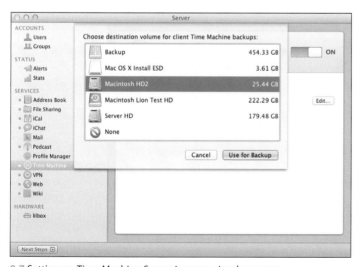

9.7 Setting up Time Machine Server is a very simple process.

The Time Machine Server pane shows the currently selected drive and the available free space.

Caution Running Time Machine Server *won't* back up your server files; Time Machine Server is a completely different service from Time Machine. If you want to use Time Machine to back up the files on your server, enable it from System Preferences in the usual way.

Caution External drives can cause issues with Time Machine. If you disconnect one or power it down accidentally, the backup files may become corrupted. Always eject a drive manually before removing it or powering it down. Ideally, use a UPS (Uninterruptible Power Supply) to protect your server and its associated disks from power fluctuations and brown-outs.

Using Time Machine Server

When Time Machine Server is running, Macs on the network can select it as a virtual disk drive in the Time Machine pane in System Preferences, as shown in Figure 9.8. Backups work as usual, but the data is automatically sent to the network drive managed by Time Machine Server. Each user has her own independent backup volume on the drive.

9.8 Using Time Machine Server in Snow Leopard. Selecting the virtual network disk in Lion is an identical process.

Network Macs can be running an earlier version of OS X. For example, Figure 9.8 shows how to select the virtual disk created by Time Machine Server in Snow Leopard.

How Can I Make My Server Appear on the Internet?

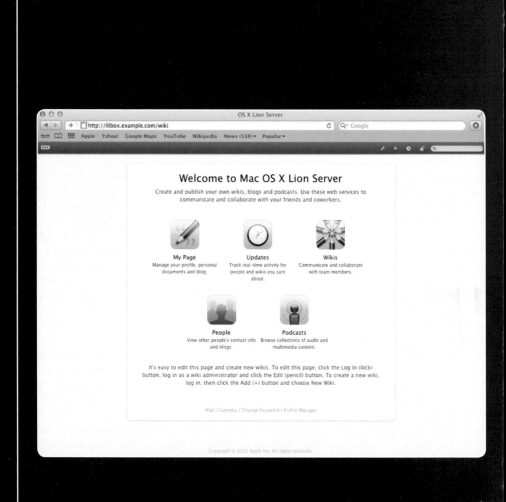

A server product like Lion Server includes most of the tools that are included in other Internet server products. Many are based on the specifications defined in the original RFC documents. You don't need to read or understand the RFCs to use the technology. But occasionally you'll find the RFCs mentioned in network documentation, and it's useful to know what the term means.

Unfortunately, the Internet doesn't have a plug-and-play feature, so before your server becomes visible online, you have to make some changes to your network. You also need to fill in some paperwork—or its digital equivalent—to register yourself, your school, company, or other organization as an Internet presence.

The key item you need to put your server online is a *domain name*—your own personal version of an Internet address ending in .com, .org, .biz, or one of the other TLDs (Top Level Domains).

Genius

Ideally, you should acquire a domain name before trying to set up your server. Then you can type the domain name during the setup process described in Chapter 2.

Understanding domain names

To recap information from earlier chapters, computers on a network need a unique IP address before they can communicate. By convention, computers on a small local network use private (local) IP addresses in the range 192.168.0.1 to 192.168.255.1.

These addresses are used on all local networks. This system works fine on a LAN, because the computers only need to find each other locally.

The Internet is more complex. Computers on the Internet need an IP address that's unique and valid for the *entire Internet*. Duplication of IP numbers isn't allowed.

Because IP addresses have to be unique, you can't pick one at random for your own use. IP addresses must be assigned by an outside authority that can ensure that addresses aren't duplicated. Typically, an ISP reserves a block of IP addresses and assigns them individually to each customer.

All ISP connections have a unique IP number, even if they're not being used as web servers. This also applies to mobile/cell connections. You can check your current IP number by visiting an IP checking site, like the one shown in Figure 10.2. Do a web search for "what is my IP" to find similar sites.

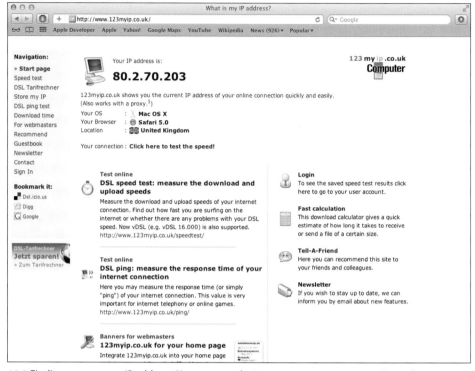

10.2 Finding your current IP address. Numerous web sites can report your current IP number.

Domain names also must be unique. For similar reasons, you can't pick one at random; you must check whether it's being used before you can reserve it and use it. Major TLDs (.com, .net, .biz, etc.) are managed by a single international agency named ICANN (Internet Corporation for Assigned Names and Numbers), whose website is shown in Figure 10.3. Country domains (.co.uk, .eu, and so on) are typically managed by smaller national agencies.

Whichever agency is in charge, you must claim the right to use a domain name. This is called *registering* a domain. After you register a domain, you have the exclusive right to use it.

Caution

To keep using the domain name, you must re-register it annually or pay up front for a bulk registration for a set number of years. If you don't renew the domain, it eventually lapses and becomes available to other buyers. (You're usually warned about this by e-mail before it happens, but note that although you'll receive regular warnings, in reality it can take almost any time period up to six months before your exclusive use expires.)

Although it's possible to claim a domain name by contacting the responsible agency directly, it's more usual to register through your ISP or through a web hosting company. Both will file the "paperwork" for the domain on your behalf and should (usually) be able to support it technically when you're setting up a link between the domain name and your server.

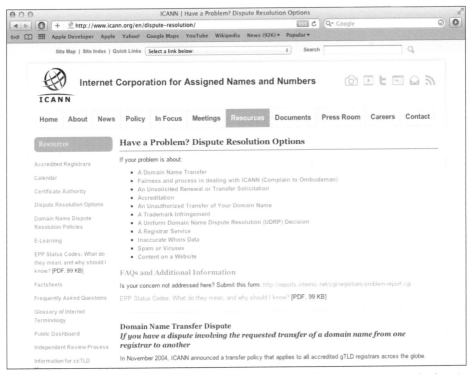

10.3 Most of the ICANN site is written for industry professionals. But if someone tries to steal a domain you own the rights to, you can contact them directly for resolution.

Getting online step by step

To put your server online, you need the following:

1. **A registered domain name**

2. **A physical connection to the Internet, with a unique IP address**

3. **An ISP or web hosting company that understands what you're trying to do and can do the work behind the scenes to put your web, e-mail, and other servers online**

When registration has worked correctly, your ISP will send traffic intended for your domain name to your unique IP address. Then you can set up Lion Server and your router to manage or respond to the traffic as you want.

Behind the scenes, the Internet relies on a network of *DNS Servers* that manage the conversion for all users. DNS may sound technical, but in fact it's a simple forwarding operation—a little like an electronic version of physical address forwarding for snail mail. When someone tries to access your domain to view a web page, send an e-mail, or to access some other service, the DNS service looks up the domain name and returns the IP number. The web browser, e-mail service, or other software uses the IP number for all communications.

Your ISP usually manages this level of DNS for you. (Lion Server includes DNS features, but it's usually better to leave critical DNS management to your ISP.) After your domain is registered and active, you can set up the Internet connection for the server from your side, as described later in this chapter.

Let's work through these steps in more detail.

Caution It can take up to 48 hours before a newly registered domain starts working, because it must be copied to every DNS server on the entire Internet. This process is called *propagation*. While it's happening, your DNS details slowly spread across the Internet, making it possible for users to access your domain. Eventually, propagation is complete, and your domain starts working for all Internet users.

Note If you're planning to use Lion Server for public web hosting, e-mail, and public services such as chat, you also should install a *security certificate*. This reassures your users that you are who you claim to be and that you're not an impostor site trying to steal useful information from them. Web browsers may display a warning message if you don't have this not-so-optional extra installed and working. For more information about getting and installing a certificate, see the section near the end of this chapter.

Registering a Domain Name

Before you can register a domain name, you must choose one you like and find out whether it's available. This can be a time-consuming process. A good domain name can make it easier to market yourself, your business, or your project. Even though the initial search can be frustrating, a good name can be a real business benefit and will keep working for you for years.

Finding a free domain name

If you run a business or work as an individual, the ideal domain name is as close as possible to your real-world business or work name. Ideally, you want a name that meets these criteria:

- **Easy to guess from your business or personal real-world name**
- **Easy to spell**
- **Memorable**
- **As short as possible**

When choosing a name, it's a good idea to make a shortlist of options before you start checking availability.

You can check whether a domain name is available for registration on numerous websites. Your ISP or existing web hosting company may have an online checking tool. If they don't, you can use a website such as www.checkdomain.com, shown in Figure 10.4.

10.4 Checking the availability of a domain name. Finding a name that isn't used can be harder than it looks.

Finding a domain name that isn't being used may not be easy. After more than 15 years of Internet growth, the most obvious and popular domain names are taken. This eliminates entrepreneurial names such as tv.com and business.com.

If you run a business or a community organization, you may find that the most suitable name is already taken too, even if it's relatively obscure. For similar reasons, you may even find that your own name or surname is already registered.

If a domain is used, you have four choices:

1. **Accept it, and look for a related but different name—perhaps with hyphens or multiple words.**
2. **Check for a different TLD suffix. For example, if .com is taken, .biz may not be.**
3. **Contact the domain's owner, and ask if they'll sell it to you (or perhaps give it away for free).**
4. **Look for a completely different and unrelated domain name.**

Technically, looking up domain name details is called *checking the whois record*. There are sites that can check domain availability for you by searching the web for "whois," as well as "domain checking." Whois is a more technical approach. A full whois record includes contact information for the domain's owner. This is useful information if you want to make a cash offer for a domain. Whois sites also are more likely to show you whether domains with alternative TLDs such as .biz are taken. Some also may suggest hyphenated and related domains, as shown in Figure 10.5.

Option 1 can work—sometimes. Hyphens aren't recommended. Prospective visitors are likely to leave them out by default, sending them to the site with the hyphen-free spelling.

But multiple words can work, as long as the domain doesn't turn into a complete sentence. For example, if you run a media company, adding *media* to the end of your business name to create a single combined word is practical.

Option 2 can be problematic for similar reasons. Users are likely to assume the domain suffix is .com by default. The one exception is national domains—for example, .co.uk instead of .com for UK domains. National domains have less prestige than a full .com, but are appropriate if you trade or work only in a single country.

To pursue option 3, use the whois record to find the domain's owner and make informal enquiries. If a domain is registered to a website that hasn't been updated for a long time, it's quite possible the owner may release the domain to you. Alternatively, if the domain is obviously busy, you can make a discretionary cash offer, with the understanding that you may need to negotiate an agreement.

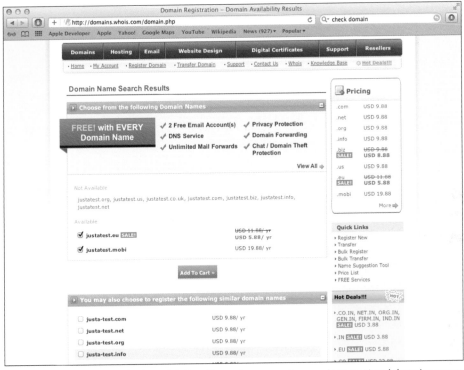

10.5 Using a whois site to check availability. Alternative suggestions and international domains appear automatically.

It's very difficult to value a domain name. Useful but non-obvious domains may be worth $100 to $500. Large corporations and entrepreneurs have been known to pay more, occasionally much more, as shown in Figure 10.6. Individual owners of neglected domains may be willing to accept a token sum of less than $100 as a sweetener.

Genius

If you buy a domain from an existing user, transferring registration is a slightly technical process. The current owner has to unlock the domain and send you an unlock code, which you enter into a website that releases it. Then you can register it yourself. If neither you nor the current owner is familiar with the process, your ISP or their ISP almost certainly is. Some ISPs will manage the transfer for you on request. Note that the seller may need to pay a small fee to release the domain.

10.6 The most popular domains are very, very expensive. But don't forget that companies have created successful online businesses with almost meaningless names such as Amazon, Apple, and Yahoo!.

Option 4 can be the most challenging. If your new name is too different from your business or personal name, it may be useless as a marketing tool. However, this may not apply if the name is unusually catchy or memorable. This option requires the most creativity and discretion.

Genius

Domain names that include an *oo* sound are inexplicably popular and memorable. Cynics have suggested that rather too many web business names sound like baby talk; there may be some truth to this observation. However, on the Internet, quirky is good. Real-world businesses can get away with being literal. But web businesses can benefit from an original and quirky name, even if it's just a short collection of meaningless syllables.

Getting started with domain hosting

After you've found an available domain name, you need to select a service to register it. Technically, this means two things:

- You now have legal title to the domain name.

- You tell your new domain hosting service to set up DNS records for the domain, so Internet users can access it.

Note For clarity, it's important to understand that domain hosting is *not* the same as web hosting, although often you can buy both from the same supplier. Domain hosting is a domain name and DNS management service. It redirects Internet traffic aimed at your domain name to your IP number, which connects to your router and your server. Web hosting is an off-site service that keeps your web pages and e-mail accounts on someone else's hardware in their datacenter.

Domain hosting means getting either a fixed IP number or setting up a service called DynamicDNS if your ISP doesn't offer fixed IP numbers. The details are covered in the next section. Don't start the registration process until you've read them, because your chosen third party will want to know which scheme you're using.

Possible third parties include the following:

1. **Your ISP**

2. **An existing web hosting company**

3. **An online registration service**

4. **A free service such as FreeDNS**

Caution It's possible to make a mistake at this point. If you register your domain name with the wrong entity, the organization or company responsible for providing DNS services may not be able to administer it correctly. After a domain is registered, it can't be transferred for 60 days, so it's important to get this right. And note that because this initial registration and setup is likely to cost money, it's worth shopping around for the best deal. You'll find a wide variation in prices and contract length.

Option 1 can seem appealing, but not all ISPs want to administer domains or have the technical skills for it. This is especially true of the mass consumer ISPs, which are unlikely to offer the technical support you need.

Option 2 is often the simplest. Even though you don't want to use physical web hosting, it can be easy and convenient to use a web hosting company for both registration and administration. Web hosting companies have plenty of experience dealing with registration and domain management issues, and they're more likely to understand the process and to manage it for you in an efficient way.

Option 3 may be the wrong solution, unless the website offering registration also offers domain (DNS) administration as a minimum. Figure 10.7 shows an example of a registration website with the features you need.

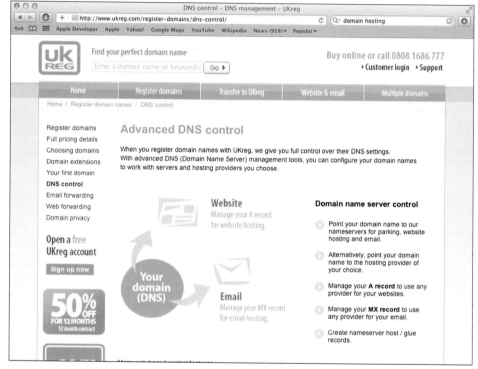

10.7 When you're hosting your own website on Lion Server, DNS management is the key feature you need when registering a domain.

The critical issue is that you need to be able to make active use of your domain. Registration without technical administration gives you legal access to the domain, but no more than that. And because of the 60-day transfer lockout, you won't usually be able to pass your domain to an ISP or hosting company who can set up administration for you.

Genius

You can use a registration-only service if you want to "park" a domain for a while, which gives you legal title to it and locks out other potential buyers. Large businesses often park competing or similarly named domains to maintain legal ownership, even when they don't plan to use them.

Option 4 is interesting for more experienced users. freedns.afraid.org, shown in Figure 10.8, offers free domain hosting (without web hosting) with many flexible options. More advanced features are available for a nominal $5 per month, although the basic features are good enough for most applications. FreeDNS is more of a hands-on option, so it needs more knowledge than a set-and-forget ISP or web hosting service. But technically it offers a competitive alternative to paid-for options and is well worth investigating.

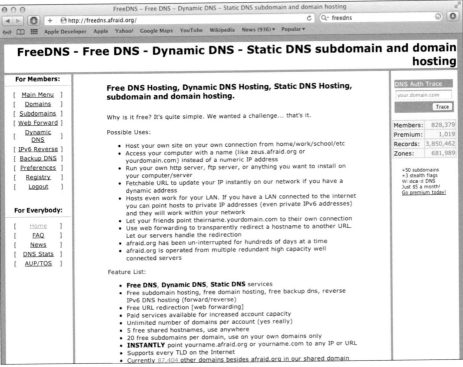

10.8 FreeDNS.org is, as the name suggests, a free DNS and domain hosting service.

Getting a physical connection

You can connect your server to the Internet in three ways:

- **Over an existing Internet connection, supplied by your ISP.** You can simply plug your server into your existing router. After your domain's DNS has been set up to forward traffic to your IP address, web requests and e-mail traffic are sent to your router automatically. After you've made some final changes to your router settings, described later in this chapter, your server is online.

- **Over a new dedicated Internet connection, supplied by an ISP.** A dedicated connection gives you better performance. It's possible to share bandwidth between external web and e-mail traffic and your own browsing and downloads. But users may find web pages are delayed if they access the server while you're trying to download a large file.

- **With a dedicated leased line.** If you use a standard consumer Internet connection, you'll be forced to share bandwidth with other users, so your connection may slow down during busy periods. A leased line is for your use only, and performance should be constant. Because leased lines are much more expensive than consumer connections (they cost hundreds or thousands of dollars a month), they're used almost exclusively by large businesses and academic institutions.

Genius How much performance is enough? Generally, a shared consumer line is fine for a casual family or light-duty small business server, and a dedicated consumer or small business line is adequate for more serious mid-weight business use. Most ISPs offer special business Internet connections that are shared between fewer users and should (in theory) offer higher performance than standard consumer connections. (In practice, businesses use more bandwidth than consumers. But they use it throughout the day, while consumer lines tend to become busy—and slow—in the evening.) A leased line is usually excessive for the kind of performance Lion Server can provide.

Genius While some businesses have run a web server off an older dial-up or ADSL connection, this is a practical option only for sites that are text-oriented and don't emphasize graphics. Modern site designs tend to use more bandwidth. Although it's not impossible to run a small site successfully with limited bandwidth, it's likely to be a very limited website.

Managing your IP address

After you have a physical connection, it automatically comes with an IP address. You must check with your service provider whether the IP address is *static* or *dynamic;* their technical support staff should be able to tell you.

Genius If your service provider can't tell you whether your IP address is static or dynamic, consider changing to a more technically literate provider.

A static IP address never changes. Even if your connection drops, your ISP always reassigns it the same address. This makes it easy to set up a server. You can use a "what is my ip" site to check the address by viewing from a browser on your server. You can then give this IP address to your domain registration or hosting company when you're ready to put your server online.

A dynamic IP address is assigned whenever your server reconnects to the Internet, and it may even change without warning. ISPs typically assign addresses from a block of addresses reserved for their exclusive use. Whenever you reconnect to the Internet, your ISP assigns you one address from this block, and it may be different from the one you used at the previous reconnection.

Dynamic IP isn't compatible with an online server. The DNS process must be able to translate your chosen domain name to an IP address, which isn't possible if the address keeps changing.

Luckily, there's a workaround, called *DynamicDNS*. DynamicDNS is built into many routers, but it must be paired with a domain hosting service that supports it, such as www.no-ip.com, shown in Figure 10.9.

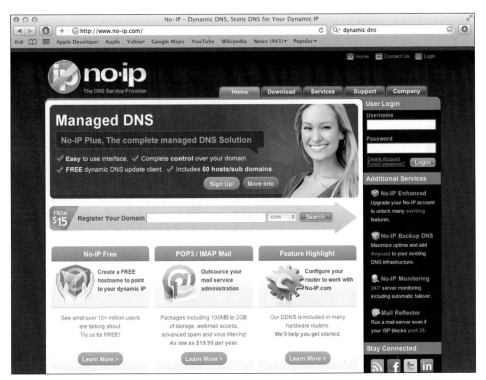

10.9 If your ISP uses Dynamic DNS, you need a DynamicDNS management/hosting service to keep your server online.

To use Dynamic DNS, you need to set it up in your router. This typically means entering the domain name of your Dynamic DNS service provider and enabling the DynamicDNS option.

Genius

If you need DynamicDNS, you can (and should) try to buy it with domain management, so you have an all-in-one solution. Although you can buy DynamicDNS from one supplier and domain hosting from another, getting the two to talk to each other can be unnecessarily complex. It's much simpler to keep everything under one virtual roof.

After Dynamic DNS is running, it's a set-and-forget task. Your domain name is mapped to your current IP number in the usual way. The only difference is that there's an extra (hidden, automatic) stage in the lookup process that finds and reports your current IP address at the time. Because Dynamic DNS is a slightly more modern technology, this happens without propagation delays.

Ordering domain hosting from a supplier

After you have an IP address and a domain name, you can contact your chosen supplier to register your domain and set up the DNS service for your server.

At this point, you're likely to encounter more jargon. When your supplier sets up a DNS record, they need to enter two types of information:

- **An "A record" takes your domain name and IP address and tells the DNS service to route most types of traffic to your server.** This sets up your server for web access and for most other types of traffic you choose to support.

- **An "MX record" directs e-mail traffic to your server.** You need to supply the same IP address and the name of the mail hosts you set up in Chapter 4—one for sending e-mail and one for receiving it. If you followed the instructions in Chapter 4, the hosts have the same name as your server; for example, if your domain name is called example.com and your server is called lilbox, both hosts are called lilbox.example.com.

Caution

Not all routers support Dynamic DNS. If your ISP supplies dynamic IP addresses and they also supply a router as part of a broadband package, check that DynamicDNS (DynDNS) support is built in. If it isn't, you may be able to buy an old cheap router and plug it into the network exclusively for DynDNS support, although clearly it's easier for you to buy a package that doesn't require this workaround.

You'll be asked about the web and e-mail settings you want to use when you create an account with your domain hosting provider. Some providers ask you to create your own A and MX records, but it's easier to hand the details to your provider and ask them to do this for you.

Genius

If you're not using your server for e-mail, you don't need to specify the MX record. It's good practice to buy a mail service from a web hosting company rather than hosting it locally. If your server crashes because of hardware problems or a power failure, or if your ISP disconnects you for any reason, your e-mail server disappears from the Internet, and e-mail bounces. A good hosted e-mail service is more reliable, because it includes resilient backups that can handle power and connectivity failures.

After the records are set up, your domain name starts propagating across the Internet.

If you want to know more about A records, MX records, and other types of DNS records, it's easy to find detailed tutorials online—like the one shown in Figure 10.10.

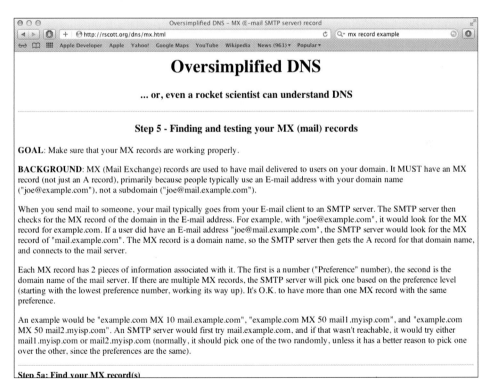

10.10 One of many tutorials about DNS you can find online by searching for "DNS tutorial." A complete introduction to DNS would be the size of this book.

Domains, sub-domains, and e-mail addresses

If your local e-mail addresses are set up to send e-mail to name@servername.domain. com, and you want your Internet e-mail addresses to be a more professional-looking address@domain.com, how do you resolve the incompatibility?

The MX record for your mail server can solve this problem.

Technically, servername.domain.com is a *subdomain*—a domain name with a prefix. So is www.domain.com.

Luckily, web servers automatically ignore the www. After you set up a DNS record for your domain, you don't need to add further records for a separate www subdomain.

Mail servers need a little more help. The MX record tells incoming or outgoing mail traffic that servername.domain.com and domain.com are identical.

Because Lion Server's own default DNS settings don't include this mapping, the DNS lookup for "domain.com" is passed to the Internet, which returns the link in the MX record.

The end result of this rather complex procedure is that you should be able to use address@ domain.com addresses locally on your network and on the Internet, and translation should happen automatically.

Genius

If you master DNS fully, you can use Lion Server's DNS feature in Server Admin to create more complex local and remote mappings. DNS mastery is a complex topic, but it can be worth learning if you want to have more precise control over the structure of your network.

Configuring a Router for NAT and Port Forwarding

At this point, you have chosen a domain name, registered it, set up a domain hosting service, and given the service the information it needs to set up a DNS record for your server.

But you're still not finished. While the DNS record is propagating, you must make some changes to your router settings to tell it to forward incoming web or e-mail traffic to your server.

Most LANs have at least a handful of computers, and unless you give your router some hints, it doesn't know which one is the server.

Note Forwarding is a problem only for incoming traffic. A router is clever enough to manage outgoing traffic automatically, which is why you can view external web pages on a LAN without issues.

Understanding NAT

The solution to this problem is Network Address Translation (NAT). *Port Forwarding* is an advanced version of NAT and is built into most routers.

Port forwarding simply sends incoming traffic of a certain type—web traffic, e-mail, chat, and so on—to one designated computer on your network. To set up port forwarding, you need two items of information:

- **The type of traffic you want to forward.** On most routers, you can select the most common traffic types from a list.
- **The local network IP address of your computer.** This is the address you set up in Chapter 2.

Genius Technically, you specify a service by selecting a *port number*. Each network service has a unique, standardized port number; for example, web traffic uses port 80. There are literally tens of thousands of possible services. Most routers include a predefined list that includes a short selection of the most popular services. If you don't know the port numbers you need, you can usually select them from this list. For more advanced setup for less popular services, you can specify the port number by typing it in and assigning a name.

Note There's more information about port numbers in Chapter 12, which is about Lion Server's firewall. If your server refuses to work after you've finished working through the instructions in this chapter, check the instructions in Chapter 12 to make sure the firewall isn't filtering out web or other traffic.

Setting up port forwarding in practice

The details for every router are different, but you're likely to see something like the option shown in Figure 10.11. This includes the following:

- **A list of active forwarding rules.** Initially, this is empty. As you add forwarding rules, they appear here.

- **A menu showing a list of services.** You can select the most options here.

- **A box for adding new rules.** You can use the menu to insert a named service with an associated port number, or you can add your own custom number and service name. Use the local IP address field to specify the local address of the server to which you want to send traffic.

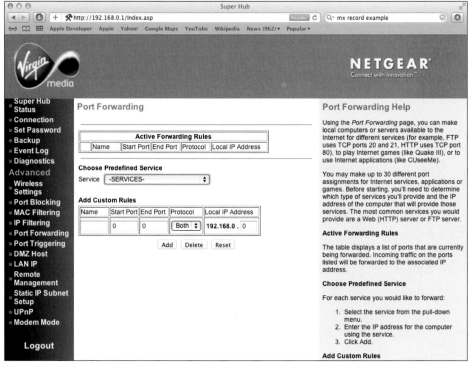

10.11 A typical port forwarding option built into a router.

Genius

Finding detailed instructions for setting up port forwarding in every make and model of router would be useful. A website called portforward.com has exactly this information.

Which ports do you need? Figure 10.12 shows a minimum configuration for web traffic, for receiving POP3 (Post Office Protocol) e-mail, and for sending e-mail with SMTP (Simple Mail Transfer Protocol). For other common ports and services, see Table 12.1 in Chapter 12.

In this example, the server has a fixed IP address of 192.168.0.99. If you've set up your server on a different address, replace that number accordingly.

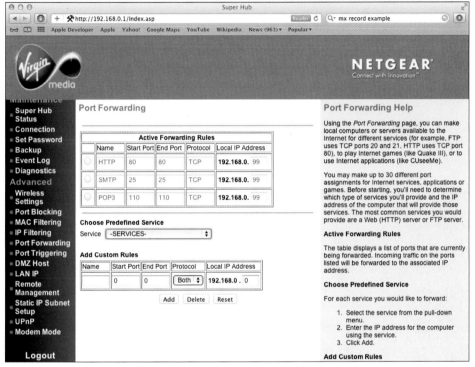

10.12 A minimal port forwarding configuration supporting web traffic and POP3 e-mail.

Installing a Security Certificate

If you've worked through the steps so far and allowed for propagation, your server should now be online. But it isn't yet a *trusted* server. Web users have no guarantee that you are who you say you are, and some browsers may include a warning message when displaying your custom web content.

To fix this, you should install an *SSL certificate*. This is a digital file that's checked by web browsers and other Internet services such as e-mail and chat. It confirms your identity and can be used to set up secure communications that send critical information including passwords in an encrypted form that can't easily be read by a third party.

Certificates have two components:

- **A self-signed certificate.** You can create this yourself on your server.

- **A full SSL certificate.** This takes your self-signed certificate details and wraps them in a further layer of security provided by a *certification authority*—a third party that specializes in online security and confirms the validity of your certificate on demand.

Genius

Certification support is built into most web browsers. Behind the scenes, your browser checks the SSL certificate of most sites it visits by downloading the certificate from the site, forwarding key details to the certification authority that certified it, and receiving formal notification that the certificate is valid. This process is automatic. If it fails, your browser displays a warning.

Note

As of Lion Server 10.7.2, certificates aren't yet working properly. Installing a certificate for the web server forces encrypted web access. (Technically, all http:// requests are converted into https:// requests.) This isn't correct behavior. Until this bug is fixed, the rest of this section is a provisional description of how you *should* use a certificate, but it's better to turn off certification for now.

Creating a self-signed certificate

Follow these steps to create a self-signed certificate for local use or to begin creating an SSL certificate for Internet use:

1. **Launch Server.app.**

2. **Select your server under Hardware in the Server app sidebar.**

3. **Click Settings.**

4. **Click the Edit button to the right of SSL Certificate.**

5. **Choose Manage Certificates from the Action pop-up menu.**

6. **Click the Add button (+).**

7. **Select Create a Certificate Identity from the pop-up menu, as shown in Figure 10.13.**

8. **In the Name field of the Certificate Assistant, enter your server's host name (for example, server.example.com).**

9. **Check the following settings:** Identity Type should be Self Signed Root; Certificate Type should be SSL Server; "Let me override defaults" should be deselected, as shown in Figure 10.14.

10. **Click Continue, and then click Done.**

11. **When you see a dialog asking you to export your new key to the keychain, click Always Allow.**

10.13 Launching the Certificate Assistant by asking for a new Certificate Identity.

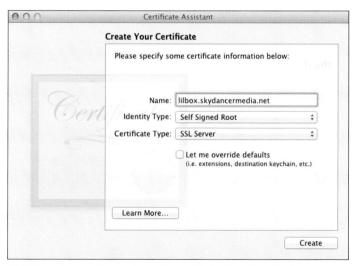

10.14 Creating a self-signed certificate with the Certificate Assistant.

Note

If you've changed the host name—and you almost certainly have—you can ignore and delete the default certificate created by Lion Server during its initial setup. Select it, and click the - (minus) icon.

Creating a Certificate Signing Request (CSR)

The previous steps add a new certificate to the list that appears in the Manage Certificates dialog.

A CSR takes the information in this file and creates a new file that you can send to a certification authority (CA). The CA may take some other details when you e-mail your request, and it may also perform a full identity check.

If all details are correct, the CA converts the CSR into a full SSL certificate that you can install in Lion Server.

To convert your self-signed certificate into a CSR, follow these steps:

1. **Repeat steps 1 to 5 in the preceding list to show the Manage Certificates feature.**
2. **Select the self-signed certificate you've just created.**
3. **Click the gear icon, and select Choose Generate Certificate Signing Request (CSR).**
4. **Save the CSR file, as shown in Figure 10.15.**

Creating a signed SSL certificate

Various certificate authorities exist. Most of the signed SSL certificates they create cost money, which can be as much as a few hundred dollars. And certificates must be replaced every 90 days or 365 days.

In this example, we use the FreeSSL service at RapidSSL (www.freessl.com) because it offers a free 30-day certificate service with an almost instant turnaround by e-mail after an automated phone call to confirm identity. (Other CAs can take up to a week to create an SSL certificate. They may also demand various identity checks.)

The exact steps you follow to obtain an SSL are different for each CA. Figure 10.16 shows the first stage of the FreeSSL sign-up process.

Whichever CA you choose will have clear instructions that you can follow. Note that you may need to open the CSR file you created in the preceding section in a text editor and copy its contents manually into the web form.

10.15 Saving a CSR.

Caution

As a further security measure and to check that you own the domain you claim to, certificates are usually e-mailed to an address at the domain name you specify in your paperwork. This can become complicated if you haven't yet set up e-mail on your server. Ideally, you'll have external e-mail hosting set up for your domain already, and you can start moving it to your new Mac server after the SSL certificate arrives. Sometimes, you can use an alternative authentication option, but this may involve faxing paperwork to the CA.

Caution

A CA typically assumes you're a corporation or small business, and it asks for a company name. If you're an individual, you may need to confirm identity in some other way.

10.16 Getting started with FreeSSL.

Installing a signed SSL certificate

Your signed certificate usually arrives as a file attached to an e-mail. To install it, save it to a convenient location with a .crt extension, and follow these steps:

1. **Open the Manage Certificates dialog following the steps earlier in this section.**

2. **Click the Action (gear) icon.**

3. **Select Replace Certificate with Signed or Renewed Certificate.**

4. **Drag and drop the file you saved earlier onto the sheet, as shown in Figure 10.17.**

Caution   Sometimes certificates arrive as plaintext in an e-mail. To create a certificate file, copy the text to a text editor and save the file with the .crt extension. Make sure you save the file as plaintext, with all formatting removed, and not as rich text.

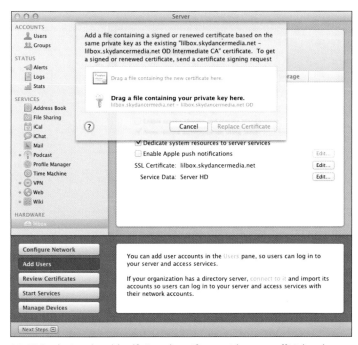

10.17 Replacing the old self-signed certificate with a new official and web-ready CA-signed version.

Note

When the certificate expires, you need to request a new one using the same CSR and install it over the old one in the same way.

Using the certificate

By default, the certificate is valid and active for all relevant services and websites. You can enable it selectively by clicking Edit next to the SSL Certificate box (as before) and selecting custom from the Certificate menu. Then you can enable the certificate for selected services. You also can use the None option to turn off SSL support altogether.

Genius

You can use this option to select different certificates for different services—for example, if you have different websites on different domains running on the same server.

Putting It All Together

For clarity, here's a recap of the stages in this chapter, in the order you're likely to do them:

1. **Use a domain checking website to find an available domain name.**

2. **Set up a physical connection.**

   If your connection has a static IP address, skip the next step.

3. **Set up DynamicDNS for your dynamic IP address.**

4. **Contact a domain hosting service, and tell them your domain name and static or dynamic IP addresses.**

5. **For web hosting only, tell them to set up an "A record" on their DNS server.**

6. **If you're hosting a mail service, tell them to set up an "MX record," and supply the subdomains used for mail by Lion Server.**

7. **Obtain and set up a security certificate for Lion Server, and enable it for web, e-mail, and other services.**

8. **Set up port forwarding for your router.**

9. **Wait until DNS propagation completes.**

Internet users should now be able to access the web and e-mail services running on your server, with full online security and authentication.

How Can I Connect to Lion Server Remotely?

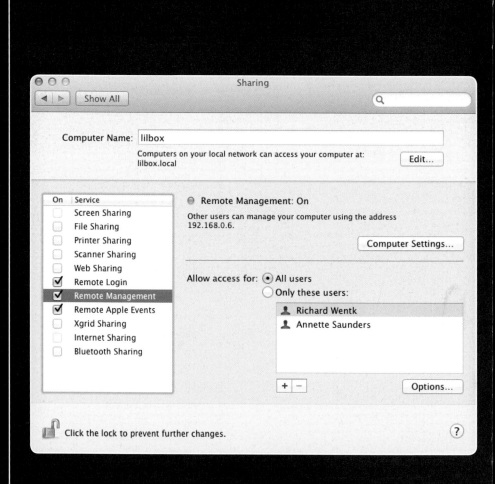

It's useful to give users remote access to your server so they can log in and access your network from a remote location. Administrators also may need to administer the server remotely or manage and control users' computers. OS X Lion and Lion Server include a selection of remote access tools that support these options.

Understanding Remote Access

Unlike local applications, network services are usually designed for remote access. Services run on a server, but they're accessed from other computers, either locally on the same network or remotely over the Internet.

But it's also useful to support more direct kinds of remote access. For example, you may want to administer your server remotely while you're away from your usual base—perhaps to update pages on your web server or to add a new network user.

It also can be useful to control networked computers from the server. OS X includes a selection of remote control features that make it possible to view a Mac's screen over the network and send it commands via a mouse and keyboard, just as if you were sitting in front of it.

Table 11.1 summarizes the remote control and remote access options that are available for OS X Lion and Lion Server. The rest of this chapter introduces these options in more detail.

Table 11.1 Remote Control and Remote Access Options

Option	Description
Screen sharing	Control any Mac from any other Mac.
VNC (Virtual Network Computing)	Control any computer from any computer.
Remote Administration with Apple Remote Desktop (ARD)	Manage and control networked Macs from your server. (Note: ARD is an optional extra purchase for Lion Server.)
VPN (Virtual Private Network)	Create a secure remote link over the Internet to connect a Mac to your network. The Mac operates as if it were connected locally.

A note about port numbers

If you use the Lion Server firewall, you must remember to allow traffic for the services mentioned in this chapter. If you don't set up the firewall so it passes this traffic, the features mentioned in this chapter won't work.

For more details about ports, services, and setting up the firewall to manage them correctly, see Chapter 12.

Understanding Screen Sharing

The Screen Sharing application isn't exclusive to Lion Server; it's built into OS X Lion. Screen Sharing does what the name suggests; it displays a remote Mac's window, tracks your mouse movements and mouse clicks, and sends them to the remote computer, which responds as if you were operating it locally.

You can use Screen Sharing with any Mac on your local network. Performance is limited by network speed, but even over WiFi, you can view SD video. On a faster network, you can stream HD video from one screen to another.

You can access remote Macs by name or by IP number. In OS X Lion, Screen Sharing has been built into Finder, making it even easier to access another Mac remotely.

Setting up Screen Sharing

To set up a Mac for remote access via Screen Sharing, follow these steps:

1. **Select ⇨ System Preferences to open System Preferences.**

2. **Select Sharing.**

3. **Check the Screen Sharing option, as shown in Figure 11.1.**

11.1 Setting up screen sharing in System Preferences.

4. **If you are setting up screen sharing on your server, leave the Computer Name field unchanged.** See Chapter 2 for more information about the computer name.

5. **Ignore the Computer Settings button for now.** For more information about the features, see the section about VNC later in this chapter.

6. **Optionally, click the Only these users: option in the Allow access for: field.** Use the + (plus) icon to add one or more named users from the list that appears. You can use this feature to enable screen sharing for specific users; this is recommended, because the default All users setting allows anyone on the network to view and control your server's screen.

You can now access the Mac remotely from another Mac, as described later.

Caution

Clearly, Screen Sharing can be a security risk; it gives direct access to a Mac. After a user has logged in on a Mac, you can use Screen Sharing to view everything they do, and "drive" the Mac remotely. Typically, you'll be very selective about Screen Sharing permissions. It's useful to give network administrators access to another Mac's screen. But you won't usually want to enable access for most users. For similar reasons, you should warn users not to enable Screen Sharing, or if you've enabled Screen Sharing with limited-access settings for your own convenience, warn users not to change the settings.

Using Screen Sharing

When Screen Sharing is enabled, Macs with a shareable screen appear automatically in Finder, as shown in Figure 11.2. To access the remote Mac, click the Share Screen… button.

Genius

You also can launch the Screen Sharing application manually from System/Library/Core Services—although it's easy to use this feature in Finder and Safari, so you won't often need to do this.

Note

Although Screen Sharing, File Sharing, and other sharing options are grouped together in System Preferences, they operate independently; from a user's point of view, they're not particularly closely related. You can enable the various sharing options as needed; they don't interact with each other.

By default, the remote Mac appears in a window that duplicates the original aspect ratio (the ratio of the width to the height) as shown in Figure 11.3.

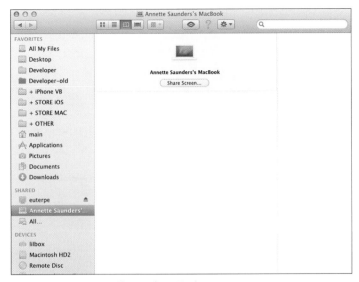

11.2 Accessing Screen Sharing from Finder.

Unless your Mac's display has the same aspect ratio as the remote Mac's display, you'll see gaps at the top and/or bottom of the window. If you resize the Screen Sharing window, the remote image is scaled automatically to maintain the aspect ratio.

11.3 Viewing and controlling a remote Mac.

Although Screen Sharing is a simple application, it has many options. Figure 11.4 shows the application preferences. You can turn off the automatic scaling, enable encryption of all data—including screen images—for extra security, and show the screen at full quality. Because the remote Mac may have a larger screen than your Mac, you can control what happens when you scroll to the edge of the screen. Screen Sharing can scroll through the remote window automatically or on request.

Understanding VNC

Although the Screen Sharing application is limited to Macs, it uses a technology called VNC (Virtual Network Computing). VNC isn't platform-specific; it can be used with Windows and UNIX/Linux computers as well as Macs.

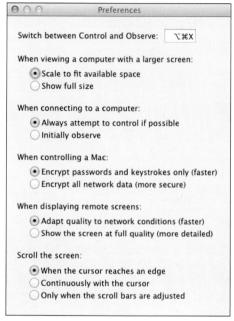

11.4 Screen Sharing preferences.

A VNC system has two components. A *VNC server* provides remote access. When you enable Screen Sharing on a Mac, you're setting up Apple's own VNC server, which runs behind the scenes. Other platforms have their own corresponding VNC servers.

A *VNC client* or *VNC viewer* connects to the server. The Screen Sharing application that runs when you connect to a remote Mac is Apple's own VNC client. Again, other platforms have their own corresponding clients.

VNC relies on IP numbers. On a local network, you can use standard local addresses. If a server is available on the Internet, you can use its online IP address to control it remotely. [You may need to set up NAT (Network Address Translation) on your local network before this works for your server. See Chapter 10 for details.]

Potentially, you can use VNC to operate your server, or your home Mac, from almost anywhere in the world.

Because VNC isn't platform-specific, you can operate a Mac using other clients running other plat-forms. You also can operate the desktop of any computer running a VNC server with Lion's Screen Sharing application.

OS X, Windows, and Linux all offer a selection of VNC server and client tools. Some are free. You can find a list by searching the web for VNC client and VNC server. Figure 11.5 shows one exam-ple—Screen Sharing on Mac displays the desktop of a Windows XP desktop running a free VNC server called Tight VNC.

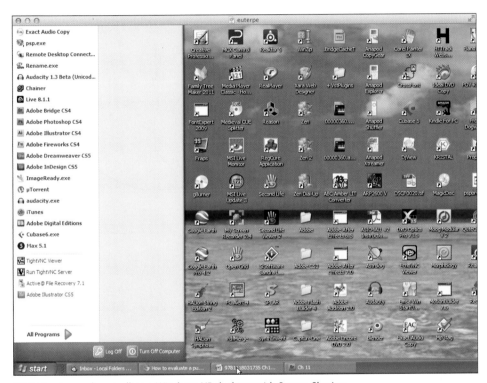

11.5 Viewing and controlling a Windows XP desktop with Screen Sharing.

Because Screen Sharing is compatible with VNC, you can use it to administer Windows and Linux computers on your network. But the process may not be as smooth as Mac to Mac remote control; there can be big differences in speed and efficiency when sharing across platforms. Apple's Screen Sharing is optimized for Macs and provides very good performance. Other clients and servers can be much slower; they may be so slow that they're difficult to use.

Genius

VNC is included in Safari. The easy way to launch Screen Sharing for any remote computer is to open Safari and type vnc://[remote IP address] or vnc://[domain name]. Safari launches the Screen Sharing application and attempts to create a connection to the computer with the specified address.

Genius

VNC also works on mobile platforms. Client apps are available for iOS devices, Android, and other mobile devices. Search the App Store for VNC to find some free examples.

Setting up VNC

When you enable Screen Sharing in System Preferences, VNC is enabled by default. But you can set up some extra options that are specific to VNC and can provide further security. You can view these options by clicking the Computer Settings button, as shown in Figure 11.6. You can do the following:

- **Control which users are allowed to use screen sharing**

- **Set a password**

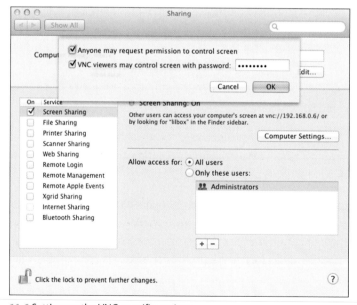

11.6 Setting up the VNC-specific options.

Controlling access

The operation of the check box labeled Anyone may request permission to control screen isn't obvious, nor is it explained in the online help.

If you leave this box unchecked, users are asked to supply a username and password when they attempt to share a screen. Access is filtered through the Allow access for settings in the main dialog. If the username and password matches those in the settings, the user is given remote access.

If you check this box, any user on any Mac can attempt to share the screen, but if they're not in the list of allowed users, they must ask for permission. The owner of the target Mac must accept the request before sharing is enabled.

Setting a password

The VNC password is an optional extra security feature. When a user attempts to share the remote Mac, they're asked to enter the password set here. Sharing is enabled only if the password is correct.

All VNC clients support password protection, so you can use this feature to limit access from all networked computers, not just from Macs.

Introducing Remote Management

Apple sells an optional product for network administration called Apple Remote Desktop (ARD), shown in Figure 11.7.

In spite of the name, you don't need to use ARD to control a remote computer; the free Screen Sharing application can do that for you.

ARD is much more sophisticated. You can use it to view and control multiple Macs simultaneously, with an optional "curtain mode" that hides your actions from the remote user. You can take screen shots and even read and write the remote clipboard.

ARD is also ideal for rolling out software across a network. Instead of installing the same software on multiple Macs manually, you can create a single packaged installation with a scripted installer, and the installer runs automatically. You can schedule the installation to run at a convenient moment, and the installer can wait for powered-down Macs and run the installation automatically when they become available.

ARD also includes a set of automation scripts that can set each Mac's wallpaper, configure preferences, and so on.

11.7 Using ARD to manage a single Mac remotely.

Genius

ARD sells for $299 for a network with up to 10 Macs, and $499 for a network with an unlimited number of Macs. But robust time-limited pre-release versions are available as an additional download for the Mac Developer Program, which costs $99 a year.

Getting and installing ARD

ARD is available as a download from the Mac App Store. Installation is simple; the application downloads and installs itself like any other Mac app, and it appears in the /Applications folder.

Because ARD isn't built into Lion Server, a full introduction to its features is outside the scope of this book. But ARD is well documented, and as long as you understand the principles of screen sharing and remote control, the basic features are very easy to use. Advanced administrators can use it to perform more complex automated tasks and to control Macs remotely from the command line.

Enabling Remote Management

However, before you can use ARD effectively, you must enable it on the remote Mac. To enable Remote Management, follow these steps:

1. **Select ⇨ System Preferences to open System Preferences.**

2. **Select Sharing.**

3. **Check the Remote Management and Remote Apple Events options, as shown in Figure 11.8.**

11.8 Enabling Remote Management in System Preferences.

4. **Optionally, set up a list of permitted users.** You can follow the same steps you used to set up a list of users for Screen Sharing, described earlier in this chapter.

5. **Optionally, click the Options button and select the permitted remote management features available to all users, or for specific users, as shown in Figure 11.9.** The figure shows the two most useful options: Observe and Control. The other options are subsets of the full Control features and can be used when more specific control is needed.

If you click the Computer Settings button, you see two options that aren't available in Screen Sharing.

You can choose to show the Remote Management status in the remote Mac's menu bar. This tells users when Remote Management is active and lets them know when their Mac is being observed or controlled.

You also can type some custom text into four info fields. ARD can collect reports from the Macs it monitors, and these text fields are custom information you can add to each report—for example, to give each Mac a different name, room number, or some other unique text id.

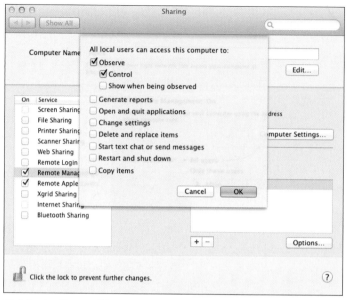

11.9 Setting Remote Management permissions, to define what remote management is allowed to do.

Note

Because Remote Management is an enhanced version of Screen Sharing, its settings override those of the Screen Sharing feature. In fact, you can't make changes to the Screen Sharing option when Remote Management is enabled.

Getting started with SSH and Remote Login

SSH (Secure Shell) is a remote control option for advanced users with command-line experience. You can use it to send text commands to a remote Mac; the Mac runs the commands just as if you ran Terminal and typed commands into it directly.

Note

You can skip this section on a first reading if you're not already familiar with command-line control. Although command-line control can be powerful, it's an optional extra for experienced users. You won't miss any essential features if you ignore it for now.

The key benefit of SSH is that commands are encrypted. Passwords and other important details can't be read even if the messages sent between computers are intercepted.

Setting up SSH

Logically, SSH should be labeled "SSH" in the Sharing System Preferences. In fact, it's labeled "Remote Login," which is a more descriptive name, but a less familiar one.

To enable SSH, follow these steps:

1. **Select ⇨ System Preferences to open System Preferences.**

2. **Select Sharing.**

3. **Check the Remote Login option, as shown in Figure 11.10.**

4. **Optionally, you can define a list of users who are allowed to use SSH on that Mac.**
   The Allow access for: field works like the equivalent fields in Remote Management and Screen Sharing.

   You can now send text commands to that Mac remotely using the instructions in the next section.

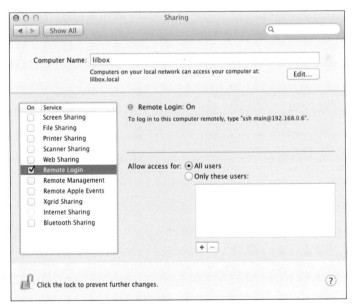

11.10 Setting up Remote Login/SSH on the target Mac.

Using SSH

SSH is an industry-standard tool, with many options and features. (See http://en.wikipedia.org/wiki/Secure_Shell for a complete description.)

But you can use SSH in a very simple way, simply by logging in remotely. The login process is similar to the standard Mac login, except that you type a username directly into the SSH command and then type a password when asked for one.

It's possible to access a Mac using any valid login account—or any account included in the access list set up for that Mac. Typically, you log in using your own name or an account with a generic name like "main."

To log in to a remote Mac, you must know its IP number. SSH works equally well over local networks and the Internet, although Internet response times can be slightly slower.

To send commands to a remote Mac, follow these steps:

1. **Launch Terminal from the /Applications folder.**

2. **Type *ssh username@IPaddress*.** For example, if the username is admin, and the remote IP address is 192.168.0.99, type ssh admin@192.168.0.99.

3. **If the remote Mac doesn't have a valid certificate (see Chapter 10), you see the warning message about authenticity shown in Figure 11.11.** Type yes to skip past it.

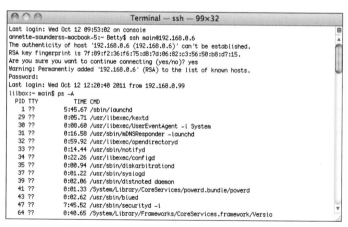

11.11 Using SSH to log in to a remote Mac and send it a command to show all running processes.

4. **Type the password for the remote account you're using.**

5. **After a few moments, SSH logs you in.** You can now type commands, and the remote Mac will respond to them. The figure shows what happens when you type a command to show all running processes.

Note

An alternative command-line tool called telnet is similar to ssh, but without the security. You can use telnet to connect to your server remotely over your local network. Type telnet [ip address:port number]. Because telnet accepts port numbers, you can use it to log in to a specific service, which can be very useful when checking that services are working correctly, because you send commands to them manually.

Introducing VPN

Lion Server's VPN feature is perhaps the most powerful of all the remote control options. VPN technology can seem complex, but the concept is very simple; instead of connecting a Mac to your network via WiFi or an Ethernet cable, you can connect to it remotely over the Internet.

The key difference between VPN and other technologies is that VPN becomes a *virtual cable*. The remote Mac appears to be on the local network, just as if it were physically connected. It even has a local IP number, and it can access all local network services.

But the Mac can be anywhere on the Internet. For security, the connection is encrypted. Sensitive information can be sent safely, and there's almost no chance of it being intercepted.

Like VNC, VPN uses a client and a server to create this link. A VPN server is built into Lion Server, and you can enable it to support remote access.

Both OS X Lion and iOS include free VPN clients, so you can use VPN for free with any Mac, iPhone, or other iDevice.

Note

Also like VNC, VPN software is available from third parties. Some VPN tools are free, but many aren't. VPN is widely used on corporate networks, and the more complex VPN tools are priced accordingly.

Caution Snow Leopard Server's VPN features were moderately challenging to set up, but fairly robust. As of version 10.7.2, Lion Server's VPN features are more challenging to set up and far less sturdy. Although it's possible to get VPN connections working, VPN in Lion Server isn't outstandingly reliable. In fact, it may not work for you at all. The instructions in the rest of this chapter are as reliable as they can be, but if you need to rely on VPN, you may want to consider alternative client and server solutions or wait for an Apple update.

Setting up VPN

The VPN pane shown in Figure 11.12 is misleadingly simple, because if you flick the giant switch, VPN almost certainly won't work for you.

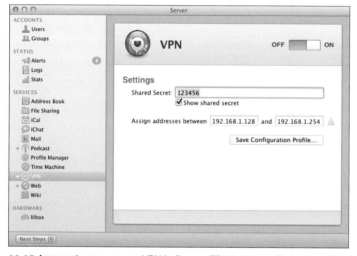

11.12 Attempting to set up a VPN in Server. (This is very unlikely to work.)

Server Admin contains a more useful setup tool that creates settings more likely to get VPN to work. But for maximum reliability, it helps to isolate the VPN traffic from the rest of the local network and force Lion Server to give it special treatment.

Note I based these instructions on the clever solution devised by the people at Macminicolo.net (www.macminicolo.net).

The easiest way to do this is to create a Virtual Network (VLAN) in your server's Network Preferences, run the setup tool in Server Admin, make a manual command-line change, and then restart the VPN service.

If you're using an external router or modem, you also need to change its port forwarding/NAT options to support external VPN.

These steps are outlined in this section.

Genius

A VLAN is an obscure feature in Network that creates a virtual router. You can use this router to create custom DHCP, DNS, and NAT settings exclusively for the VPN. (For an introduction to DHCP and DNS, see Chapter 2. For information about NAT, see Chapter 10.)

Creating a VLAN

To create a VLAN, follow these steps:

1. **Open System Preferences.**

2. **Select the Network item.**

3. **Click the gear at the lower right, and select Manage Virtual Interfaces.**

4. **Click the + (plus) icon at the lower right of the sheet.**

5. **Click New VLAN to add a new item, as shown in Figure 11.13.**

6. **Optionally, type a new name in the dialog, or just use the default.**

7. **Click the Create button at the lower right.**

8. **Click Done.**

Now that you have a VLAN, you can create a virtual network around it. The details of this network will change later, so enter placeholder values for now.

Follow these steps:

1. **Select the VLAN in the Network pane from the list at the left.**

2. **Select Manually in the Configure IPv4 field.**

3. **Type 10.0.0.1 into the IP Address field.**

4. **Type 255.255.255.0 into the Subnet Mask field.**

5. **Type 10.0.0.1 into the Router field, as shown in Figure 11.14.**

6. **Click Apply at the lower right.**

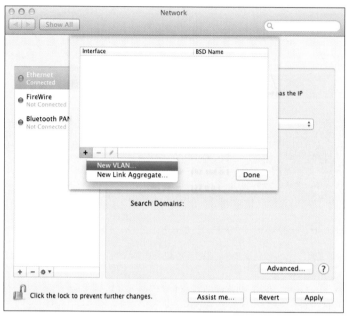

11.13 Creating a VLAN.

11.14 Setting up the new VLAN.

The VLAN is now active, and you can set it up for use with VPN.

Setting up VPN with Server Admin

It's not at all obvious that Server Admin includes an Assistant that can help you set up DHCP, DNS, NAT, and VPN settings. In fact, it does, and using it is more likely to get VPN working than using the simpler switch in Server.app. So this is one instance where Server Admin is an essential install, not an optional extra.

Caution As explained in Chapter 2, it's likely you'll use your router's DHCP and DNS features. However, if you're more experienced and have set up Lion Server's internal DHCP, note that you'll have to add your custom settings again after the Assistant finishes because it will overwrite them.

The Assistant is buried inside Server Admin's NAT settings. To use it, follow these steps:

1. **Launch Server Admin if it's not already running.**

2. **Make sure DHCP, NAT, DNS, and Firewall services are visible in the list at the left of the window.** If they aren't, click the server name at the top of the list, click Settings, click the Services tab, and check these services in the list.

3. **Click the NAT item in the list at the left.**

4. **If it isn't already visible, select the Overview icon at the top.**

5. **Click Gateway Setup Assistant at the lower right.** You see the first page of the Assistant, shown in Figure 11.15.

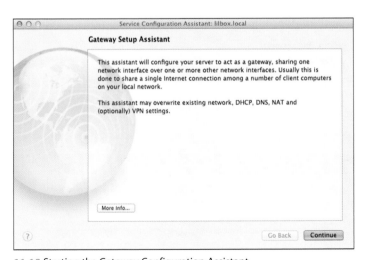

11.15 Starting the Gateway Configuration Assistant.

6. **Click Continue.** Confirm that you want to overwrite existing DHCP subnets.

7. **On the next page, select Ethernet, as shown in Figure 11.16.** (Do *not* select VLAN here.)

8. **Click Continue.**

9. **On the next dialog, check the VLAN box.**

10. **Click Continue.**

11. **On the next dialog, check the Enable VPN for this server box.**

12. **Type a Shared Secret.** This should be a very long string of letters and numbers. (Lion Server supports a maximum secret length of 56 characters. Stick to letters and numbers because other characters can confuse it. Make a note of the secret because you need it later.)

13. **Click Continue, and then click Continue again to skip past the information screen.**

14. **Wait a moment while the Assistant makes your changes.**

15. **Click Close to close the Assistant.** The Assistant sets up the DHCP, DNS, NAT, and VPN services to use the information you entered.

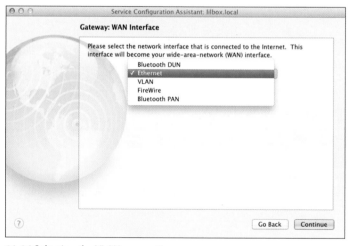

11.16 Selecting the VLAN connection.

Turning off the firewall and resetting DNS

The Assistant has made some changes you may not want. One change is that the firewall is now working. Chapter 12 includes more information about configuring the firewall. Leave the firewall turned off until you work through that chapter. In Server Admin, click the Firewall item in the list at the left. Click the Stop Firewall button at the lower left of the window, as shown in Figure 11.17.

The other change is that you may need to reinstate your DNS forwarder settings. This feature tells Lion Server's DNS service where it can look up domain name IP addresses on the Internet when it can't find them locally. Typically, you enter your local router address if you have one (usually 192.168.0.1). You also may need the addresses of your ISP's DNS servers, which you can get from your ISP's technical support.

Figure 11.18 shows some typical settings. Note that the 194… addresses are DNS server settings provided by your ISP. If you're not sure what these numbers should be, ask your ISP.

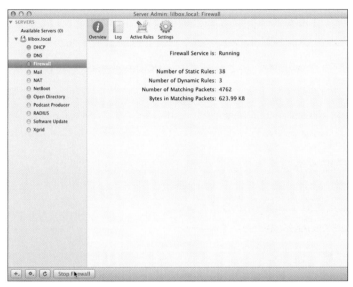

11.17 Turning off the Firewall.

Setting the VPN address range

You can now return to the VPN setup options in Server.app; open Server.app, and click the VPN item in the list at the left.

When a VPN connection dials in, Lion Server assigns it a unique IP address. The address range shown in Figure 11.19 does two things: It specifies the actual addresses that are used, and it tells Lion Server how many simultaneous VPN connections you want to allow.

If you're the only person likely to use VPN, use the same address in both boxes. To support more users, make the second address larger than the first. The range is the maximum user count; once Lion Server runs out of addresses, it rejects incoming VPN connections. The figure shows a range of five, which supports five simultaneous users.

Genius

These are *simultaneous* connections, so you can potentially support a larger total number of users. Lion Server won't start locking out users until all available addresses are being used *at the same time*. The total number depends on the usage pattern; it will be larger if users log in randomly throughout the day, and smaller if they log in simultaneously at a set time.

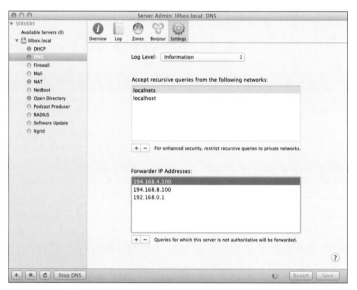

11.18 Fixing the DNS settings.

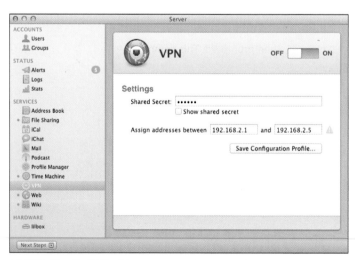

11.19 Setting the VPN address range and user count.

The other element is a workaround. For VPN to work, the addresses should be in the range 192.168.2.1 to 192.168.2.254. This setting will change later, but for now type in the range shown in the figure.

Finally, replace the shared secret with the one you entered when running the Assistant in Server Admin. Optionally, you can check the Show shared secret box to confirm that you've entered it correctly.

Genius

In this example, Lion Server actually assigns each VPN connection two addresses—one on the VLAN and one assigned dynamically from the address range you select in Server.app. If this seems complicated, it is. A VPN server would usually pick an IP address from the latter pool of addresses. This double-address workaround is necessary to get Lion Server's VPN address management working correctly.

Fixing VPN addressing

If the VPN service was running, click the switch to turn it off. Wait a minute or so while your changes register, and then click the switch to turn it on again.

The next step requires a command-line tweak to fix Lion Server's VPN addressing issues. Navigate to /Applications/Utilities and open Terminal.

Type the following very carefully on a single line; I've had to break it to fit it on the page, but don't add breaks while typing. Make sure you copy the punctuation exactly:

```
sudo serveradmin settings vpn:Servers:com.apple.ppp.l2tp:DNS:OfferedServerAddres
    ses:_array_index:0 = "192.168.2.1"
```

Press Return, and enter your password when prompted. This command makes a key change to Lion Server's internal configuration.

Enabling the VPN service

Click the switch to turn off the VPN service in Server.app. Wait a minute or so, and then turn it on again.

Check your Internet connection using Safari. (You *must* use Safari for this step.) If you see a message saying that Safari can't connect to the Internet, click the Network Diagnostics button. Select the Ethernet option, confirm that you are using manual addressing, make sure that the router field has your router's IP address, and watch as Network Diagnostics repairs your connection, as shown in Figure 11.20.

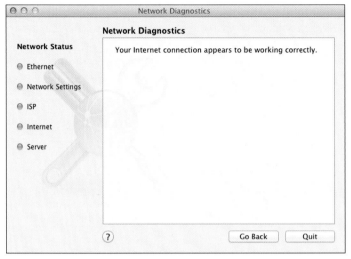

11.20 If the previous steps break your server's Internet connection, Network Diagnostics can repair it.

Setting up your router to support VPN

You must add port-forwarding (NAT) settings to make sure that traffic that arrives at your router isn't filtered and is sent to your server. The process is similar to that described in Chapter 10; for more details, see the example for web traffic.

The details vary from router to router, but basically, you must open the ports shown in Figure 11.21. (Not every port is essential for VPN, but you're more likely to succeed with VPN if you set them up as shown.)

Using VPN

As mentioned earlier, a VPN connection is similar to a cable connection, except that data is sent securely in both directions over the Internet.

Caution

Although you can connect to your VPN from a local Mac or iDevice, this is only a partial test. For a full test, you must be at a remote location. One common problem is attempting to log in via the Internet while still on your network. For example, if your online IP address is 123.231.34.45, you *can't* use this as the server address while you're still on your local network; it may confuse your router. You can, however, go to any location with a different IP address and a different router, and test your connection by logging in remotely from there. Alternatively, you can disconnect your iDevice from local WiFi and connect over a cellular data connection.

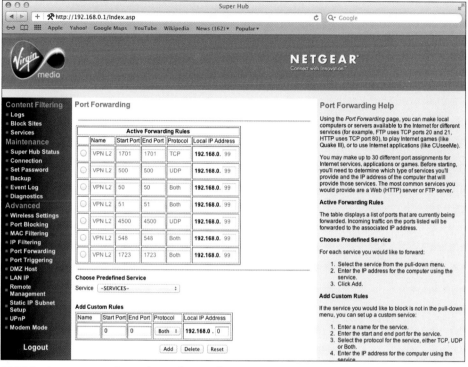

11.21 Setting up a router's port forwarding to allow VPN.

To use the VPN feature, you must set up your Mac's built-in client. Follow these steps:

1. **Open the Network pane in System Preferences.**

2. **Click the + (plus) icon at the lower left of the window.**

3. **Select VPN in the Interface field.**

4. **Make sure L2TP over IPSec is selected under VPN type.**

5. **Optionally, change the Service Name.** This is for display only.

6. **Click Create.**

7. **Select the new VPN connection, and type the values shown in Figure 11.22.** The Server address is your online server domain name. The account name is the account used to connect to the service. Each user can use her standard Lion Server login account. Alternatively, if your users access mail and wiki information via the web interface, you can create a single shared generic login account for them.

8. **Optionally, check the box beside Show VPN status in menu bar to display the connection status.**

283

11.22 Creating a VPN connection using the built-in client.

9. **Click Authentication Settings.**

10. **Click the Password radio button, and enter the password for the user account.**

11. **Click the Shared Secret radio button, and paste in the shared secret you set earlier.**

12. **Click OK.**

13. **Click the Connect button.**

The client should connect to your server. If it doesn't switch the VPN service off in Server.app, run the command again in terminal, wait 30 seconds or so, and turn the VPN service on again. You may need to repeat this several times before the change "sticks."

Genius

You can type your server's IP address directly into the server field for all VPN clients. This saves a DNS lookup and can (slightly) increase the connection speed.

Note that iOS devices also support VPN connections. You can find the VPN setup options in Settings ⇨ VPN. Set them up as shown in Figure 11.23.

11.23 Setting up VPN on an iPhone.

How Do I Secure Lion Server?

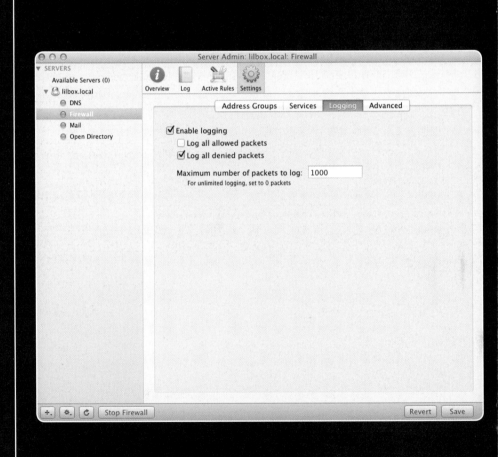

Security is a critical element of network administration. If you use your network for business or if you keep sensitive information at home, security is an issue you can't afford to ignore. Lion Server includes security features that can limit unauthorized access to services and files, and help keep your server locked down from external attacks. Setting up these services requires an introduction to network security, which is the purpose of this chapter.

Getting Started with Online Security

A server is the hub of a network, and keeping it secured from possible attacks is a critical challenge for network administrators.

Servers often hold sensitive personal and commercial information. E-mails, address books, calendars, web development projects, user databases, and even podcasts can all be valuable to outsiders, as can personal and shared files. And losing a server completely can be catastrophic.

On a local network, passwords provide a reasonable basic level of security. But networks that can be accessed from the Internet require more sophisticated measures.

Hackers have many possible ways to attack a server. Large corporations employ skilled security staff who are familiar with the most common kinds of attack, and they keep up with the latest security information, manually updating and customizing the server software to maximize security.

This isn't possible on Lion Server—at least, not for beginners. But it is possible to apply basic security measures that provide enough security for less demanding applications.

Caution Lion Server is sold as-is, and you should assume that Lion Server *isn't* a commercial-grade secured server. If you need secure computing—for example, for high-volume eCommerce—consider an alternative solution. With Lion Server, the best security is provided by not being an interesting enough online target for professional hackers to bother with, which means not keeping credit card information or other obviously valuable data on the server.

Analyzing online threats

Threats can take two forms and can cause many types of damage, from a defaced website, shown in Figure 12.1, to information theft.

Technological threats are flaws in the software running on the server or flaws in the way it has been set up. Threats and flaws such as viruses are known to almost anyone who uses a computer. Others are known only to hackers and security experts. A small number are very obscure; they may be known only to security researchers who deliberately test software to destruction as an academic exercise. But because the Internet is so good at spreading information, obscure threats can become known to attackers and security experts very quickly. And both security experts and hackers mingle to share information at conferences, like the one shown in Figure 12.2.

12.1 You don't want to see this on your server.

Social threats are the result of poor training, poor security policies, or limited user skills. For example, a poor password policy that encourages users to select simple and obvious passwords is a social threat. A less obvious example is provided by hackers who phone from outside an organization, impersonating other staff and asking for secure password information.

Security has its own jargon. It's useful to know some of the words that are used.

- **Vulnerability.** A political or technological flaw. Technological flaws often are built into software and can be fixed only by updating ("patching") the software.

- **Exploit.** A hacker action, such as defacing a website or stealing credit card details, that makes use of a vulnerability.

- **Patch.** A software update that fixes a vulnerability.

- **Malware.** Software that damages a server or other computer.

- **Black hat.** A malicious hacker who hacks for fun and profit.

- **White hat.** A security expert or academic researcher.

289

12.2 The Black Hat Briefings are one of the largest security conferences and include both white hat and black hat attendees.

Understanding practical threats

It's impossible to create a definitive list of security threats, because new threats develop regularly. But these are some of the common threats:

- **Denial of service (DoS) and other flood attacks.** A hacker swamps a server with bogus traffic that crowds out useful traffic, preventing it from functioning. It's difficult to protect a server against this kind of attack.

- **Code injection.** A hacker attempts to find flaws in a website's database or web server software. He can then use the flaws to run malicious software. Regular server software updates are the best protection against code injection.

- **Port scan.** A hacker runs software that looks for unsecured services running on a server. The more services that are open and available, the more likely it is that a hacker will find a way in. You can minimize the risks of a port scan by using a traffic filter called a *firewall*.

- **Password attack.** A hacker attempts to "guess" an important password by running software that checks the most likely possibilities. Some examples are shown in Figure 12.3. Use secure passwords, and limit the number of access attempts—where possible—to protect against password attacks.

- **Viruses.** A hacker infects a computer with software that makes it vulnerable to further attacks. In the worst case, a virus can take over the computer completely and force it to run unauthorized software that generates and sends spam, scans the hard disk for useful documents and information, and creates a "back door" through which a hacker can access the computer directly. Lion Server includes built-in antivirus software called ClamAV, discussed later in this chapter.

- **Mail relay.** E-mail is created by spammers, but forwarded through a legitimate mail server to hide its origin. For details, see Chapter 4.

- **Phishing scams.** A hacker impersonates a known and trusted site or organization to steal valid usernames and passwords. This topic is covered in Chapter 4.

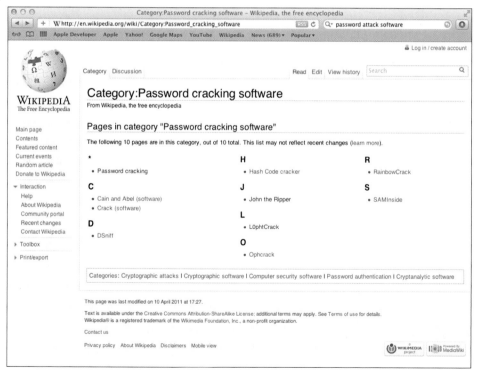

12.3 Password attack software is easy to find. Even Wikipedia lists some of the more common options.

Obviously, creating a fully secured server is very difficult. Some threats are relatively easy to guard against. For example, long random passwords are relatively secure as long as they're not accessible by indirect means and staff are trained to manage them securely.

Other attacks are more difficult to avoid. DoS attacks are best avoided by using specialized filtering hardware. It's almost impossible to protect against them with more basic equipment.

Many exploits have been standardized; they can be run by hackers with very little experience who download and run free exploit software, also known as scripts. Expert hackers dismiss these beginners as "script kiddies," but scripts can be powerful, and untrained hackers can still do lots of damage with them.

Standardization means that some exploits can be self-replicating in the form of *worms*—independent software fragments, similar to viruses—that can propagate across multiple networks and servers. Worms can run a set of exploits on a server, copy themselves to another server, and eventually spread across much of the Internet.

While it isn't possible to secure a server against every possible threat, Lion Server includes security features that make some of these attacks less effective.

Genius

Computer security can be fascinating. A common professional technique is *penetration testing*—a deliberate attempt to hack your own server. Corporations sometimes hire hackers to perform penetration testing, but it can be revealing to search for common hacking scripts and run them against your own installation. Be careful though; black hat websites often harbor viruses and attempt exploits of their own. It's a good idea to download and run scripts from an isolated computer at a remote location that has no connection to your network, and to make sure you have good antivirus software installed.

Understanding Security in Lion Server

Security in Lion Server has five elements:

- **Passwords for user logins and feature management.** It's impossible to access many of Lion Server's features without a password. Passwords management is introduced in Chapter 2.

- **SSL certificates for automated authentication.** Certificates don't protect the server directly, but they can reassure users that the server isn't being impersonated by some other computer. Certificates are described in Chapter 10.

- **Mail relay control and virus filtering.** These features limit e-mail to authorized traffic and are described in Chapter 4.

- **The ClamAV antivirus system.** This is integrated into Mail Server, as shown in Figure 12.4, and provides protection against e-mail viruses (but not against other kinds of virus attack).

- **An application firewall.** This firewall accepts or denies traffic for separate applications. It's set up from System Preferences and is described later in this chapter.

- **A port filtering firewall.** This firewall accepts and denies traffic based on port numbers and IP addresses. It's also described later in this chapter.

12.4 Mail Server's antivirus tool uses ClamAV, an open source antivirus solution.

Caution Note that this is a limited list and doesn't provide a complete security solution. Lion Server does *not* include protection against DoS attacks, code injection, or social attacks. Enabling its security features does *not* protect you from these threats. Note that some features also can be accessed by automated password attacks, although if passwords are very secure, this becomes less likely.

Outlining firewall technology

A firewall is a utility that blocks certain kinds of network traffic. Imagine that a server is a large building with many doors. Each door provides access to one specific service and its associated traffic—e-mail, web traffic, chat, and so on.

Most server users don't realize that there are literally thousands of possible doors, and by default many of them are open to outside traffic.

Technically, doors are called *ports*. Each port is a number tied to a specific network service. For example, web traffic is always transferred on port 80. E-mail traffic typically uses ports 110 and 25, although it may also use others, depending on its configuration.

An open port doesn't mean that a hacker can gain instant access to a server. But many network services have built-in vulnerabilities. The more open ports a hacker can find, the more easily he can find an open vulnerability to exploit. You can use the firewalls built into Lion Server service to manage traffic in two ways. The simpler firewall hides port numbers and service names from you. You can use it to manage traffic for specific applications—for example, to filter out remote connections to iTunes on the server.

The other firewall manages ports and services explicitly, as shown in Figure 12.5. You can use it in three ways:

- **To filter traffic to and from unused ports, for external security.**

- **To filter traffic for applications such as illegal file sharing or certain games, which you may not want to support on your network.**

- **To filter traffic to and from certain IP addresses.** Internally, you can use this option to limit network access from a specific computer. Externally, you can filter out troublesome IP addresses used by spammers or hackers.

Filters are also called *rules*. A rule defines the source and destination IP number of the traffic you want to protect yourself from or disable for other reasons. It also defines the service—via the port number—you want to control.

Ideally, you should open only the ports you need for the services that are critical on your server. For example, if you use Web Server, you should leave port 80 open; otherwise, you can't serve web pages. But if you're not using Web Server, you can use the firewall service to lock down port 80 and make it secure.

Similarly, IP address filtering can eliminate threats from certain addresses. But this may not be as useful as it sounds, because hackers often use *proxies*—pass-through servers that disguise their true IP address. Proxies are free, widely available, and often short-lived, so hackers don't need to use them more than once. Lists of proxies are easy to find, as shown in Figure 12.6.

Note

Although it's possible to discover and ban proxy access automatically on certain servers, this feature isn't built into Lion Server, and it can't easily be added.

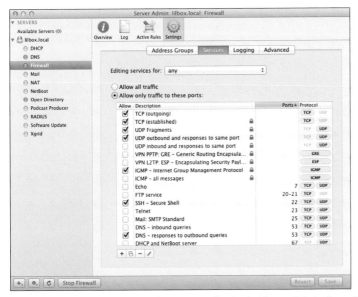

12.5 Filtering ports and services by port number in the Server Admin firewall.

12.6 This is one of hundreds of websites that list proxies. New proxies appear daily.

More about ports and services

When the Internet was developed, the port system was invented as a simple way to route traffic to a given software service. For example, a web server always "listens" to port 80. When a request arrives on port 80, it responds to it, but it ignores traffic sent to all other port numbers.

The port numbers used by services are fixed and somewhat standardized.

The first 1023 ports are *well-known ports.* Not all computers support every service in this range, but all computers support at least some of them.

Ports between 1024 and 49151 are *registered ports.* Manufacturers can reserve a port with an organization known as the Internet Assigned Numbers Authority (IANA). If the request is successful, the port is permanently reserved for that service. However, some ports in this range are unofficial; they're not formally registered with IANA, but they're often used by games or by popular open-source free software.

Port numbers in the range 49152 to 65535 are unreserved and used more or less randomly, as required.

Ports can be difficult to understand. Services are listed as an alphabet soup of acronyms, and if you don't already know what they do, you can only find a description by searching online. But you don't usually need to know the details; if you don't recognize the name of a service, turn it off in the firewall. If something important stops working on your network, turn it on again.

Using a hardware firewall

Many standard routers and broadband modems include a firewall feature service of their own. If you enable this feature, it runs independently, with separate settings and options.

You can choose to use both firewalls, either, or—if you don't mind limited security—neither. Using two firewalls occasionally provides an extra layer of security. In theory, both firewalls should work the same way and give the same results. But a router firewall protects your server from traffic external to the network. The firewall in Lion Server also can manage and protect local traffic and is more likely to protect your server if a computer on it is infected with a virus.

Because every router is different, it's impossible to provide standard setup instructions for a hardware firewall. For details, see your router's instructions. However, if you understand the principles of ports and services, you often can make an educated guess about how to set up the firewall. Figure 12.7 shows one example of traffic filtering, built into a rebranded Netgear router.

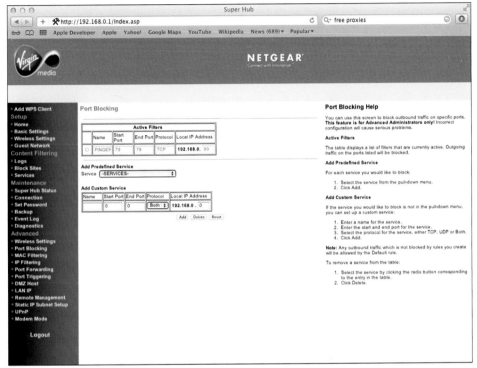

12.7 Use this to set up traffic filtering in a router. Internet users are unlikely to need to access the Finger service on your network, so it's been turned off in this example.

Genius

Having a separate external firewall can sometimes help with DoS or flood attacks. An effective hardware firewall can filter out the traffic flood, allowing a relatively leisurely trickle of traffic onto the local network. There may be a small performance penalty in using two firewalls, but this isn't usually large enough to be a significant drain on network resources.

Genius

If you're using a router as a firewall, don't forget to change the default admin password! Routers are easy to identify, and hackers interested in your network will try the default password as a matter of course.

297

Setting Up Lion Server's Application Firewall

The application firewall built into Lion Server is almost identical to the standard OS X Lion Firewall. To set it up, enable it in System Preferences as follows:

1. **Open System Preferences.**

2. **Select the Security & Privacy item in the top row.**

3. **Select the Firewall tab.**

4. **Enter your password to authenticate.**

You can now access the firewall dialog, as shown in Figure 12.8.

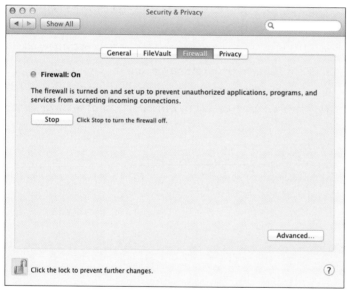

12.8 Accessing the firewall standard OS X Lion firewall.

Although this firewall doesn't deal specifically with network services or port numbers, it's an essential security tool. You can use it to lock down the server to prevent some very blatant types of unauthorized access that could potentially leave it wide open to hackers—or to unscrupulous local users.

Enabling the firewall

To turn the firewall on and off, click the Start/Stop button near the top left. Although this isn't a standard big Lion Server toggle switch, it works in a similar way.

Selecting the Advanced options

To set up application filtering, select the Advanced… button at the lower right. The four main options are shown in Figure 12.9:

- **Block all incoming connections.** *Don't* check this box; it will kill useful network traffic. The firewall in Server Admin gives you much finer control over specific selected connections.

- **The application list.** The applications shown in the figure can't be removed here, but you can add new applications to the list, as described in the next section.

- **Automatically allow signed software to receive incoming connections.** If you have a valid security certificate installed (see Chapter 10), checking this box should guarantee that mail, iChat, iCal, Address Book, and the web server are accessible to the rest of the network.

- **Enable stealth mode.** Check this box to help hide the server from hackers. The Server Admin firewall includes a more powerful stealth mode tool. This option on its own doesn't do much to protect the server, but it can help guard it from worms and automated attacks.

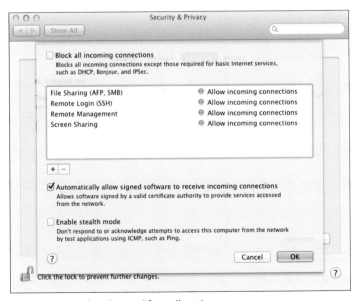

12.9 Setting up the advanced firewall settings.

Controlling application traffic

Although you can add applications to the list in the pane, this feature has limited usefulness. You can add only applications with the .app file extension, so you can't use it to manage network services, which typically run in the background and aren't listed in the /Applications folder.

However, you can use it to block client applications such as iChat and Facetime. You may want to do this as a parental control feature on a home network or to minimize external access to your server while it's visible on the Internet.

To block an application, follow these steps:

1. **Click the + (plus) icon under the list.**
2. **Select an application from the /Applications folder when it appears.**
3. **Click the Add button at the lower right of the window.**
4. **Click Allow incoming connections to the right of the application name.**
5. **Select Block incoming connections from the floating menu.**

Note

Lion adds some applications automatically—for example, when you enable some of the file sharing features described in Chapter 6.

Setting Up Lion Server's Port Filter Firewall

The firewall feature can be accessed only through the Served Admin application or from the command line. There's no way to access it from Server App.

Caution

The firewall is *disabled by default*. If your server is visible on the Internet and you don't have a hardware firewall, your server is completely open to port-based attacks. But note that enabling the firewall without customizing it filters many useful services and stops them working. You must customize some of the firewall's settings to use it successfully, as described later in this chapter.

Adding the firewall to Server Admin's list of services

Before you can set up and enable the firewall, you must add it to Server Admin's list of services, as follows:

1. **Launch Server Admin.**

2. **Login to your server.**

3. **Click the server name at the top left.**

4. **Click the Services tab, as shown in Figure 12.10.** (If no services appear, click the '+' icon at the lower left.)

5. **Check the Firewall item.**

6. **Click Save at the bottom right of the pane.**

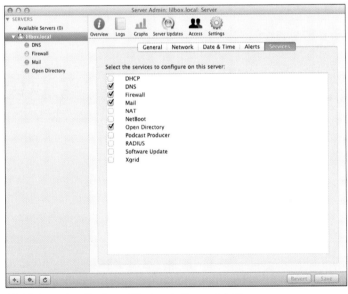

12.10 Accessing the firewall feature in Server Admin.

You should see the firewall service added to the list at the left. You can then access the settings shown in the figure, as described in the next section.

Introducing the firewall control panes

Like the other elements in Server Admin, the firewall feature includes a selection of related control panes that provide status information and make it possible to access settings.

To view these panes, select the Firewall item from the services at the left of Server Admin. You see four icons at the top of the window:

- **Overview.** This is a simple and minimal status summary. It tells you whether the service is running and includes a brief summary of the firewall settings and current filter status.

- **Log.** This is a list of events. By default, security events *aren't* logged. Unless you change this in the Settings/Logging tab below, this list displays regular maintenance events.

- **Active Rules.** This is a list of low-level filters. The Packets and Bytes columns summarize the amount of traffic that has been filtered by each rule.

- **Settings.** This icon shows a pane with four tabs—Address Groups, Services, Logging, and Advanced—that define the rules (traffic filters) created by the firewall.

Starting and stopping the firewall service

To start the firewall service, click the Start Firewall/Stop Firewall button at the bottom of the window and confirm your choice in the alert box, as shown in Figure 12.11. When the firewall is stopped, all filtering and logging features are disabled, and your server is open to port-based attacks.

Note

By default the firewall is set to pass all traffic. Traffic won't be filtered until you make the further changes described in the remainder of this chapter.

Packets on the network

Although it's not obvious, network and Internet data is sent as *packets*—small bursts of data extracted from a larger data stream, each of which is like a small digital envelope with its own content. Packets are sent separately over the network—each packet can potentially take a different route—and reassembled by the receiver to recreate the original stream.

Packet assembly and disassembly is a fairly complex process. Luckily, it just works, so you don't need to know the details. When setting up the firewall, you simply need to know that all traffic is *packetized* and that some of the firewall's logging and reporting features count the number of packets that are sent and received.

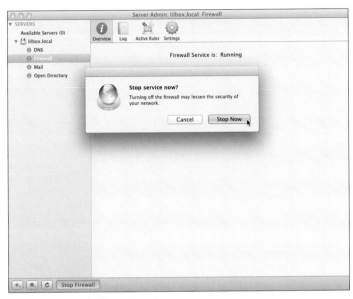

12.11 Stopping the firewall service.

Understanding Address Groups and Services

The server firewall is far more powerful and customizable than the standard OS X Lion firewall. You can filter and manage traffic in two ways:

- **Address Groups.** Use this feature to create different filters for different network addresses. You can specify individual IP numbers or address ranges.

- **Services.** Use this feature to create different filters for different services/port numbers.

Typically, you define or select address groups first and then create a different set of filters for each address group. If you don't want to use the address group feature at all and you want to apply the same rules to all traffic irrespective of IP number, you can use the default Any address group, which is a simple wildcard.

The default address groups, shown in Figure 12.12, include the following:

- **Any.** This means all traffic, from anywhere to anywhere.

- **10-net.** This address range is used for local addresses on larger corporate networks. You can ignore it on a typical home or small office network.

- **192.168-net.** This address range includes all the addresses on a typical local network.

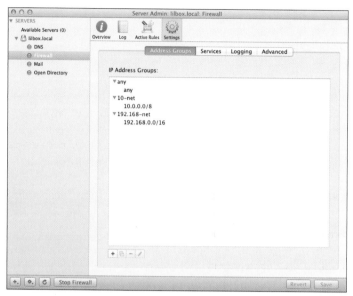

12.12 Using the reveal triangles to show the address ranges in each address group.

Genius

If you click the reveal triangles next to the three items, you see that each range is defined with a *network prefix*—a base address followed by a slash and a number. Technically, the network prefix is a bit pattern that counts from the left of the address. So 192.168.0.0/16 is a terse way of indicating the address range 192.168.0.0 to 162.168.255.255. The 192.168-net default is already set up for you, so you don't need to understand network prefixes to use this feature. Creating your own ranges can be complex, so there are various calculators online that can clarify the relationship between address ranges and prefixes—for example, http://www.csgnetwork. com/ipinfocalc.html.

Caution

In practice, because of NAT (see Chapter 10), incoming Internet traffic is indistinguishable from local network traffic. To filter local and remote traffic in different ways, you must put the firewall *before* the NAT service, which may mean putting it on the far side of the router, running on a separate server.

You can create your own address groups—for example, to limit the services available to one particular machine on the network. Initially, it's easier to experiment with filtering services for the Any group. You can return to address groups after you understand how to set up basic filtering.

Enabling the service filters

By default, you should disable as many services as possible and allow only those that are needed by your users. All other services should be filtered.

It's always more secure—and more convenient—to list *allowed* services than to list *filtered* services. This may seem quirky, but it's the most practical and efficient way to manage the firewall.

The design of the Services tab in the Settings pane reflects this. You can create a list of ports (or services) that accept traffic. Services (port numbers) that aren't in this list are filtered and don't work.

Note that by default *many useful services are disabled*. If you turn on the firewall and enable service filtering, you'll find that mail, web, chat, and other services stop working. To illustrate this, and to explain how to use the Services tab to enable them, follow these steps:

1. **If it isn't already running, launch Server Admin.**

2. **If you haven't already added the firewall to the list of services, follow the steps earlier in this chapter.** See the text before Figure 12.10 for details.

3. **Click the Firewall item in the column at the left.**

4. **Click the Settings icon.**

5. **Click the Services tab, as shown in Figure 12.13.**

6. **If it isn't already selected, choose the Any item from the Editing services for: menu.** The changes you're about to make will apply to traffic to and from any address.

7. **Click the Allow only traffic to these ports: radio button.**

8. **Click Save at the bottom right.**

9. **Click Start Firewall near the bottom left of the pane.**

You have now enabled the firewall, and the default settings mean that many useful services are *disabled* and inaccessible from other computers.

To test this, make sure the web service is running, as described in Chapter 4. Go to any computer on the network, open a web browser, and type in your server's URL.

Note In this example, we've used an old PC running Google Chrome on Windows XP. You'll see an equivalent message on Mac, Windows, and Linux computers. The exact text depends on the browser you use.

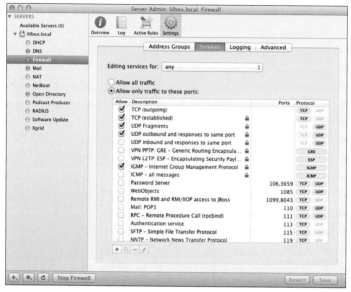

12.13 Enable services by allowing traffic to selected port numbers. By default, many useful services are *disabled* by the firewall.

Without the firewall, you would see the default Lion Server web page, the Wiki Server login page, or perhaps your own web page, if you've set one up.

But because the firewall is now blocking web traffic, you see some variation of the message shown in Figure 12.14. The web server can't be accessed, even though it's still running behind the firewall.

Genius

If you try to access the web server from your Lion Server Mac, you'll see it's still available and hasn't been filtered. This is because the firewall filters only *external network traffic*. The web server is *inside* the firewall. Localhost traffic isn't filtered, so you can view web pages hosted on the server from the server in the usual way.

Re-enabling access to a service

You have now comprehensively crippled your server. Web, e-mail, chat, and other services are no longer accessible from the rest of the network.

To re-enable access to these services, check the corresponding port number in the Allow column at the left of the pane. As an example, follow these steps to re-enable access to the web server:

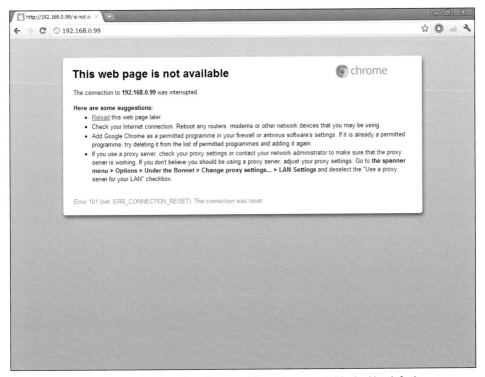

12.14 Once the firewall is running, web traffic to and from the server is blocked by default—even though the web server is still running.

1. **Open the Settings/Services tab in Server Admin, if it isn't open already.**

2. **Click the Ports column header.**

3. **Scroll down the list to find Port 80.** You see the description to the left says "HTTP - web service."

4. **Click the Allow check box in the column at the left, as shown in Figure 12.15.**

5. **Click Save at the bottom right.**

If you try to view web pages hosted on the server, you should now find they're accessible again; web traffic is getting through in both directions, and you no longer see the message shown in Figure 12.14.

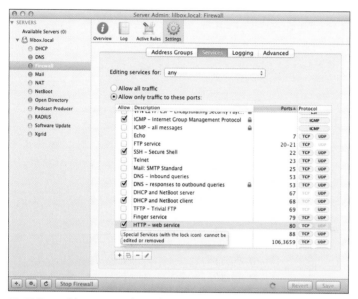

12.15 Re-enable access to the web service by making sure the firewall is set up to allow web traffic.

Follow the corresponding steps to allow traffic to other services. If you're not sure which services to enable, Table 12.1 includes some suggestions. Note that you can leave the Protocol column unchanged for all these services.

Caution

Remember that you should leave services *disabled* unless you need them. For example, if you don't use your server to serve web pages, leave port 80 closed.

Genius

The quick and easy way to find the port numbers associated with each service is to click the Description column header to sort services by name. The descriptions include the service name, and clicking the Description header lists them in alphabetical order.

Note

Services marked with a padlock are essential to network operation and can't be changed. Note also that Table 12.1 doesn't list the services that are checked by default. Don't change them; they're critical!

Table 12.1 Useful services and port numbers

Service	Port Number	Function
FTP	20-21	Leave this disabled unless you've set up a legacy FTP server.
SSH	22	This allows password protected and encrypted remote command-line access. Leave this disabled unless you administer your server from a remote location.
Telnet	23	This is a less-secure version of SSH; it's best left disabled.
DNS	53	Allow this if you use your server for network-wide DNS. (See Chapter 2.)
DHCP	67, 68	Allow this if you use your server for network-wide DHCP. (See Chapter 4.)
Mail	25, 110, 143, 465, 587, 993, 995	Allow this selectively for e-mail.
Web	80, 443	Allow this for web access and secure web access respectively.
AppleTalk	201-208, 548	Allow this if using AppleTalk file sharing.
LDAP (Open Directory)	389, 625, 636	Allow this to support remote Open Directory traffic. (It is usually necessary only on a more complex network.)
iChat	5190, 5223, 5269, 5297, 5298, 5678, 5060, 5222, 7777	Allow this to support the full range of features available in iChat.
iCal Server	8008, 8443	Allow this to support remote access to iCal on the network.
Address Book Server	8800, 8843	Allow this to support Address Book on the network.

Creating a custom address group

Now that you know how to filter specific services, you can use address groups to apply filters selectively to certain IP addresses.

The previous example creates filters for the Any address group, which means the filters apply to all network traffic. If you select 192.168-net group in the Service dialog, you can set up a different set of filters that apply only to local network traffic.

Occasionally, it's useful to apply custom filters to a specific computer; for example, you may have a computer in a publicly accessible location that should offer only very limited access to your network. Or if your server is directly connected to the Internet, you can apply custom filters to a specific Internet address range—for example, to ban certain ISPs from your mail service.

To set up a custom address group, follow these steps:

1. **Click the Settings icon and the Address Groups tab.**

2. **Click the + (plus) icon at the lower right of the window.** You see the sheet shown in Figure 12.16.

3. **Type a Group name.** This is for display purposes only.

4. **Click the default Any item in the Addresses in group box.**

5. **Click the - (minus) icon at the right of the sheet to delete the Any item.**

6. **Click the + (plus) icon at the right to add a new item.**

7. **Type the IP address you want to apply rules to.** If you're familiar with network prefix notation, you also can type an address range.

8. **Click OK to save the new address group.**

You can now select the address in the Services tab and apply custom filters to it.

Enabling logging

It's often useful to see how the firewall is performing. The Logging tab, shown in Figure 12.17, enables the firewalls logging feature. By default, nothing happens if you check the Enable logging box. The most useful setting is shown in the figure. If you log all denied packets, you get a summary of packets that have been filtered.

It can be useful to log all allowed packets when setting up your firewall to see what traffic is arriving and to check whether it needs to be filtered. But note that leaving this setting permanently enabled affects server performance, because it introduces significant overhead.

You can view the logs in two ways. If you select the Log icon at the top of the Firewall pane, you see a list of filter events—packets that are either allowed or denied (filtered) depending on your logging settings. You also can view events in your Mac's console application, which is in /Applications/Utilities.

A firewall log entry, shown in Figure 12.18, has a standard format as follows:

- **Date and time.**
- **Server name.**
- **ipfw[(number)].** This tells you the log is for a firewall event. ipfw is the firewall service. The number is your Mac's internal process number, which you can ignore.

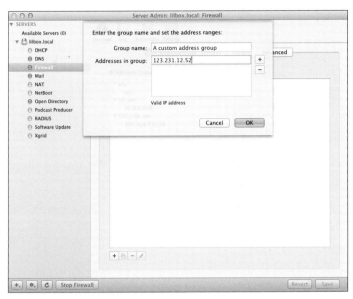

12.16 Creating a custom address group.

12.17 Enabling firewall logging.

- **The advanced rule number.** This is usually 65534. Advanced rules are very low-level filter options. You can edit them under the Advanced tab, but you don't usually need to change the defaults, and a full discussion of advanced rules is outside the scope of this book.

- **The event type.** Either Allow or Deny.

- **The protocol.** Usually either TCP or UDP. This tells whether the event used standard packets (TCP) or packets optimized for media streaming (UDP).

- **The source IP number and port, separated by a colon**. This is the IP number and port of the computer from which the packet was sent.

- **The destination IP number and port.** For example, 192.168.0.99:80 tells you that the packet was sent to a server with the IP address 192.168.0.99 and was a request for a web page.

- **In or out.** Literally an incoming or outgoing packet.

- **Via *xxx*.** *xxx* is a physical network connector, often en0, which indicates your Mac's first Ethernet port.

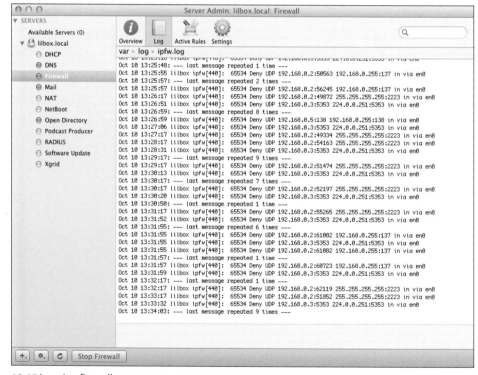

12.18 Logging firewall events.

Note

The log also includes regular *flush events* for IPv4 rules and IPv6 rules. These are records of internal server housekeeping. They're not firewall events, and you can ignore them.

Genius

If events are repeated, the log shows a note 'last message repeated X times', where x is the number of repeats. This is an automatic feature, and helps keep the log uncluttered.

Enabling stealth mode

Although a full introduction to the features and settings of the Advanced tab is beyond the scope of this book, this page includes *stealth mode,* a simple but powerful feature. Stealth mode is similar to the equivalent stealth mode feature in the main Lion firewall, but it has a couple of extra options.

To enable stealth mode, check the two boxes at the top of the window, as shown in Figure 12.19. Services filtered by the firewall are now invisible. They don't send an acknowledgement or failure message when checked; they simply don't respond at all.

Note that some network services rely on stealth mode. Experiment with it to make sure that enabling stealth mode doesn't break anything critical on the network before leaving it permanently enabled.

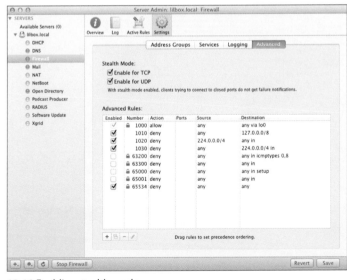

12.19 Enabling stealth mode.

How Can I Fix Problems and Get More from Lion Server?

When something goes wrong, you can use Lion Server's logs to examine problems and errors. The logs are rich in information, and you can use them as a starting point for web searches that can direct you to other users with a similar problem who may have fixed it. Troubleshooting is an advanced topic, but it's also an excellent way to find out more about the internal workings of Lion Server. After you learn how to edit configuration files by hand, you'll have earned the title of expert administrator.

Getting Started with Troubleshooting

Lion Server is a complex piece of software. As of version 10.7.2, some elements may not work entirely as advertised, while others work only with some coaxing.

When you're trying to fix problems, there are two main difficulties. The first is that although Server. app has a very simple user interface with limited options, Lion Server is a complex patchwork of interacting elements. Many elements depend on others, and if one of these critical features isn't set up correctly, some or all of the features in Lion Server may not work.

The second is that there's no simple way to check settings and troubleshoot problems. More advanced users can experiment with low-level management techniques. Beginners may find them challenging, because they assume experience with servers, networks, and command-line control.

Luckily, there are ways to minimize problems and to simplify troubleshooting. The tips introduced in this chapter won't guarantee that you can fix any issue, but they can give you an insight into some possible first steps and help you toward making a successful solution more likely.

Setting up Lion Server correctly

A big problem for new users is that Apple doesn't provide clear instructions for setting up Lion Server as a whole. For best results, follow these steps in order:

1. **Understand what's available.** Skim this book to understand what you can and can't do with Lion Server. Note which services you can delegate to third parties (such as web hosting and e-mail management) and which services require extra computing power (such as podcast production). Consider the alternative software solutions listed in Appendix A.

2. **Plan your services.** Decide which features you want to use in Lion Server. Consider the server as a whole, and buy hardware that is powerful and fast enough to meet your needs. (See Chapter 1 for more information.)

3. **If you plan to make Lion Server visible on the Internet, register a domain name and set up domain hosting.** Use this option if you want to offer public access to a web server, as shown in Figure 13.1, e-mail server, chat facilities, VPN (Virtual Private Network), and other online features. (See Chapter 10 for more information.)

4. **Create a base default installation of Lion Server, and save it.** Use the instructions in Chapter 1. (You also can create a disk image as described later in this chapter.) Use this base installation as your initial starting point. If something goes wrong, you can wipe all your settings by returning to it. Include Server Admin in your installation.

13.1 Using Lion Server as a web server on the Internet.

5. **Set up Lion Server as either a local network or an Internet domain.** Follow the instructions in Chapter 2. This should automatically set up DNS (Domain Name Services) correctly.

6. **Set up Open Directory.** Follow the instructions in Chapter 3.

7. **Create at least one administrator, at least one network user, and at least one group.**

8. **Set up other features as required.** Follow the instructions in the rest of this book.

9. **Test features with your initial users.**

10. **If there are problems, fix them.** Follow the hints in this chapter.

11. **When there are no further problems, add real users and groups and make the server "live" on the network and/or Internet.**

12. **Monitor performance regularly. You can use the performance graphing options shown in Figure 13.2.** For example, check how long it takes e-mail to work its way through your system. Check how quickly web pages appear from the Internet.

13. If there are performance issues, consider moving some services to a different solution. For example, you may want to move web and e-mail services to an external host.

Genius A useful—but expensive—option is to install Lion Server on two separate Macs. You can use one as a production server while experimenting and testing features on the other.

Genius To use the graphing features in Server.app aunch Server App, and click Stats in the list of items at the left. (Server Admin has an equivalent feature. Click the server name at the top of the list at the left. The Overview icon shows a summary of the server status.)

13.2 Checking performance using the Status Graphs in Server.app.

Monitoring operation

When a feature isn't working, there are three ways to try to diagnose the problem:

- **Server.app logs.** This feature displays a log—a list of important events—for some of the services in Lion Server.

- **Server Admin logs.** This feature is similar to the Server.app logs. But because Server Admin supports services that can't be controlled from Server.app, you can extra detail in Server Admin.

- **The Mac Console application.** This utility application that lists error messages and updates created by applications and services as they run.

We'll look at finding and viewing these logs before explaining what they mean and how they can help pinpoint and fix problems.

Viewing the Server.app logs

To view the logs, launch Server.app if it isn't running already and select Logs from the list of items at the left. Server.app can display logs created by various parts of Lion Server. To select a log, click the menu at the bottom of the pane and select a feature or service from the list, as shown in Figure 13.3. Table 13.1 outlines the function of each log.

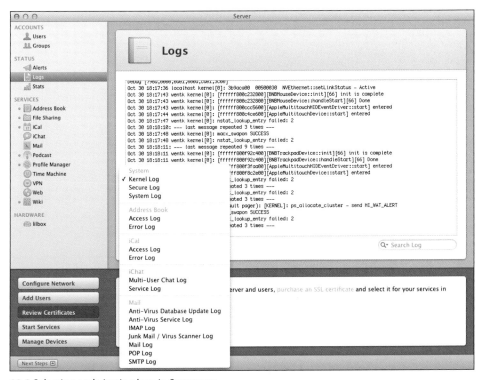

13.3 Selecting and viewing logs in Server.app.

Note

The grayed out items in the menu are the names of each service. Black selectable items are different logs for each service.

Table 13.1 Services and their logs

Log	Service	Function
Kernel	System	Core low-level system messages. Messages here describe hardware problems, network issues, and general errors.
Secure	System	Authentication and security issues. This includes user login events.
System	System	Application and service messages and events.
Access	Address Book	Users or services that have accessed Address Book server.
Error	Address Book	Address Book server problems and issues.
Access	iCal	Users or services that have accessed iCal server.
Error	iCal	iCal server problems and issues.
Multi-User Chat	iChat	Users or services that have accessed iChat server.
Service	iChat	iChat server problems and issues.
Anti-Virus Database Update	Mail	Update events for the ClamAV antivirus tool, which is built into the mail system.
Anti-Virus Service	Mail	General messages generated by ClamAV about its status.
IMAP	Mail	Messages generated by the IMAP sub-service in Mail.
Junk Mail/Virus Scanner	Mail	Messages generated by the junk mail and virus scanning system.
Mail	Mail	General mail-related messages and issues.
POP	Mail	Messages generated by the POP sub-service in Mail.
SMTP	Mail	Messages generated by the SMTP sub-service in Mail.

Note

For an explanation of the acronyms used by the mail service, see Chapter 4. Note that the mail logs show the messages for each sub-service. For example, when you try to send e-mail, it usually goes through the SMTP sub-service. If SMTP can't send your e-mail, because it isn't set up properly or because you've used an invalid user account, you can find out more about the problem by looking at the SMTP log.

Genius

Some logs don't appear in Server.app; for example, there's no logging for the web server. You can view logs created by other services using the Console, which is described later in this chapter.

Viewing Server Admin logs

To view the logs for each service in Server Admin, select the service from the list at the left and click the Logs icon at the top of the window, as shown in Figure 13.4. Many services include sub-logs, like the ones in Server.app. There are too many logs to list here, and some are highly specialized, but it's useful to know they're available.

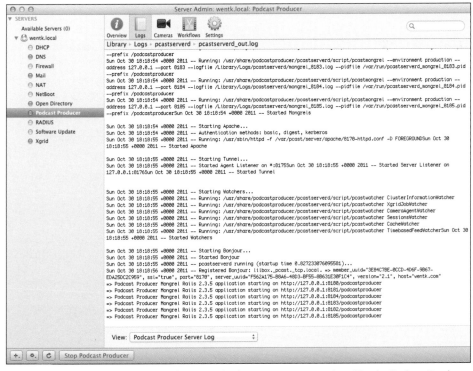

13.4 Viewing a log in Server Admin. This example shows messages produced by the Podcast Producer service.

Using Console

Console is a utility application available in OS X Lion and Lion Server. To launch it, double-click it in /Applications/Utilities.

Console provides system-wide logging of errors and system events. The left of the Console window includes a list of items you can select. By default, Console shows the complete System Log, which is identical to the System Log feature in Server.app.

It's often more useful to view application and service logs. There's no explicit list of services, but if you click the /var/log item at the bottom of the list at the left, you see a long list of services. You can ignore most of them, but some are useful. For example, the apache2 access.log shown in Figure 13.5 shows a list of IP addresses that have tried to load a web page.

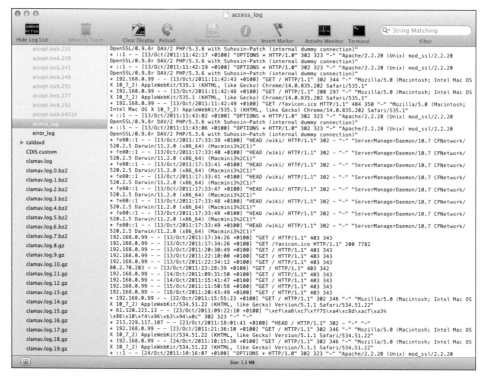

13.5 Viewing the apache2 (web server) log in Console.

Finding problems

Fixing problems is a creative process rather than a mechanical one. You need to know the following:

- **How to read logs and extract useful information about errors and issues**
- **How to search the web for help about these errors**
- **How to make changes to Lion Server settings**

As you may have realized, making deep changes to Lion Server settings can be a complex process. Before looking at the details, let's find out more about log files.

Note This chapter includes a section about log files because they provide more information—and more useful information—than the errors and alerts you see in Server. app. Most of the latter amount to "something isn't working," which doesn't give you much of a start when you're attempting a fix.

Understanding logs

A log is simply a list of messages, recorded as they're generated. There's no single standard format for logs, but most include a *timestamp*—a date and time marker—and a message or alert text. Most also include the name of the service that generated the message.

Few Lion Server services have obvious names. You might expect the web server would be called something like webserver. But most service names are more…creative. Table 13.2 lists some common services and the jobs they do.

Table 13.2 Common Services

Service name	Function
apache (or apache2)	Web server
caldavd	iCal
carddav	Address Book
clamavd	ClamAV anti-virus
collabd	Wiki server
dovecot	E-mail
ipfilter	Firewall
jabberd	iChat
launchd	Automatic service launcher; often "respawns" (restarts) services if they crash
raccoon	VPN (Virtual Private Network)
servermgrd	Master Lion Server management service
slapd	Open Directory
xscertd	Certificate management and authentication

Note Service names may be prefixed with Apple's com.dot notation; for example, the full name of the apache service is 'org.apache.httpd'. The extra words are used for internal housekeeping, and you can ignore them.

Genius

The *d* at the end of some of these names is short for daemon, which is short for "a process that does something useful and runs in the background, so you can't see it working." Most network services are daemons. (But not all of the daemons running on a Mac are network services.)

Genius

If you see a name that isn't in this list, you can do a web search for it. Remember that Lion Server is made from a kit of software parts, many of which are used in other non-Apple contexts. Don't be surprised if you find references to projects and products that don't seem to have anything to do with your Mac. They may still be relevant.

Finding errors in logs

Not all log messages are errors. Some are *diagnostics*— information about what a service is doing. Diagnostics can be useful, but they're not critical. Sometimes they simply waste space. (The jab-berd service is particularly verbose.)

Generally, if a message includes the *words fail, error,* or *can't [do something]*, it's almost certain to be an error.

If a service isn't working, you can sometimes prompt an error message with some or all of the following actions:

- **Turn the service off.**
- **Turn the service on.** Both actions should generate a block of diagnostic messages.
- **Interact with the service.** For example, you can try to view a web page or send an e-mail and check what happens in the corresponding logs.

Some errors also appear repeatedly while your Mac is running. For example, as of version 10.7.2, Lion Server regularly reports the following message, as shown in Figure 13.6:

```
kernel: nstat_lookup_entry failed: 2
```

Note

Log files can include a line that says "last message repeated *n* times" (where *n* is a number). This means what it says; the message occurred more than once, but to save space, the log file window didn't list every occurrence.

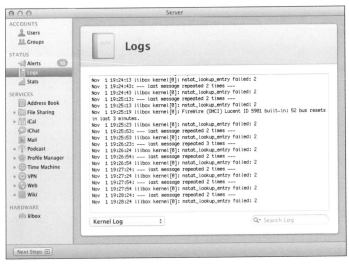

13.6 Viewing a repeating error in the kernel log.

Looking up errors online

Not all errors are critical. If a service is working as it should, it may still generate the occasional error, but you can ignore it.

Otherwise, you have two options: You can try to make sense of the message yourself, or you can search for it online.

The DIY approach depends on your background knowledge. If you have plenty of experience with Macs or other computers, log files will give you useful clues. If not, it's easier to search for the message online. You can see if other users have had a similar problem, and if they've found a solution. Errors aren't usually unique: If you're having a problem, other users likely are too.

To search, simply copy and paste the message from the log window into the search field of a browser. You'll almost always see some hits, of the kind shown in Figure 13.7.

If you get no results, try the following:

- **Add the words *Mac, Lion,* or *Lion Server* to your search.**

- **Try searching for the name of the service and *bug* or *error*.**

Errors are discussed in many places online. Apple's own online user communities regularly appear in search results, but you can find results from personal blogs and developer sites such as Stackoverflow (www.stackoverflow.com).

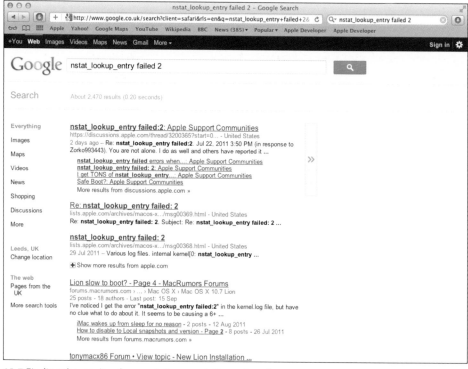

13.7 Finding the results of a search for more information about an error.

But just because an error is mentioned online doesn't mean that a solution is available. At worst, you'll get reassurance that you're not the only user with the same issue. But it's not unusual to get some hints for solutions. And at best, you may find a detailed step-by-step fix.

Note

If you search for the nstat_lookup_entry error mentioned earlier, you'll find that no one is sure what causes it. Some users appear to have solved it, and there are some clues about which parts of Lion Server are causing it. But there's no reliable fix. Sometimes, users simply have to wait for an update from Apple that fixes the problem.

Fixing problems

Some problems are easy to fix, but other discussions assume expert skills and knowledge. On a forum, you can usually ask for polite clarification if you don't understand abbreviations and ideas.

You're likely to get basic help, but you'll have to supplement this with further research and background reading.

Don't assume that all suggested solutions work. Even experienced users regularly stumble around trying possible solutions at random. Solutions may work for one person and not for another, especially if there are obvious differences in configuration and setup.

Generally, troubleshooting is an inexact process, far outside the realm of simple step-by-step guides.

Understanding the command line environment

Before going further, it's important to know that some suggested solutions require command-line control. You need to know three things before you attempt this:

- **You can use a utility called Terminal to control Lion Server from the command line.** Terminal is shown in Figure 13.8. You can find it /Applications/Utilities.

- **Parts of your Mac's file system are hidden from Finder, but visible in Terminal.** The hidden files include the configuration (setup and management) files that control the services in Lion Server.

- **To fix problems, you may need to edit the configuration files by hand.** This sounds easy, but it isn't. TextEdit won't show the files you need to change. Even if it did, you don't have the privileges needed to change them. Luckily, there are ways around both issues, which are described in the next few sections.

13.8 Getting started with Terminal.

Genius

Technically, accessing the command line is called "using the shell"; the shell is the software that interprets your typing and sends it off for processing. Shell commands date from computing's prehistory, and they're almost completely counterintuitive. For example, the command to show the files in a directory isn't "show files" or "directory"; it's 'ls'. Many commands are long and include extra characters and punctuation, especially dashes. You *must* get these right, including capitalization and case, because the command line is completely unforgiving. Commands that aren't typed perfectly either won't work as expected, or they won't work at all.

Finding configuration files

As an exercise with Terminal, we'll enter a command that forces Finder to display the files it usually hides. Start by adding the Finder icon to the Dock, if you don't have it there already; you'll need it later.

Launch Terminal from /Applications/Utilities, and type the following:

```
defaults write com.apple.Finder AppleShowAllFiles TRUE
```

End the line with Return, and type the following command:

```
killall Finder
```

You've now killed Finder. Restart it from the Dock. Navigate to your main hard disk, and you see that Finder is now displaying extra folders and files in gray. You can click some of these folders to see their contents, as shown in Figure 13.9.

Genius

You can hide files again by typing the same two lines, replacing TRUE with FALSE.

These are the critical folders:

- **bin.** Short for binary, it's a list of some of the commands you can run from the shell. This folder holds the software that runs the commands. You can look up what the commands do by searching for them online.

- **etc.** This stores settings for most services in named folders. Configuration or .conf files can be edited in a text editor. This is the most useful folder and the one you're most likely to work in when troubleshooting.

- **var.** This contains live working data for services. There's nothing editable here.

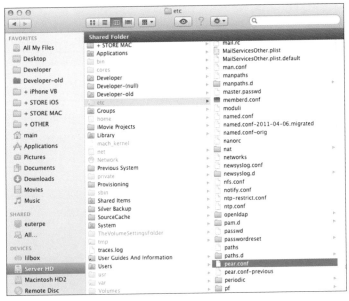

13.9 Viewing hidden files in Finder.

Some commands have a help option. Many don't. You can find out more about commands by typing "man [command name]" in Terminal; *man* is short for *manual*. This displays a highly technical page about each command. The man pages are useful references for experienced users, but they're largely useless for beginners because they're packed with jargon and the explanations make no attempt to be reader-friendly. Figure 13.10 shows an example for the mkdir (make directory) command, which lists the command and the various options you can add to it, selected by typing a minus sign followed by a letter. Hold down ctrl and type Z to quit from man.

Viewing configuration files

When you find suggested fixes online, they often specify a configuration file. The chances are good it's in one of the folders in /etc. As an example, let's look at the webserver configuration settings, which are in the httpd.conf file in the /apache2 folder in /etc.

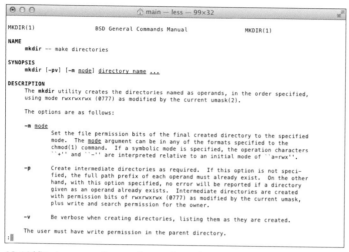

13.10 Viewing a man (manual) page from the command line.

Click etc in Finder, click apache2, and select the httpd.conf file. Because the extension isn't known to Finder, you can't open it by double-clicking it. But you can right-click it, select Open With and Other, and navigate to TextEdit in /Applications. This loads it into TextEdit, as shown in Figure 13.11.

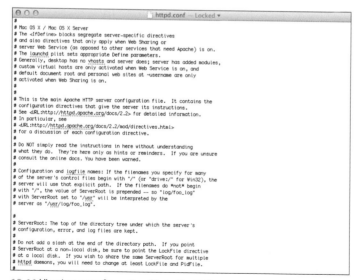

13.11 Viewing a configuration file in TextEdit.

Caution

Unfortunately, hidden files can't be found with Spotlight, even after they've been displayed in Finder. If you can't find a configuration file, you have to search for it manually.

If you try to save it, you'll find it's locked. This is a deliberate security feature built into Mac OS X. Only one user is allowed to make changes to critical files—the superuser, also known as root.

Note

The superuser is *not* the same as the network administrator. Even if you have network administrator privileges, you're still not allowed to edit critical files.

Editing configuration files

When an online search for fixes suggests editing Lion Server's configuration files, you can use the techniques in this section to make the changes you need. If you're new to this level of control, don't attempt to understand the contents of the configuration files, because they can be highly technical. But if you find clear instructions for changes online, they don't usually require more than a line or two of changes. You can do this successfully without modifying the rest of the file.

Before going further, you need to know that there's an easy way and a difficult way to edit configuration files.

Editing the difficult way

The difficult way—which is also the way used by most experienced users, including those who post solutions to problems online—is to launch a text editor from the command line. Typically, you use one of two editors: vi and nano. If you're used to TextEdit, you'll find them quirky and crude, because *everything* is done from the command line.

To use these editors, do the following:

1. **Navigate to the correct (hidden) folder.** Use the cd command to enter and exit a directory and ls to list the directories you can access.

2. **Type sudo su to give yourself superuser privileges.** Enter your password when asked.

3. **Launch the editor, typing the exact file name.**

4. **Make changes as needed.** All editing uses a combination of Control key and standard key combinations.

5. **Quit when done, saving the file.**

Navigation is challenging, because you can't see where you are in the file system. And after you launch one of the editors, there are no menus and you can navigate through and edit the document only with the cursor keys because *there is no mouse support.*

We won't say more about vi and nano here, except to add that nano is the more intuitive of the two editors, and if you want more information, you can find instructions and tutorials at www.nano-editor.org.

Editing the easy way

The easy way to edit configuration files is to log out of your Mac as a normal user and log in as root. You can then edit every file on your Mac, without restrictions.

Caution Editing configuration files is unlikely to damage your Mac's hardware. But if you make a mistake, you can destroy critical settings. This probably won't trash your installation. But…it might. If you're not comfortable with the possibility that something may go so badly wrong that you'll need to reinstall your server from a backup, *don't do it.* Otherwise, back up your system—or at the very least create safety copies of the files you change—and *proceed at your own risk.*

Caution To add to the confusion, Server.app regularly overwrites configuration files. Whenever you change a setting in Server.app, it's likely to have made a change to a hidden configuration file. After you start editing configuration files, it's useful to keep a backup of your changes and to avoid using Server.app unless you have no other option.

The all-powerful root account is disabled by default, so you must enable it manually before you can use it. Log in with your administrator account, and follow these steps:

1. **From the (Apple Symbol) menu at the top left, select System Preferences.**
2. **Select Users & Groups.**
3. **Click the lock, and type your password into the box.**
4. **Click Login Options….**
5. **Click Edit… or Join… at the bottom right.**
6. **Click Open Directory Utility….**
7. **Click the lock in the Directory Utility window.**

8. **Enter an administrator account name and password.**

9. **Click OK.**

10. **Select Edit, and Enable Root User.**

11. **Enter a password for root in the Password and Verify boxes, as shown in Figure 13.12.**

12. **Click OK.**

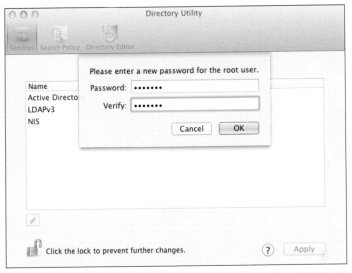

13.12 Setting a password for the root/superuser/system administrator account.

To use your new account, log in with the username root and type the password you chose. Hidden files are still invisible to root by default, so you need to open Terminal and enter the commands given earlier in this chapter to reveal them. After the files are visible, you can open and edit them using TextEdit, as shown in Figure 13.13, although you still need to right-click and select TextEdit as the editing application.

Caution

In addition to .conf files, configuration information is stored in .plist files and in files with no extension. You can edit most configuration files of every type with TextEdit. But be very, very wary of editing .plist files by hand. The format is very structured (technically, it's called XML, eXtensible Markup Language), and it's very easy indeed to break a .plist file. Don't attempt manual editing unless you're absolutely sure you know what you're doing—from knowledge rather than guesswork!

Caution

Don't use the root account for day-to-day administration. Because the account has superpowers, it makes your Mac very vulnerable to both accidental and deliberate damage. It's good practice to use root only when you really need to and to log in again with your usual network administrator account when you've finished troubleshooting.

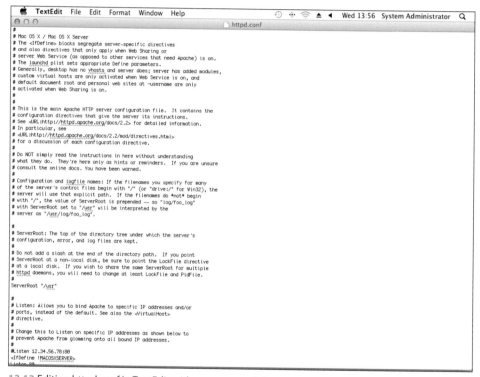

13.13 Editing httpd.conf in TextEdit with superuser privileges.

Going Further with Lion Server

Although this book tells you everything you need to know to get started with Lion Server, there's always more to learn. A full introduction to every possible feature and setting would need a book at least twice the size. But this last section introduces some other features in Lion Server—or more specifically, in Server Admin.

Figure 13.14 shows the supporting applications in the /Server folder, which includes Server Admin. You may find them useful, so we've included very short introductions as a starting point for further exploration.

13.14 The full Server Admin toolkit.

- **Podcast Composer.** This application is described in Chapter 7.

- **Server Admin.** This application is described throughout this book.

- **Server Monitor.** Use this application to check performance, hard drive status, and other critical features of a remote server. It's designed for use on multi-server networks; it isn't useful if you only have a single server.

- **System Image Utility.** This application is described in the next section.

- **Workgroup Manager.** Use this application to edit the list of users and groups on your server, as described later in this chapter.

- **Xgrid Admin.** Use this application to set up and manage an Xgrid. (If you set up Podcast Producer, as described in Chapter 7, Xgrid is set up for you automatically.)

Introducing System Image Utility

System Image Utility, shown in Figure 13.15, is used for copying and automatically installing operating system boot disks. This is useful for Mac Lab teaching and demo situations where Macs have to be wiped after each use and reinitialized with a clean install of the lab's software.

You can use System Image Utility in three ways:

- **Remote boot.** Instead of booting from a version of OS X from a local disk, Macs can boot from a disk image (a copy of the OS) on the server. The boot process is repeated every time the Mac restarts, so the Mac is always "clean" with the same software and settings.

- **Remote install.** This option installs OS X from a disk image. Remote install is typically done infrequently. After installation, users may (optionally) be allowed to customize their Macs with their own software and settings.
- **Remote restore.** This option makes a copy of existing software and settings. A user can then restore her Mac to that configuration.

For smaller server owners, Remote Restore is the most useful option. If you have multiple Macs, you can use it to back up your complete Lion Server installation, creating a disk image on a remote Mac that can be used as a restore point. This isn't necessarily more convenient than using Time Machine to perform server backups, but if you do it manually, it can add an extra independent safety copy.

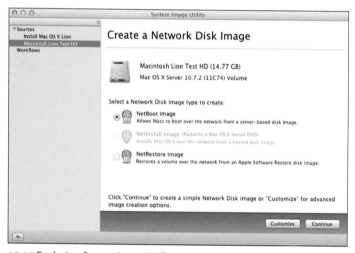

13.15 Exploring System Image Utility.

Note System Image Utility uses a feature called NetBoot. You can set up NetBoot options and manage disk images using the NetBoot service included in Server Admin.

Introducing Workgroup Manager

Workgroup Manager, shown in Figure 13.16, is a larger and more powerful version of the Users and Groups editor in Server.app. You can use it to list local users, local contacts from the server's address book, and network users.

It's not essential for smaller networks, but on larger networks, it's a convenient way to manage users and groups from a single application, because it includes control features and settings that aren't included in Server.app.

A key feature is the group selector, which appears as a tiny reveal triangle under the Server Admin icon. Click this to show a menu with a list of different user locations.

The default local option shows users local to the server—in other words, the list of users you can see and change from the Users & Groups pane in System Preferences. The /LDAPv3/127.0.0.1 option shows the Open Directory listing of users with network accounts.

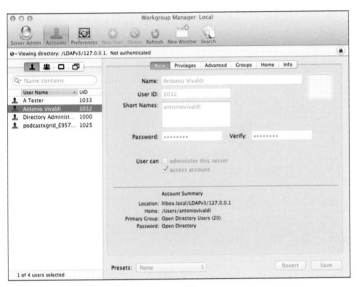

13.16 Experimenting with Workgroup Manager.

Genius

One of the useful features in Workgroup Manager is the ability to selectively enable applications options for each user. Select a user, click Applications, click the Preferences icon at the top of the pane, select the Applications tab, and click Manage: Always. You can now add a list of applications the user is allowed to run. You also can customize access to Dashboard widgets and Front Row. In fact, you can customize almost any aspect of each user's System Preferences and some of their application preferences too.

Appendix A

Lion Server Extras and Alternatives

Both Lion and Lion Server can be extended and modified. Experienced web developers, bloggers, and system administrators can add these extras to enhance the basic features of Lion Server. For some applications, alternatives may be closer to existing industry standards. They also may be more flexible and easier to customize.

Note that some of these options can be added to Lion as well as Lion Server. For certain applications, Lion Server may not be necessary at all. Note also that certain applications can be administered only from the command line.

The following lists aren't completely comprehensive—many, many more products and options are available than I have space to discuss here—but they provide an introduction to some of the ways in which Lion Server can be customized or extended.

Alternatives to Lion Server

The following items provide alternatives to some of Lion Server's standard services.

www.mamp.info

A Mac-centric version of the industry standard LAMP (Linux, Apache, MySQL, PHP) package, used as a standardized web platform by many web developers. Available in free and commercial versions.

www.apachefriends.org/en/xampp-macosx.html

An alternative to MAMP, which bundles Apache 2, MySQL, PHP, and Perl into a single package. (Note: This may no longer be current. You should check XAMPP on a spare Mac before using it commercially.)

www.dovecot.org

A free mail server. Dovecot forms the core of Lion Server's e-mail server, but it also can be installed on a Mac running Lion. Administration is from the command line.

www.igniterealtime.org

A collection of free chat servers with supporting Java libraries. OpenFire is chat only, Spark provides live collaboration tools, and SparkWeb is a web-based version of Spark. Mac versions are available.

www.addressbookserver.com

A useful alternative to Lion Server's address and calendar-sharing tools. Address Book Server offers more flexibility and support for more complex sharing options. A free 10-user license is available.

www.mediawiki.org

The most popular web-based wiki software application used by Wikipedia and other high-profile internet sites. Mediawiki is free but requires command-line skills. Compatibility with Lion Server's PostgresQL database system isn't quite perfect—MediaWiki was written for MySQL databases—but is robust enough for basic use.

www.basecamphq.com

An online web-based project management, collaboration, and file-sharing service. Basecamp isn't a server product and isn't free. But it has become very popular with small businesses that use it for collaborative communication, sharing, and project management.

Extras for Lion Server

These extras add features to Lion Server that extend or replace the basic Wiki features with more advanced blogging and content management or add further media streaming features. Because Lion Server uses the PostrgresQL database system instead of the more common MySQL technology, these extras may need to be hand-optimized for use with Lion Server or enhanced with special compatibility plug-ins.

http://wordpress.org

The industry standard blogging platform, which can be used to provide a personal blog, a set of product pages with occasional updates, or other more highly customized but easy-to-modify web pages.

http://wordpress.org/extend/plugins/postgresql-for-wordpress

A plug-in that makes Wordpress compatible with the PostgresQL database used in Lion Server. Wordpress relies on MySQL, an older database format no longer used in Lion Server.

http://drupal.org

A content management system (CMS) that can provide more complex collaborative web content management than Wordpress. Unlike competing CMS alternatives, Drupal can work with the PostgresQL database technology used in Lion Server.

(For a comprehensive list of content management systems compatible with PostgresQL, see http://en.wikipedia.org/wiki/List_of_content_management_systems.)

www.logitech.com/support

Offers the free Squeezebox Server system for OS X, which supports media streaming to a variety of media devices made by Logitech and other companies. (The download location for Squeezebox Server varies, so search the support site for the latest details.)

www.pulptunes.com

A free, easy-to-use web-based iTunes server. Access your iTunes library remotely from anywhere on the Internet. It works with Lion and Lion Server.

www.dropbox.com

A web-based file sharing and manual backup service that's a popular alternative to iCloud's backup features. The first 2GB of storage are free.

Glossary

127.0.0.1 A special reserved IP address that always maps to the local host.

192.168.x.x A special reserved range of addresses used exclusively on small local networks; *x* stands for any number between 0 and 255.

A record A DNS address record type used to translate domain names to *IPv4* addresses.

account name The internal username used by *Open Directory*, which doesn't include spaces. (See also *display name*.)

address An identifier that uniquely identifies a computer on a network.

administrator A user with special privileges who sets up and maintains a network server.

Apple Filing Protocol (AFP) An older technology used to share files between Macs on a network.

AirPort Apple's WiFi technology; used in Macs and in standalone network products.

Address Book Apple's contact management tool, which has links to e-mail, calendar, wiki, and other services in Lion Server.

alias A network address or identifier that redirects traffic; for example, an e-mail alias collects e-mail for a dummy address and forwards it automatically to a user's real address.

Apache 2 The second-generation open-source web server used in Lion Server. For details, visit www.apache.org.

Apple Remote Desktop (ARD) Apple's remote control tool for network users, which makes it possible to view and interact with the screen on one Mac from another.

Authenticated POP (APOP) An extension to the POP3 e-mail protocol, with improved security.

authentication A security process that checks whether users and network services are allowed to access other network features, usually with a password or some other identity check.

backup A safety copy of information kept on a server or user computer.

bandwidth A measure of network speed, usually defined in bytes per second.

blacklist A list of servers and e-mail sources collected by ISPs and other key Internet users and monitored for spam, hack attacks, and other antisocial behavior. Blacklisted servers may be barred or filtered. (See also *whitelist*.)

blog A web page with entries arranged in date order. Often used for personal diaries, project updates, and general discussions.

blogger Someone who blogs.

Bonjour A protocol borrowed by Apple (from a project called Zeroconf) created to make it easier for computers on a network to connect to each other, discover each others' capabilities, and exchange information.

boot The sequence of events and instructions that happens when a Mac or other device is powered up and begins working.

browser A piece of software used to view pages on the World Wide Web.

certificate A file that contains a digital key that securely identifies a web server, mail server, or other network service.

chat See *instant messaging*.

command line A text-based interface that offers powerful and direct control of a server, but relies on typed commands instead of windows and menus.

client A software application that uses some feature of the network; for example, a mail client provides the user's view of a mail service. (See also *server*.)

Console Lion Server's log reader, which shows a list of events and errors and updates the reader as they happen.

display name The human-friendly username on a network, typically first name and surname with a space between.

Domain Name Server (DNS) A network service that translates domain names into IP addresses.

domain name A human-readable easy-to-remember computer address, defined by words with periods between them.

Dynamic Host Configuration Protocol (DHCP) A network service that assigns IP addresses to computers when they connect to the network and keeps track of which addresses are being used.

e-mail server A computer that provides the e-mail service for a network.

encryption A process that converts information that anyone can read into secured information that can be read only with a key. On a network, encryption may be hidden and automatic.

file sharing A system for making files on one computer accessible from another.

firewall A tool for filtering network traffic for security reasons. Specific IP addresses and ports can be filtered to prevent unauthorized access.

File Transfer Protocol (FTP) A popular technology for copying files from one computer on the Internet to another.

group A collection of network users, often set up with common privileges.

Globally Unique Identifier (GUID) In the context of disk storage, a disk format that a Mac can boot from.

hacker An Internet user who spams, phishes, or attempts to break into or take down useful network services.

host A computer running one or more network services.

Hypertext Transfer Protocol (HTTP) The system used on the World Wide Web that sends pages between web servers and web browsers.

iCal Apple's calendar server; a tool that manages schedules for groups and users, and integrates with other services such as Wiki Server to share them visually.

iChat A free IM and chat client built into Lion Server.

instant messaging (IM) A set of protocols, services, and software that makes it possible for users to exchange text messages, live audio, and live video between two or more computers. It is used for entertainment and for collaboration.

Internet Message Access Protocol (IMAP) A technology that collects messages from an e-mail server and copies them to an e-mail client. (See also *POP*.)

IP address A machine-level network address, used by computers when they communicate over a network.

IPv4 The current specification for IP addresses: four numbers between 0 and 255 separated by periods.

IPv6 The next-generation specification for IP addresses: eight groups of four hexadecimal digits separated by colons. IPv6 supports a much larger total range of addresses than IPv4.

Kerberos An authentication service built into Lion Server that runs behind the scenes and can be used by Mail Server and certain other services.

key A very long number built into a certificate. Keys are split into a public part that is available to anyone and a private part that is known only to the key's owner. During authentication, public and private keys are combined to check online identities.

Lightweight Directory Access Protocol (LDAP) One of the components of Open Directory, used to manage a database of network users.

.local The domain suffix used to access services on a local server.

localhost The technical term for "this computer."

Local Area Network (LAN) A small local network limited to one geographical location.

log A list of events and errors created by a network service for diagnostic purposes.

mail exchange (MX) record A DNS record that specifies a mail server.

Media Access Control (MAC) address A unique address that specifies one particular network address on a device. Unlike an IP address, a MAC address corresponds to a specific physical connector, such as an Ethernet socket.

mailing list An optional mail server feature that supports grouped and themed e-mail discussions.

mirrored A RAID option that makes two identical copies of information on two or more disks to improve reliability.

mount To make a directory, disk, or device available for access.

MySQL A popular database technology, built into previous versions of OS X Server. It was replaced in Lion Server by PostgreSQL.

name server A server that keeps a list of domain names and the IP addresses associated with them. (See also *DNS*.)

network A collection of computers connected together so they can exchange information and access common services.

Network Attached Storage (NAS) A relatively slow system for connecting disk storage to a network. (See also *SAN*.)

Network Address Translation (NAT) A network service that converts Internet address into local addresses, and vice versa, making it possible for Internet users to access the network.

network service A software application that provides useful features for network users. Unlike a conventional desktop application, a network service can be used by many computers and may not have an easily accessible user interface.

network user A user with permission to access network services.

Network File System (NFS) A technology used to share files across a network; used almost exclusively by older Apple products.

Network Time Protocol (NTP) A technology used to synchronize the time setting of computers on a network.

offline A device or service that either isn't working or isn't connected to a network.

online A device or service that is working and connected to a network.

Open Directory A database of users that manages network logins and access to other services including e-mail, wikis, Address Book, iCal, and so on.

open source Software that is supplied with the original source code—the instructions created by a programmer—that can be modified and extended by anyone who understands how to program.

Post Office Protocol (POP, often known as POP3) A simple technology for copying e-mail from a server to an e-mail client, with limited features.

partition Part of a hard disk or other storage device; often used to split hard disks into smaller working areas.

password A hidden word or sequence of characters used to identity a user and gain access to one or more network features.

phishing An attempt to trick users into giving away their password and login details by impersonating a valid website with a fake copy.

podcast Originally an audio or video recording that can be downloaded to an iPod; now used to mean almost any audio or video content distributed online.

port A number associated with a certain type of service on a network. For example, web traffic is usually sent and received on port 80. Effectively, it's an extra optional part of an IP address.

privilege The right to access a restricted network service.

Profile Manager A tool that makes it possible for a network administrator to restrict access to certain network services from certain devices, optionally for certain users. For example, some Mac users may not be allowed to install their own software.

protocol A formal set of rules that defines how users or network services must exchange information.

public key cryptography The technology used to check identities on the Internet by combining public and private keys.

push notification A technology that sends notifications to devices whenever a network event occurs. The notifications can be received in various ways, but they often appear as pop-up messages.

QuickTime Apple's movie playback and editing technology; used in the creation of podcasts.

quota A limit set by a network administrator to ration network resources, such as disk space.

Redundant Array of Inexpensive/Individual Disks (RAID) A technology that combines multiple physical disks into a single volume to improve speed, reliability, or both.

relaying A process that forwards e-mail through a server. "Open unless secured" means that open relaying can be used by spammers to fake the original source of an e-mail.

Remote Authentication Dial-In User Service (RADIUS) An authentication technology used to identify users who connect to a network wirelessly.

root A network or computer account with all possible privileges and no restrictions.

router A dedicated box that connects computers and networks together. Routers often include basic services such as DNS, NAT, and DHCP.

Terminal The Mac application used for command-line control of Lion and Lion Server.

Time Machine Apple's automated backup tool for Macs.

Time Machine Server Apple's optional centralized backup tool, which creates a common virtual backup disk on the server for all network users.

Samba A technology used to share files between computers that use different operating systems.

Simple Message Block (SMB) The technology used by Samba.

server A computer on a network that provides network services to network users. For example, an e-mail server manages a network's e-mail facility.

Server App Lion Server's simplified server administration tool.

Server Admin Lion Server's optional more complex server setup tool, with access to extra features and settings.

Secure Shell (SSH) Secure command-line control over one computer from another computer on the network.

Secure Sockets Layer (SSL) A security system that encrypts information sent over a network. Authorized users can read it without problems; unauthorized users can't.

Shell The software that responds to command-line control and converts user commands into actions.

Simple Mail Transfer Protocol (SMTP) A technology for copying e-mail from a client to a server, so the server can send it on to its destination.

spam Junk e-mail, sent out indiscriminately to millions of network users.

Storage Area Network (SAN) A very fast technology used to connect remote disk drives to a server or other computer; often used by corporations and media companies.

stripe A high-speed option used by RAID drives to increase speed by interleaving data across two physical hard drives.

TCP/IP (Transmission Control Protocol/Internet Protocol) The low-level technology that moves information between computers on large and small networks.

Thunderbolt A new, very fast technology used to connect computers to external devices.

Universal Serial Bus (USB) A popular but slow technology used to connect computers to external devices.

Virtual Network Computing (VNC) A non-proprietary and popular system for controlling one computer from another.

Virtual Private Network (VPN) A tool for accessing network features from the Internet over a secured connection.

Web-Based Distributed Authoring and Versioning (WebDAV) A technology for reading, editing, and modifying web pages while a website is running.

whitelist A list of trusted servers and e-mail sources, known to be reliable and safe.

Wide Area Network (WAN) A network that connects computers in many different geographical locations.

web server A computer that sends pages to users' web browsers on request.

wiki A collaborative document that can be edited by anyone who has permission to make changes.

Wiki Server 3 A component in Lion Server that manages wikis, blogs, shared documents, and user's personal web pages.

workgroup A set of users with a common purpose, who may also have identical network privileges.

zone transfer A system used by DNS servers to replicate data between them.

Index